Getting The Girl

Moving Beyond the Pick Up Artist, Changing Your Life and Attracting More Women

Jack Hickey

Edition – 1st

Copyright

Dedication

No man is an Island. This book could not have been made possible without the support of my friends, family, and work colleagues. I thank you all for your support before, during, and after writing.

Special thank you to Guy & Paul for giving me a chance to learn marketing and PR and to practice my skills in town every week. Thank you to Danny for giving me my first taste of working in town and understanding the power of networking. Thank you to Reg for giving me even more opportunities to hone my craft on a Saturday night, we have had some laughs.

I wish to extend my thanks to Jack the best wingman I ever had, Gaz the best of friends one could ask, George my first mentor, Cubbie my manager, Ben my editor, my great work buddies – Kristian, Paulo, Tommy, and others. Karlton the fitness coach. Tayla my illustrator. To David my friend and mentor. Thanks to Tom and Scott for always being true friends and giving me the truth.

To the rest of my friends and all the women along the way that helped. Thanks a lot.

I hope this book helps someone out there to change their life for the better.

The book is about helping you on your journey to get to a different place. To give you the confidence to do new things and step out of your comfort zone. I am fortunate in life I have had some great teachers that allowed me to do so. From: Mr. Tedd to Mark, and Anthony.

The others who helped me get to where I am: Mum, Dad, Les, Brady, Sian, Ellie, , Sarah, Julie , Metty, Colin, Joe, Mikey, Lord Hayward, Will, Mr. Briscombe, Lee, Jason, Tim, Minty, Izzy, Paige, Gemma, Lisa, Elise, Lillie, Charley, Kelsey, Zara, Buster, Aaron, Rory, Alice, Mia, Jess, and Sophia. The lads from Thurnby Rovers, Houghton Rangers, St Patricks. Raynze, Scott, Possum, Zak, John, Sancho, Jordan, Narinder, and probably many more I have missed. Thanks a lot. Also, a special mention to my niece and nephew – Carter & Amaya. To my grandparents – Jack, Mary, Jackie & Bobby.

I hope you enjoy reading it as much as I enjoyed writing.

Foreword

The book has been written to help men out there. In the modern age and the modern world, men's role in the world has become blurred. The book itself helps to bring together the latest in research and experience. In order, so you may map out ways in which to improve your life. We also jump deep into the subconscious mind of the woman so we can demonstrate just how to attract more women.

Now, more than ever we need a plan of action and a set of tools to use to help us navigate this varying and changing world. It is tough for men out in the modern world. You are left on your own expected to know the answers to everything with very little guidance given. Often we men get the blame for all of society's wrongs and none of its rights.

With mental health, a growing concern, and male suicide the largest killer of men under 40 such a book is needed to help men combat loneliness and come up with a plan to turn around their lives.

We will look at exactly what to say, how to say it, and when to say it. We will look at the psychological impact of your words and how to climb inside a woman's head.

Each chapter will help you understand more and more about how to better your chances with women. We will look at online, offline, first impressions, mental preparation, and more.

The book takes you from before you meet a woman through to make her attracted to you, then closing the deal and even a chapter on sex itself. Aren't you a lucky boy?

The book contains cultural references that aren't necessary to follow the book but helps make it read better, don't worry if you don't understand any of them. They aren't needed to get the book and the theorem around them, but you may decide to read up on them at a later date. If nothing else, it gives you some new and cool things to talk about.

In the book, there are a few QR codes that are there to enhance the experience. A modern book has a modern take. You do not need to use or access them for the book to work, they are just additional information around people I have written about or video clips of things in practice. All that you need is contained within the book itself. The book is designed to be read more than once and referred back to, you may decide to scan the QR codes on the second time of reading or if you have the time, you may do it the first time around. Often the code may be a link to a short clip or a long documentary. Watch these if and when you have time, but they are not essential to the book.

All of the references for each chapter are at the end should you wish to look up the research yourself.

The book is a journey so be prepared. As you move through chapters each section has been carefully scaffolded to underpin one another. You build upon your knowledge chapter after chapter. You understand the theory that supports why you should behave in a particular way. I will explain complex issues in the simplest of forms. Transforming the way, you think about situations.

There are diagrams to help illustrate points and many references to other places you can seek help or advice to continue your personal development. The book allows you to acquire skills you can use in many situations throughout life from negotiation, sales, and networking right up to conflict management.

I bring the greatest modern minds, the most relevant research and literature, and a wealth of personal experience altogether to create this modern guide for the modern man.

By the time you are finished reading, you'll have everything you need to be a modern-day Casanova.

Ready?

Then let's begin.

Contents

Getting The Girl

CHAPTER 1
Why the Modern Man is Wrong

"The tragedy of modern man
is not that he knows
less and less about the meaning of his own
life, but that it bothers him
less and less"

Vaclav Havel

Chapter 1 – Why the Modern Man Is Wrong

The modern man according to the mainstream media is many things; sensitive, empathetic, understanding, and above all else anti-toxic masculinity. The problem lies in this is not a man, this is a narrow view of a small subsect of "third-wave feminism" that wishes to impose their meaning of manhood onto the opposite gender. The worse of this being that many don't even like men so why on earth would you want to appeal to them?

Toxic masculinity was introduced to us by Shepherd Bliss, the Mythopoetic Men's Movement activist who was active within the 1980s in his mission for men to become more in touch with themselves pre-industrial revolution. Since then the term has made the rounds on social media, as flocks of scorned women tweet and post until their heart's content as they feel wronged by a former lover.

Just as another famous phrase the line from William Congreve's 1697 poem The Mourning Bride **"Hell hath no fury like a woman scorned"** is a paraphrase (although many would argue accurately) so too has toxic masculinity been twisted and formed to suit a meaning with which to bludgeon all men that behave in a way which does not resemble the level of worship they think they deserve according to their favourite Instagram account.

The prevailing question from this however is – "Why are women so attracted to it?"

This my friend I can explain.

Buckle up. Take a deep breath.

We are about to take a deep dive into the truth.

Contrary to popular belief we are not too dissimilar from our prehistoric ancestors. In fact, our internal hardwiring is almost the same. We share the same two innate fears now as we always have: the fear of falling and the fear of loud sounds. The fear of falling is an instinct necessary for the survival of many species. The fear of loud sounds triggers what's called your Acoustic Startle Reflex, this is the phenomenon where you duck down and cover your head.

Such internal hardwiring is necessary to our survival and eventual replication. It however isn't the only one and men and women have different needs.

Women are blessed with a purpose in life since the day they were born. They naturally possess something no man ever has or ever will. The ability to reproduce. Women are therefore born with **replication value**.

Men this purposeless creature spend an aeon attempting to figure out what they are useful for and their meaning whilst on this earth. Since the pre-historic times, men however brought with them one unique trait that made them worth keeping around. That is their ability to help themselves and others survive. Men, therefore, have **survival value**.

It makes sense then that each gender seeks to help balance its inadequacies. Women, historically, sought survival value in men. Men seek replication value in women.

Women used to need men.

Men still need women.

Here we see the power imbalance. As modern technology and the changing of the industry have meant that women have broken free of the "shackles of marriage" and can now work, feed, clothe and survive pretty well all by themselves, many men have felt lost.

But fear not, all is not lost. Women still seek survival value in men just as you seek replication value in women. They however are no longer so desperate in their pursuit nor so urgent is their need. It is however hardwired into them to seek such value and we will describe how we look for this value next.

When men see replication value in a woman this trip their **Attraction Switches** just as when a woman sees survival value in a man it trips hers.

Replication value in women is easily presented. Men naturally seek an array of things that point to a woman having high replication value. The following are indicators of health. They suggest that a woman will be more successful in giving birth and producing healthy children with which a man can continue his genetic pool. After all, he cannot do it himself so he must seek a mate that can help.

Long hair is a definer of health, it shows to a man that a woman is healthy and will probably survive childbirth. Have you never seen tangled? Long hair has throughout history been drawn, sculptured, and painted to indicate beauty on a woman. Not attracted to women with long hair. Fine, the global hair wigs and extension market is expected to grow at over 8% during the period 2018-2024 this means the global hair extension market is expected to reach over $5 billion by 2024. Do you think women would be spending so much money if they thought it lowered their chances to attract guys?

Facial Symmetry is another one of the Male Attraction Switches. Since the publication of "Facial Symmetry and The Perception of Beauty" in 1998, we have long known that both genders find someone with a more symmetrical face more aesthetically pleasing. Here again, women are way ahead of men on knowing how to use this to their advantage. Even before the rise in aesthetic procedures, since Egyptian times, women have managed to manipulate their faces to drive men wild. Enter here – Makeup.

If you thought the hair extension market was surprising, then wait until you get a load of this. In 2024, the global make-up market is estimated to be worth about 85 billion U.S. dollars. Even today be the most recent census in 2016 the U.S. cosmetic industry is projected to generate revenues of more than 60 billion U.S. dollars and employ about 63,816 people as of 2016.

The rise of YouTube and Tik Tok has allowed women to share skills, talents, and tutorials to enable even the most amateur of appliers to contour their face so well that they can resemble almost anything they so wish.

Many a man has been lured in by an artisan's talents at makeup only to find out the next morning with a hangover they look utterly different. Is it wrong? Of course not, they are only flicking your attraction switches because they know exactly how to do it. Don't fret soon you'll know how to flick theirs.

Another attraction switch that signals replications value in a woman is childbearing hips. Now hang on before I hear you screaming "I have never once looked at a woman and thought what lovely childbearing hips!". This is almost certainly true.

And if you did frankly, I would be worried. However, we have spoken about how this is hard-wired into your brain. It's in the subconscious and it manifests itself very simple. Your attraction switch for childbearing hips presents itself as your admiration for a *nice booty*.

That's right, men like women with nice butts. Those things right around where your hips are. Who'd of thought it! Crazy isn't it.

Now I know what you're thinking, Jack this is great, but I ALREADY KNOW what I am attracted to, I want to know what flicks women's attraction switches. Patience we will get there, but it is vital to understand your enemy (I jest). To properly stimulate her attraction switches you must first see how she does it to you.

The final and perhaps the most well-known of these attraction switches are often staring us in the face. Right below women's noses. I am of course referring to men's fascination with breasts. Now Freud would give us some disturbing rant on why men love boobs very much, and he may be right, or he may be wrong.

One thing we do know is that men do not naturally have boobs. Unless they are very overweight. Even then they are not the same as those wonderfully formed objects on a female's chest. The opposite sex is of course aware of the mystic powers that boobs have over men and have done many things over the years to take full advantage of the spell they can cast. Unbuttoned tops push up bras, breast implants, and the newest of trends the under-boob top.

All of this alludes to maximise the power these assets have over men.

Hardwired speaking there could be two distinct reasons why men love breasts. One, simply, we don't have them. We want what we don't have. Women have breasts and Men in their infinite jealousy want to enjoy them as well.

Another and perhaps more plausible theory is that in the relationship between the breast nurturing children. Men seeing larger breasts as being able to nourish offspring. This goes back to men seeking replication value in a woman as they cannot do this themselves. The main job of breasts, of course, is to feed offspring. Some researchers think that sexual interest in breasts simply hijacks the breastfeeding circuitry and uses it for another purpose.

I am not alone in this. Dr. Larry Young of Emory University who is a professor in the field of psychology has written on the neurological basis of complex social behaviours. In doing so he believes that human evolution has harnessed an ancient neural circuit that originally evolved to strengthen the mother-infant bond during breastfeeding. This has now been hijacked to strengthen the bond between couples as well. The result? Men, like babies, love breasts.

In fact, a quick google search will bring up a multitude of journal articles on the studies of men's fascination with breasts. Something for some late-night reading. One interesting study however is on how breasts as a symbol of fertility may be almost right. A 2004 study in the Proceedings of the Royal Society B even found that women with large breasts have higher levels of the hormone estradiol mid-cycle, which could increase fertility. Maybe there is a method in the madness and our ancestors had more to them than a mildly strange obsession with two fat deposits on a female's chest.

We will come back to this later when we compare men and female attraction switches. Hint men are very visual. Women are not.

Females as stated before do not seek replication value in a man as they have no need. They can replicate fine all by themselves (with a donor). They instead seek survival value in men. Now cast your minds back to life in prehistoric times. You are a woman of value and you are seeking a mate, what is your number one aim when finding a mate? Probably to choose one that's going to help you survive and who is going to survive themselves.

Why? Well for starters back then when you became pregnant and probably for the first few years after childbirth, you were extremely vulnerable. You could not hunt and forage for yourself as you needed to look after your offspring. Now I am yet to hunt in general, but I imagine it would be somewhat difficult to track deer, avoid sabretooth tigers and breastfeed all in the same hour. There are of course remarkable women that anthropologists have shown that can carry their young and hunt and forage, but these almost always work together in large groups and are in no way isolated. Often these are part of larger tribes with males in. In these cases, the women hunt because the men are off making war, so society's not devoid of men.

Back to the cave now. You're a woman and you've decided to lay down with a man who you think has got a good chance of keeping you alive. How did you come to this decision? Well, he ticked a few of your **Attraction Switches** of course. Let's explore these now.

Men as we have explored are very simple. The good news is women aren't that much more complicated. You've just got to know what their **Attraction Switches** are.

Women's attraction switches differed from men as they are not looking for men to demonstrate the ability to replicate, after all, we can't. Instead, they are looking to see signs that this particular male that's swooned over the bar after downing his "woo woo jug" from Wetherspoons can survive out there in the real world (note never actually approach a woman like this). So how do they determine this? Well, they are hard-wired to pick up on social cues and notice triggers that turn on that emotional circuitry that's been around since they were deciding whether to let Barney Rubble take them out or not.

So, what kind of things are they looking for? What's going to make their bedrock? Let me explain.

Leader of men – The Alpha Male is a great demonstration of survival value in men. Why? Think back to the early days let's say you're a woman in Mongolia and you've decided now would be a great time to find a mate and have a child. You could mate with the pretty boy with nice eyes, after all, you've noticed him looking at you OR you could go with the tribe leader, you know the one that has 50 men armed to the teeth with curved bows that they can fire off horseback and kill a man (especially pretty boys with nice eyes) from 200 yards. Which one is going to have the best chance of surviving? You guessed it pretty boy is fucked.

Women are selective over who they decide to breed with and so they should be. Nothing harms a woman and her offspring's chances of survival than laying down with the village idiot who's going to get bludgeoned on a Friday night for saying something he shouldn't. Then she's left with a small child and got to fend for herself again. Nope. No Thanks. Much better to wait until a suitable mate presents himself.

Getting The Girl

So how does a woman determine who is an alpha male, a man of value, a leader of men? The answer – she doesn't have to.

You see women are geniuses in this regard, they don't even bother to do so. Like every good woman, they just let men do the work. That's right. They let men sort themselves out into their hierarchies and then choose from there.

Brilliant isn't it.

Men have hierarchies everywhere: Grand Chess master, Captain of the football team, Hardest lad on the estate, UK Fortnite champion. You name it. If it can be ranked, then men will almost certainly rank themselves and they'll be sure to let others know where they rank.

So, all women need to do is just wait for males to organise themselves and then select from the top. Simple, yet highly effective.

The research supports this Dr. Jordan Peterson the renowned clinical psychologist has presented the findings on this at length.

There is a much higher probability that a man at the top of a dominance hierarchy will reproduce and pass on his genes. The idea of the successful male is therefore encapsulated in biology. The species in this case humans win and pass on their genes. So, then males begin to adapt to this selection process.

An example most commonly found in the UK. Footballers. There is an obsession with footballers amongst the working class especially. They are how to break free and become rich. They are valued highly by males for their exceptional talents. They are valued highly by females because males hold them highly and they are handsomely rewarded for their talents.

The hierarchy is not created by females but by men themselves. All the women do is wait until the best ones emerge then say – yeah, he's alright.

In school, we have an example of hierarchies in all areas from drama, sport, intellectuals. Hierarchies sort themselves from which women pick men. Whether you the Captain of the Debate team your every day Steven Fry or you're the Fresh

Prince of Bel-Air the coolest in the cafeteria women will always gravitate to the top of the chain.

Now, this doesn't mean you need to start learning chess and learn the floss but what it does mean is that through competence comes success.

Hierarchies are found in all aspects of life from work to play. The best thing is studies of hierarchies show us that being at the top releases extra serotonin which makes you feel better. Feeling happier is going to naturally make you more attractive as well as giving you the confidence to approach women in the first place.

Now I know what you are thinking. Excellent theory Jack but how can I use this to trigger a woman's attraction switch as I am not an Olympic-level athlete nor am I a world champion poker star. Well, the good news is you don't have to be.

The attraction switch for being a leader of men or an alpha male does have a low bar. There are many ways you can show you can be a leader and it doesn't have to be complicated. It is the act of being decisive and people listening and following that can stimulate the attraction switch.

An example could be being the person who organises things. If you have a talent for being good at organising, then overseeing a club can show leadership qualities. All you are doing is showing that people can listen to you because you have something worth saying.

There are numerous examples of job roles where people display authority all the time that women gravitate towards: fireman, policeman, doctor, bouncer (well who doesn't want to see someone able to make a man change his shoes to get in). These are situations where they get listened to. Women see other guys listening and decided -well they must be worth listening to.

There are numerous ways you can use this to your advantage and we will explore these later in the book but for now:

- Asking fellow men to do something for you and having compliance
- Running clubs, committees, companies, being in a position of authority at work

- Being above average in any given field – competent people get listened to – being a great mechanic means you'll always have people begging for your advice

- Having a social group with which to do activities
- Being someone, people come to for advice
- Having a talent in a sport or discipline of any kind – especially those with rankings. karate, basketball, rugby

So, we have explored one Attraction Switch in women. That being that showing you're an alpha male or a person which other men value will, in turn, make you more valuable to women. Wow, controversial stuff aye. Probably not but understanding the theory behind it may help you in the way in which you interact in the world and it will almost certainly help with the later chapters.

Remember if this doesn't apply to you right now then great! We know one area we can immediately work on. Maybe we need to try and join a few new clubs or target promotion at work. It may be finding a new friendship group that values you or it may simply be learning something people find valuable to come and find you for advice. All of this is in your hands.

The best thing about all the Survival Value Switches is that they are in your control.

You'll probably never see this on a girl's Instagram quotes, but you'll almost certainly see it in the pictures of the guys they date. Remember as the phrase goes: people vote with their feet.

Meaning what they say they want and what they go through with is vastly different.

Now onto Attraction Switch number 2.

Protector of Loved Ones. If SHE aligns with him, she too will be and feel protected. This one is much simpler to understand. If he already protects those, he cares about then what is he going to do with you? Exactly. DING DING. Her ovaries will begin to glow like sonic rings boy.

There is an easy way to do this and it doesn't involve carrying around a sword to show you are a stringent follower of the chivalric code. Simply talk about situations in which you have stuck up for someone you care about and almost certainly do not bad mouth others, especially friends.

This gives them an example of how you will behave about them when they are not around. Are you going to have their back and talk about how good a person they are or are you going to reveal all their secrets and flaws when you argue?

Think carefully about how you behave as you are demonstrating to others if your actions match your words.

There are lots of examples of how you can do this:

- Do you have a pet that you look after? Well, guess what you can protect something you love. If you've never seen a woman talk about her love for puppies, then you must be from the Chinese food market kid. The best thing is you don't even have to own a pet you may just have one you treat well. People that are mean to animals are normally mean people. Don't be that guy

- Have family? treat them well. I know this can be hard if they don't do the same, but do you stoop to their level or rise above. As always cut off people that make your life a misery but if you can have a good relationship with your family then you are showing that you know how family structures work

- Have any friends? Get some. There are people out there always willing to make new friends from all walks of life. A friend can be a great way for someone to share time with and show you care. The best thing is you can choose your friends, unlike your family. Showing you care about your friends stimulates those attraction switches.

- Defend a maiden's honour by defeating a troll under a bridge. I know what you're thinking, he's lost it. Not quite. Defending others, especially those that can't defend themselves triggers the same response as defending a loved one. It shows your prepared to put yourself in potential harm's way to protect others. Now I am not saying become a masked vigilante and call yourself JACKMAN running around attempting to attract women by taking bullets and stopping muggings. What I am saying is that if you see a situation perhaps at work that doesn't sit well with you then speak up. You'll be amazed how many relationships start this way.

Like the previous attraction switch, this is again well within your control. You can easily bring this into your life and by doing so you will begin to flick female's attraction switches. Now a word of caution must be uttered you may very well meet your nagging NANCY who says things such as " I don't need you to hold the door open for me" or " I didn't need you to stick up for me" in these situations the response is a cool, calm and collected " I know have a good day ". It is as easy as that. We do not get bogged down with such negativity and showing it doesn't affect us anyone else watching holds us in higher regard.

If you are following the pattern you are noticing that very little about how we look is playing a role in ticking females attraction switches, that's not to say it doesn't play a role it does. It just isn't as important as we give it weight to in our minds. You have no doubt often seen couples and thought how on earth has he done that? Well he probably knew just what switches to tick or he probably bought this book **Successful Risk-taker. The operant is successful.** This one can display itself in many ways and we aren't just talking about the man's ability to get red on the roulette wheel right. Wealth is often a demonstration of someone who has successfully taken risks. After all, money is just a way of keeping the score. Now me telling you that someone who is very rich has wider access to women is nothing ground-breaking, but have you ever considered how successful the same person would be if the value of the money suddenly plummeted? Probably not but I think you would agree they would have far fewer options as they become a "less successful risk-taker".

Risks can be many things:

- Completing university
- Completing an apprenticeship
- Starting your own business
- Going self-employed

- Quitting school to become a successful YouTuber, boxer, and music star (HELLO KSI)

All of which involves leveraging your bets and trying to improve your circumstances. Being successful is attractive. This is universally known, and it happens across a wide range of areas.

SO, JACK WHAT YOUR SAYING IS I SHOULD START LIVING A RISKIER LIFE!? Absolutely not.

What I am saying is if you can demonstrate you can take calculated risks and get rewards then you will demonstrate you understand the patterns for success.

We see often how this switch gets **turned OFF.** A guy loses his job – dumped. A guy loses his house – dumped. A guy loses his car – dumped. Now, this isn't because women are materialistic per se (some are) but it shows that the man has taken a risk and it hasn't paid off. Is this the type of person she wants to spend her life with? Can she entrust the running of a family to him?

Now many women will look beyond this and try to help pick a man up. This is known as the saviour complex. How many times have you heard "I can change him"? You probably can't Hun, but you'll die trying.

However just because this works for some very small section of men it does not mean it is how you should live your life. Remember a better you, attract a better next. So, as we improve ourselves, we open more doors. Now that is attractive.

Alas, we come to the final and most powerful of all attraction switches. I have left this one to the end as it is the kryptonite to Superman. It has been known to do things to women that orange soda did to Kel. It has the power to turn just about any boring genius, billionaire, philanthropist into IRON MAN (who doesn't want to be an Avenger). So, Jack what Is it?

Well ...

****

Preselection is the most powerful of all attraction switches. This is the one thigs that can send a flock of women into a feeding frenzy so what do I mean when I say it? Let me explain.

Just as we read that men have Dominance Hierarchies then so do women. Put simply if a woman higher up the food chain than herself finds you attractive then you instantly become way more attractive. In fact, if any woman finds you attractive then you become more attractive once this fact is known.

This is because it taps into our primordial fears of a scarcity of resources and good males to mate with being one of them. This is the good old FEAR OF MISSING OUT or FOMO for short.

In economic terms, scarcity is defined as – Resource scarcity occurs when **demand** for a natural resource is greater than the available **supply** – leading to a decline in the stock of available resources. This can lead to **unsustainable growth** and a **rise in inequality** as prices rise to make the resource less affordable for those who are least well-off.

In this case, the price rise is your value. When lots of people want you then your value increases. Simple.

This known truth is played out time and time again when celebrities cause fans to faint and collapse or when we see girls in a nightclub look over to the guy who is already surrounded by girls.

They think – well he must have value otherwise all these girls wouldn't be spending time with him.

Now there is magic in this. Women like us all have a lovely envious streak and a competitive edge. If they think you're a prize up for grabs my god they will go after you. Here lies the power in flipping the dynamic, no longer are you the hunter you are the hunted. As a valuable commodity watch as more women take an interest in you.

This **Snowball Effect** works wonders once you begin to have success with women. Success breeds success. Women will notice you spending time with lots of women, beautiful women especially, and think – there must be something about him.

Kezia Noble put it well in her blog

" When a woman walks into a bar on her own, whether she is beautiful or average looking, men will notice her. They will look up from whatever they are doing and look her over with a sense of interest. Why? Because she seems available. She's not with a guy, and the fact the guys in the bar have an option of talking to her and possibly sleeping with her, automatically heightens her level of attractiveness. As soon as a guy joins her, (a date, or a guy she has been waiting for) her level of attractiveness drops immediately, and the men in the venue lose almost instant interest and continue to go on with their evening without giving her a second thought.

Yet, with women, the opposite effect happens in these situations.

When a man walks into a bar on his own, women barely give him a second glance, even if he's good looking, but as soon as a beautiful woman joins him or even better, 2 beautiful women join him, he instantly becomes much more attractive, and his presence enters our radars.

Why?

When a man has noticeable female attention and is in the company of beautiful women, we automatically believe he is an 'in demand' man with high standards and high value. To add to this, we also find ourselves psychologically comparing ourselves with those very same women. We think of things such as *"what does she have that I don't have?"* This is a direct result of the illusion that the guy has created of being a man with high value and a man who he is in demand. Or in other words, A MAN WHO DEMONSTRATES PRE-SELECTION."

Now a word of caution – THIS DOES NOT APPLY TO GUYS IN THE FRIENDZONE –

Getting The Girl

This is an important point and the reason It is the next chapter. This is the place that Mufasa warned you of. The place where all hope of hitting the Jackpot fade quicker than your suntan on the plane ride home.

Back to preselection now. In our Influencer dominated world, we see how groupthink works in action, when someone speaks about a product or service and it comes from someone you value you instantly hold the product being marketed in higher regard. The same applies to men.

Pre-selection has been observed among many species of the animal kingdom and is an agreed-upon fact. An experiment by a biologist on pre-selection was conducted amongst birds. Whereas birds have long been reported to mate based upon tail length, colour, and symmetry this can often be disguised through hiding in long or tall grass. One thing that cannot be faked (other than in this experiment) is the interest of other females.

The experiment was simple; place a female-looking bird doll next to the male bird's nest and see what happens. Yep, you guessed it. He got way more attention and therefore mated more than those without a doll.

Now before you start placing an order for a fake girlfriend from Ann Summers you must remember that humans can easily distinguish between the fake and the real. If a girl is looking over at a bar for example and sees an attractive woman laughing at your jokes and appearing flirtatious then she has every reason to believe it is real.

The natural selection here has it hard-wired in a female's brain to flick that attraction trigger and signal competition for resources when she sees a male with a woman of high value.

Success, therefore, breeds success.

This may seem counter-productive to show women that other women value you, that you spend time with them, or even (depending on your circumstances) that you are dating them, but it does trigger their emotional circuitry.

Now before you think I am saying it is time to become a modern-day Casanova, on the contrary, I am simply stating that if other women aren't interested in you then why should she? You see the point.

So, Jack how do I get women in my life in the first place? How do I use my newfound knowledge of all the attraction switches to approach a woman? Why is the friendzone so bad?

Well lucky for you the answers to the above and more are just waiting in the next few chapters.

I am going to teach you how to put the theory into practice.

So, ready to change your life?

Good. I am delighted you are along for the ride.

To summarise men and women look for different things. These being a person's survival and replication value.

The purpose in life is to **SURVIVE** and **REPLICATE.**

In Ancient times it was widely accepted and for most of our past that men have higher survival value, but lower replication value. Women on the other hand have high replication but lower survival value. Now, this isn't everything. You only need to talk to a guy who can tell you about his friend who is a complete loser and ticks none of the appropriate survival boxes, yet his handsome face gets tons of attraction and he would be right.

The reason is that approximately 70% of a Woman's attraction switches are weighted towards survival value. Approximately 70% of a woman's attraction triggers are based on emotions and long-term characteristics. Men on the opposite hand are attracted to the replication values - the physical. These being fitness and looks, for replication purpose.

These have been written about extensively by Robin Baker in Sperm Wars. Baker details how women are genetically wired to mate with the most physically dominant male for the best genes but marry or stay long term with a male that has the most resources and is emotionally stable to help her raise her children.

I however believe that when Baker talks about being physically dominant this applies more to a survival value. The female seeking an alpha naturally applies in all circumstances and showing physically dominated characteristics do not necessarily refer to being aesthetically pleasing. An example of this would be a professional MMA fighter or a bodybuilder. Both have worked to become physically dominating in different ways and neither of these is genetically gifted.

One thing Baker and I have in common with other well-published journal articles such as " The ecology of human fear: survival optimization and the nervous system (2015)" is that we agree with The War On Nature as Darwin theorised that those unable to survive will not only not pass on their genes but will not be chosen to mate with in the first place. "Natural selection increases fitness by optimizing survival relevant behaviours within a given species' environment" (Mobbs, D 2015).

What I am saying is this. It does not matter if you did not win the genetic lottery. Any excuse you have previously used as to why you could not attract women is now off furlough and firmly in the redundancies pile. Don't think you're the best looking? Great be ugly in a Ferrari with a beautiful woman sat next to you. You were born vertically challenged? Fantastic be short whilst performing a rear choke and dominate in the ring and the bedroom. Decided you look old and bald? Marvellous embrace the baldness gains 3 stone of muscle and strut around like Dwayne The Rock Johnson turning heads wherever you walk.

The point is your ability to attract women is not limited by any predetermined genetic characteristics. **EVERYTHING CAN BE IMPROVED.**

If you've ever played a video game you'll know how difficult it may seem at first but after you understand the game mechanics, how the enemies move, the best moves to use, the quickest way to level up, what side quests to complete it suddenly gets a lot easier right? Yes, that's what I thought. Now guess what you've got one better than all those other guys out there who are wallowing around scared to talk to women, not knowing what to say, how to say it, or even how to approach it. You have me. I am your game guide.

And yes, we may have a few cheat codes along the way ...

R1, R2, L1, R2, ←, ↓, →, ↑, ←, ↓, →, ↑

Getting The Girl

CHAPTER 2
Friends Don't Get Laid

"Being in the friendzone is just like being front row at an awesome concert...except you're deaf"

Chapter 2 – Friends Don't Get Laid – Avoid the Friendzone

Let me guess there is a girl you like, and you thought it would be a great idea to become her friend so that one day she will realise that you are everything she ever wanted?

Boy O Boy are you wrong.

Let me tell you now when you are a girl's friend and I mean this as nicely as possible you are basically her brother.

And guess what?

Girls don't want to sleep with their brothers.

That's right, regardless of all the films you've watched. All those ROM COM's on Netflix. This just isn't the way it works in the real world. The closest you'll get to seeing her naked is when she asks you to tan her back so she can go out on a date with that guy she has been crying over for the last two days.

SO, it's time to give up on it. For now.

We need to go and reinvent ourselves and show that we are a potential mate to mate with not a mate to eat cake with (cake can also be eaten while mating, cream cakes work best).

Let's explore what it means to be in the friendzone and how you got there in the first place. Take a seat I am about to explain what your dad should have told you when he spoke about the birds & the bees. I am about to explain **the 3 stages of courtship** or to use an early 2000's term the pickup.

Erik Von Markovich was the world leader in a sub-sect community known as the PUA community. PUA in this instance stands for Pick-Up-Artist. It was a group started for men that struggled to talk to women and wanted to look at ways to get women into their lives.

He made a huge splash in the early 2000s staring in Neil Strauss's book The Game.

Here it was revealed that he had a methodical approach to the Pick- Up. He defined the three stages as Attraction, Comfort, and Seduction. Now, all that he spoke of will work and if followed will help get women in your life. He has produced a wonderful book on this which you can find online if you so wish. He was also the star of VH1's The Pick-Up Artist where he helped clueless men to talk and be successful with women. You can find it online in the remnants of YouTube no doubt.

However, I feel as if we have moved on a little in the 15 years since it has been written and therefore there will be many changes as I explain to keep things up with the time to ensure we use the Attraction Switches effectively in modern times.

In Erik's day, you met people in person way before the rise of social media, tinder, and bumble. For the record, the best way to meet people is still in person but there are other avenues to attract women which we will discuss later.

So, by my recognition in 2021 THE GAME is as follows:

There are 3 defined stages to courtship that are universally true. These are: **Attraction, Safety, and Closing**

All of these are explained in how you use them in subsequent chapters.

However, for now, let me give an overview.

The purpose of the **Attraction stage** is to build enough attraction that she finds you someone of value and this then allows you to have a conversation or send messages to one another where you get to know each other.

This should then lead to the **Safety stage** this is where she feels comfortable and safe around you in order to build rapport and spend time enjoying one another's company.

Finally, we have the **Closing stage** this is the bit where sexual relations begin and thus is the end of the Courtship Process.

Here things can progress onto a sexual relations stage, a relationship stage, or simply a parting of ways. This is usually decided by mutual agreement by both parties concerned.

A good point to mention is that if you perform both stages 1 and 2 correctly it is not uncommon for a woman herself to initiate stage 3. So, In this instance you relax and go along with her seduction powers.

Now the reason we have gone over this is by knowing this model explains why most guys get stuck in the friendzone.

Men that skip straight to the close

Skipping to the close is absolute amateur hour. Ask any girl who's been there. A guy rocks up with his cheesy lines or even worse "Hey ladies are you having a good night?" We were until you showed up kid. You're not even wearing socks go away.

Nowhere has this been worse than online. The invention of the DM has allowed many men to take absolute liabilities. Whilst we are on the topic let me categorically state sending a **DICK PIC** will only **EVER DECREASE YOUR VALUE**. Stop it. Please.

When you slide in the DMS to express "hey beautiful" what you are doing is telegraphing your interest and worse it's your poor attempt at seduction.
There is a time for seduction in the closing stage I promise but it is not before first building attraction (if she isn't attracted to you she is not going to sleep with you donut) and comfort (if she doesn't feel safe around you it's not happening either).

A common error of the fool is to start at the end it shows a blatant lack of understanding of social cues and a disregard for her comfort levels. Do not do this.

I know what you're going to do now, you are going to tell me about this one time your mate Dave got it in. Dave is the kid who grew up from the Stacy's Mom video. He spent his summers cutting grass and staring through windows until eventually, he burst into her room in all his glory hoping to make his dreams come true. It didn't work. However, Dave hasn't learned any better. He isn't helped that on occasion he has had success with his Hail Mary throw. So, he will happily remind you of the time he was down his local 4 pints of Guinness and sambuca deep before he popped in a Tik Tac and strolled across to the pool table. From there he popped on Mambo no 5 and went over to Sandra who was playing on the fruit bandit. Laden with confidence and knowing no better he said, "oi love fancy coming home for a quickie?" and Sandra (remarkably) said, "yeah alright".

Whereas this may have worked, and it does work on very rare occasions especially if the guy in question is extremely good looking do not make it your only move. This is not a lasting way to make meaningful relationships.

It is the equivalent of learning the shoot button on FIFA and hitting it from everywhere. Yeah, one day you may score a Worldie, but the game is better played and much easier if you actually shoot your shot at a more appropriate time.

So that is what happens when you start at the end but the next two are probably far worse and a lot more common so let's look at those now.

There are two ways you end up in the dreaded **Friendzone.**

One is where you are just seen as a friend straight off the bat. This is where you start at stage 2 – safety and try to move to stage 3 -closing. However, the problem is she is just not attracted to you. This is the good old:

"Hi, my name is Sam ..."

Do one Sam. Why would a woman who isn't attracted to you, care who you are, unless she must?

Getting The Girl

Here you must understand that women and attractive women especially, get hit on daily so they must develop a mechanism for weeding out these weak men or they would forever be stuck in a cycle of being " nice" to every guy that strikes up a conversation.

A woman will have her pre-determined excuses already lined up:

- I have a boyfriend
- I am waiting for a friend
- I'm just going toilet wait here (do not wait there she isn't coming back)
- Get lost
- Proceeds to pull out mobile phone

In this situation, you didn't build attraction and your first impression wasn't good enough but don't worry if this sounds like something that has happened to you there is no reason for it to carry on. There are lots of ways to approach women without triggering these responses. Even more, ways to make a better first impression. Once you understand how to build attraction, you'll start at the beginning of the **Courtship Process** just like you should.

Now the second way you end up in the **friendship zone** and most common is when a guy gets stuck after stages 1 and 2. He can't close the deal and eventually, he becomes a friend. Sound familiar? I bet.

This can only happen when you fail to demonstrate to a woman that you are a potential romantic interest. You played it too safe and didn't escalate anything. No holding hands, no flirty chats, no playfulness that borders on sexual tension. Nothing. Zilch.

She then grows so comfortable with this that she prefers it to stay this way. Next thing you know you've been relegated down to the Friendship zone and it's not like the good old Premier League where you can drop down to the championship and come back up. Oh no.

This is American franchises. No promotions.

So how do I know if it is heading towards the friendship zone? Simple. She will not give you any **Indicators Of Interest** or **IOI**s for short. Even more precisely within the first 25 minutes. If she is not showing she is interested in you then you probably won't see it.

An indicator of interest and there are many is a way a woman telegraphs she is interested in you sexually. Now one standalone means little but get a few in short succession and you can be sure she is interested. We will cover these in more depth in the chapter on attraction but for now, let me share a few.

- She asks for your name
- She plays with her hair
- When you grab her hands, she doesn't let go
- She laughs at all your remarks especially the funny ones
- She plays with the area behind her ear (this naturally gets hot and flushes due to pheromones)

We can go on but why spoil the surprise. Soon you'll be able to spot all a woman tells and know EXACTLY what she is thinking about you. Even better when you know you've managed to lead her to demonstrate these IOI's due to your mastering of the **Courtship Process.**

So, the next question you've got around the friendzone is inevitable. So, can I get out?

Straight away – no. She has assessed you at this stage and determined you do not possess the required S & R value.

What we need to do in this instance is go away and improve both. You'll come back as a new man and you get a whole new shot.

New job, new car, new style, been to the gym? Any of these may give you another shot on the wheel.

The best one – get a girlfriend. Nothing makes a woman more interested than pre-selection. You were listening in the last chapter, right?

Being in the friendzone can be painful for a guy especially if he has intense feelings for a woman but he needs to realise *"if you always do what you've always done, you'll always get what you've always got."* In other words, you need to make some changes, and this will almost probably mean spending less time with the person whilst you work on yourself. You need for her to see you as more valuable than you currently are and without going away for improvement this is not possible.

An effective strategy is to spend less time with that person if you are already close, date other people and then come back and reassess the situation. By now you are more confident, you are more experienced, and you have new values for her to look at.

Also, you would have read this book, so you'll know everything you need to know.

The phrase goes **Nice Guys Finish Last** and although they may not be exactly true, they certainly don't win.

Am I telling you anything you aren't currently aware of? Let me be very clear girls **DO NOT** like **NICE GUYS**.

A nice guy with an edge? Well, that can just about do but let me explain why women do not like nice guys.

The answer lies in one of the innate differences between men and women. That being their level of agreeableness.

It is a known fact that women score higher on the Five-Factor Model (FFM) traits of Neuroticism and Agreeableness (Costa, Terracciano & McCrae 2001). This happens at all ages amongst the genders (Chapman et al 2007). Now what I am not saying Is that agreeable men do not exist nor am I saying that there are not disagreeable women but by in large women are more agreeable than men.

Now as for the five-factor model of personality it is a hierarchical organization of personality traits in terms of five basic dimensions: Extraversion, Agreeableness, Conscientiousness, Neuroticism, and Openness to Experience. It is widely used by clinical physicians especially in therapy.

Now what do I mean by agreeableness and why is this so important in terms of being a nice guy? Well ...

****

People who are measured as being high on being agreeable are friendly and cooperative.
They are usually more liked and behave altruistically. They are the team players and those that want everyone to get along. They dislike conflict and aggression. Think the "peace-maker".

Now by comparison people who are disagreeable score lower on this dimension of personality. They are less concerned with pleasing other people and making friends. Disagreeable individuals are more suspicious of other people's intentions and likely to promote self-interest. They often show less regard for the needs of others and can focus on achieving their own goals.

If I read, these two descriptions which one would you say is the alpha-male?

Remember we are going back to these attraction switches. Which one is more likely to take calculated risks and protect their loved ones?

Hmm. Your following. Now I am not saying that you should be argumentative for the sake of being argumentative nor should you go around inciting violence. This shows a lack of social awareness and an inability to regulate oneself. Basically, you're a Neanderthal.

Probably not going to survive the ice age pal.

However what I am saying is if you do not stand up for your beliefs, if you are scared of upsetting people for voicing opinions, if you are not prepared to take a leap of faith and become a "yes man" then you will never be considering a leader and therefore will not stimulate this Attraction Switch. At best you become a token woman. Gossiping about others with your passive-aggressive tone. This is not how alpha men behave. They are direct as they want to solve problems. Therefore, in a good male friendship group, someone can slap a mate around the face, look him dead in the eyes and say, *"you're acting like a knobhead stop it".* Problem addressed. Simple.

It is the swiftness in which it is dealt the not worrying to upset someone because the goal is greater than someone's feelings that sets them apart in this regard. Now a gentleman is sensitive to someone's feelings and would not purposefully offend someone. We would address things in a polite way where possible but what he wouldn't do is hold his tongue if he saw something he found unacceptable to then post about it on Snapchat with a caption starting *"can't believe some people ..".*

The good news is as with some of the other 'Big Five' personality factors, our agreeableness levels are fluid throughout our lives, tending to increase as we grow older (Donnelan et al, 2008). We can change and become less of a wallflower and more of a rose. Pretty but with an edge.

Now I can go one further by proving that those nice guys finish near the bottom. Remember how we said people vote with their feet? Their actions always override their words. Well, sometimes there are certain things people don't talk about in public. Especially women. The things they long for. That they desire when it's late at night. I am of course talking about the one way to know what gets a woman going.

That's her porn search history.

Two maverick neuroscientists use the world's largest psychology experiment--the Internet--to study the private activities of millions of men and women around the world, unveiling a revolutionary and shocking new vision of human desire that overturns conventional thinking. The book is called **A Billion Wicked Thoughts: What the Internet Tells Us About Sexual Relationships.**

In which these two google engineers managed to break down exactly what is it that men and women search for. It is no surprise that men searched out images after all we are very visual, we already know this from our attraction switches in chapter one. Now what women search for Is perhaps a surprise to most other than those that have read chapter one of course... knowing that women are not driven by the visual ...what women searched for was literary figures.

Most women of a certain age can talk at length about this harlequin book written before the internet where women would read about romances and so forth. For those of you unsure of a harlequin book it's the dirty ones sold in airports with a cover of a couple on there.

Now the early ones, some 40 years ago hardly had any sex scenes but now we have progressed. Dare I mention 50 shades of grey? The smash-hit novel that leads to a movie.

BDSM is hardly considered vanilla but clearly, something about being tied up in bondage at the complete mercy of a man was doing something. I think that year saw more men learning rope knots than the boy scouts.

Now back to the findings on google. The engineers discovered that women's fantasies could be ranked into a standard literary plot – a well-meaning girl meets a male who's a bit of a monster and somehow, they manage to make it work or overcome the struggles together.

Now let me tell you the top 5 most sought-after males in female porn searches. (make sure you are sat down because this is slightly funny):

- Vampire
- Werewolf
- Billionaire
- Pirate
- Surgeon

Yep, you read that correctly. SO, NO MATTER WHAT THEY TELL YOU, google doesn't lie. But does this really come as a shock to anyone? Think of the impact of the following series: Twilight, Vampire Diaries, 50 Shades Of Grey, True blood, Teenwolf, Buffy the Vampire Slayer, The Order, Being Human, 365 days on Netflix, Pirates of the Caribbean, Greys Anatomy, ER and so many more. We see it staring us in our eyes daily.

The question is why? Why are women fantasising over these characters? Well one of them is that they are at the top of their dominance hierarchies. They have predatory dominance. The Billionaire is more abstract but it's an indicator of high success. On the other hand, there is a desire for aggression.

Tom Hardy is seen as a modern-day sex symbol, it is not a coincidence that most of his roles involve violence. He epitomises the tamed beast. From portraying a British gangster to biting off people's heads as Venom. He is seen as an alpha male with a capacity to reach his goals by any means. He even reads CBeebies stories late at night (protector of loved one's switch).

Gangsters, criminals, fighters, and hitmen are other examples of caged violence that stir up emotions within women. I do not condone any of these behaviours and if you are a current hitman then I hope you appreciate the free publicity I am giving you.

You do not need nor should you become any of those in the previous paragraph, but I am merely highlighting how the use of attraction switches often lends itself to certain professions. We can of course tick these in far better ways of which we will explore.

I also think a werewolf would probably beat a gangster in a fight. So, what's the point in aiming low boys? Ask Professor Lupin it may not be as bad as you think.

Let's not forget the classic Disney – Beauty & The Beast. Women have a natural affinity to want to "Tame".

When chaos manifests itself when things go really wrong who do you think they want to be "protected" by the tame individual or the one who can fight back. To use channelled aggression to protect his loved ones. The aggression is therefore vital and necessary. The female in these romances seduces and tames these creatures to make them more civil. Here we see how a partnership is formed. They are there to help support one another. To both bring something to a relationship.

Here lies your answer to why nice guys finish near the end. It's because they are not seen as useful especially if the female is already nice. What does she need someone who isn't going to challenge her, to support her, to protect her, a goal-getter to drive them forward?

Now I am not saying nice guys can't do this. I am just saying that you won't even get the chance. You won't of ticked enough attraction switches to prove you can.

The good news for you is that you don't need to start applying fake blood, wearing a cape, or stop shaving to make the most of this. What you do need to do is to start embodying some of these traits. The first being developing a backbone. You may find it easy to not argue, to avoid conflict but in the end, you **promote what you permit.**

If you are saying to her that your opinion is never of value, then you are saying you are not a person of value and why would she want to settle with that person?

Use this to know that standing up for yourself is a good thing. It is important that you can show a willingness to face confrontation at times and not worry what others think. Now that is very attractive.

If you find this is not quite you yet, then don't fret. The next chapter is all about the inner game. Developing from the inside out. We are going to work on transforming your mind before we begin on your first impression. After that's done, we will be ready to approach a woman.

Get ready because Professor X is about to dig deep into your mind and turn you from a plain old Jane Grey into a Phoenix. Let's begin.

Getting The Girl

CHAPTER 3
Inner Game - Rebuild Inside Out

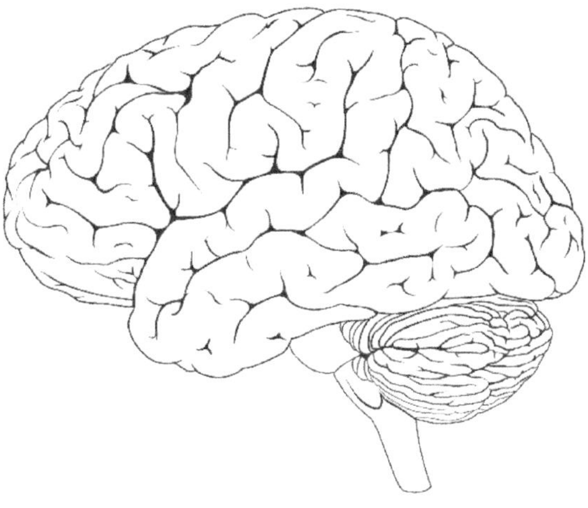

"Whether you think you can or you think you can't, you're probably right"
Henry Ford

Chapter 3 – Inner Game – Rebuild Inside Out

There is a book that has sold over 100 million copies. In which it has the secrets to being successful. It will teach you within 13 steps how to achieve financial fulfillment. I am talking about *Think and Grow Rich by Napoleon Hill.* The book is over 75 years old but has some key ideas that in today's modern society can be extrapolated and applied today. In preparing for the modern world we have given a modern approach to a classic and essential guide for improvement. This section is heavily influenced by the book and chosen deliberately to do so. The key ideas have been taken and transformed for you in the modern age.

Think and Grow Rich is the result of Hill's study of over five hundred self-made millionaires and it all starts in the mind.

This is also where we must start. Within the mind.

The reason for this is because **whether you believe you can or believe you can't then you're probably right.**

YODA – DO OR DO NOT THERE IS NO TRY.

I am going to attempt my best to summarise each chapter as it is invaluable to transforming your mind to understand what you can achieve.

Chapter 1 Faith: Visualization of, and Belief in the Attainment of Desire

Through affirmations or repeated suggestions to the subconscious, you can develop the emotion of faith, which is necessary to transmute your desires into their physical or monetary equivalent.

We use this in The Game by telling ourselves some universal truths.

For starters – **No-one is out of your league**.

I mean it. The league system is a creation of the mind. Mostly created by yourself. You have ranked yourself according to a score. This exists only in your mind and nowhere else.

Let me explain.

Men as we have covered seek replication value more than survival value. Women it's the opposite they seek survival value more than replication value.

Now men can quickly rank women due to their ability to trip their triggers. As we have covered, we know what men look for in women:

- Boobs
- Bum
- Symmetrical face
- Long hair

All of these can quickly be judged at a glance. I also want to introduce another thing that men look for. This is called the hip to waist ratio. The ideal hip to waist ratio for a woman is 0.7. This magic figure is something our subconscious minds can quickly process.

Science has narrowed down the perfect body, and according to one theory, it comes down to this: 1.618. This number represents the Golden Ratio, a thousand-year-old theory that goes back to the ancient Greeks.

Now as for the Hip to Waist Ratio it is usually defined as 0.7 for the ideal waist-hip ratio (WHR). Let me list all of the know celebrities with this golden number:

- Jessica Alba
- Kelly Brook
- Katy Perry
- Rita Ora
- Kate Moss
- Helen Mirren
- Kim Kardashian
- Scarlett Johansson
- Salma Hayek
- And finally, Marylin Monroe

As we can see such a figure is universally appealing throughout the ages. There are many more celebrities that fit this bill that if I began to list them all I fear I would get so lost in my imagination I may never finish the book.

The point is as a guy you can immediately judge someone's attractiveness as you can assess whether they tick your attraction switches.

A woman cannot do this.

Therefore, where you sit on her RANKING system is not easy to distinguish. Basically, you still in with a shot kid cause there's no way she can judge whether you are:

- A leader of men
- Protector of loved ones
- Pre-selected (unless you're with a woman)
- Successful risk taker (although how you dress may, and we will cover that in the next chapter)

So do not panic. Although you have ranked her, she probably hasn't ranked you.

This is where visualisation and belief come into play. First, you've got to believe you deserve to be with a woman. Cause why not? You have a lot to give. You are a wonderful person; she just hasn't had to opportunity to meet you yet! How unlucky is she! But fear not, because you're such a great guy, you **are going to allow the opportunity to meet women to happen**. In your mind, you are going to visualise yourself talking to a woman. Now when you talk, she is enjoying your time. In fact, she wouldn't want to be anywhere else other than right here. She had no idea you were so interesting! You are like nobody she has ever met before.

I want you to pause and hold this image in your mind. You in a freeze frame with a woman (not one you know) in mid-conversation. You may be at a bar, a beach, a swimming pool or just the supermarket. You see her smiling, playing with her hair, and laughing at you. Her eyes are warm, she is making lots of eye contact. You have relaxed your shoulders are down and back there is an air of confidence and calmness from you.

Freeze just here.

Now we need to save this emotional state you are currently in. This is the state we want you to be able to enter at will. Soon your body will naturally slip into this and it will feel as comfortable as your favourite coat. Until then, we will produce a trigger for your subconscious mind to take you to this confident and calm state.

Triggers are used for buyers as sales techniques all the time. It is when somebody screams *"I want one!"* throws their hands in the air and it causes a Mexican wave of buys.

Our trigger is much simpler we are going to tap into the body's natural endorphin release. The famous outward V pose.

This is the pose you have seen expressed by a cyclist, runners, sprinters, tennis players, and so forth right after the victory. It is where they put both arms into the air in a wide V shape.

Research of Olympic athletes has proven that raising our arms overhead is hard-wired in our DNA. Raising the arms embodies a gold medal performance while slumping the shoulders in defeat is also a natural response to loss. In a study of athletes who were blind from birth, researchers found they too exhibited these responses to wins & losses.

Some nonhuman primates use the exact same posture. This animal display seems related to the position in a group – Remember we spoke about alpha males? Anecdotal evidence suggests the alpha male gorilla in a group will raise its arms in a gesture to make itself look bigger. The expanded posture and outstretched arms associated with pride may have originated as a way of appearing larger, allowing for the assertion of dominance, and attracting attention.

What I am saying is this gesture is already hardwired into your genetic makeup to perform when you win. So, let us hack the system. You are going to close your eyes, imagine the scenario and raise your arms wide in the air as you have just won a race. Perfect. Hold this.

What we are doing is programming your mind and body to believe you are already a winner. You are already successful with women as your mind thinks you have been successful previous.

Congratulations we now have fixed in our toolset a gesture and visualisation to get us into the required state to talk to women.

For lots of guys, the mere thought of talking to women is nerve-wracking and if we focus our negative energy on this, we give it life and it becomes a self-fulfilling prophecy.

In order to avoid this, we only focus on the positive and being successful.

This mind tip will work in all areas of life. We visualise then we make it real.

We combine visualisation with the power of Auto-suggestion.

Auto-suggestion: The Medium for Influencing the Subconscious Mind

Eddie the Eagle knew the power of influencing the subconscious mind when he willed himself to the Winter Olympics since being a boy. By his admission and that of many professional Ski Jumpers, Eddie was not the most talented, but my god did he believe in himself. He believed in his heart of hearts and won a nations heart by his appearance.

You do not have to be the best to believe in yourself. If you want to saw like an eagle you must first believe you can fly.

Auto-suggestion refers to the use of self-directed communication and self-administered stimuli to channel thoughts from the conscious mind to the seat of the subconscious. Because the conscious mind often acts as a barrier to sensory impressions, auto-suggestion must be used to create thought patterns conducive to translating your desires into their physical equivalent.

By putting together the visualisation with the following affirmation we seek to change the way our brain works.

Repeat the following affirmation once a day for an extra boost.

" No Woman Is out of my league , there are so many women out there that haven't been lucky enough to talk to me yet, but I will give them the chance to meet me , I deserve to have women in my life because I am a great person. Today someone may be lucky enough to meet me"

You must have every faith in yourself and your ability to be successful. I have every faith in you.

The reason it may not have worked so far is because you didn't believe and you didn't have the correct skills to approach, maintain conversation and move things forward. I can teach you all the later but you're going to have to help me with the former. The next chapter Hill speaks of is self-explanatory.

Specialized Knowledge: Personal Experiences or Observations

General knowledge, or that typically taught in schools, will not help you accumulate riches, nor will specialized knowledge on its own. Rather, you must learn how to organize and use knowledge after you acquire it. If you lack the specialized knowledge necessary to build your business or attain your goals, you can supplement your own knowledge with that of other individuals by forming a "Master Mind" group.

Luckily, you possessed one fantastic observation or specialised knowledge. You either observed you are shit with women or at least need improvement or you had the specialised knowledge to use amazon and order this bloody book.

As in the next chapters, I will give you the specialised knowledge based upon my personal experiences, my observations, and those of many other men out there that have been successful with women. I will tell you what things to say, how to say them, and when to say them. If you follow my advice the only regret, you'll have is that you didn't have this book when you were younger.

See it is not just knowing the knowledge but putting it into practice and bringing it all together where the true success lies. I have spent my time bringing together the information into one place for you with signposts for you to find additional information if you so wish.

It is not just obtaining the knowledge but putting it into practice that will lead us on our path to glory, my friends!

Imagination: The Workshop of the Mind

The imagination is the unique faculty of humankind that shapes, forms, and gives action to desire. Hill distinguishes between two modes by which the imagination functions: the *synthetic imagination*, which does not create but rather arranges old concepts, ideas, or plans into new combinations; and the *creative imagination*, which, when stimulated by strong desire, picks up thought vibrations from other humans and from the ether, connects with Infinite Intelligence, and develops new ideas.

This is how we work in the comfort building stage; we tell stories that demonstrate we are high-value individuals and we share interesting things. It requires a degree of imagination to turn the mundane into a learning experience or a way to convey a message.

What message are you trying to convey in your story: is it humorous, is it that you are a high-value male, is it that you protect the ones you love? What are we trying to get across in our interactions with the opposite sex?

I'll give you a hint it's not – I want to get you naked as quickly as possible.

Being imaginative is one of the wonders of dating, it enables you to try new things to explore new places. A person with an imaginative mind can make even a trip to the supermarket fun. As you explore the world food section of Tesco you speak of what they like to eat, where they want to visit, or even what the differences in cultures are.

You showcase you are a valuable male by making things exciting fun and informative.

Remember, there is a time and a place to get into deep and meaningful discussions, like is it weird that Luke Skywalker kissed his sister in Star Wars? (pretty weird if you ask me) and it is probably not in the cereal aisle. Save such talk for after you have established a connection.

Organized Planning: The Crystallization of Desire into Action

To translate desire into its physical or monetary equivalent, you must form a definite, practical plan and put it into action. This chapter details how to build plans and ensure they are functioning to your advantage.

Plans are the route to success. It is not enough to just think and believe you will be successful when talking to women. To have a definite plan is the way we translate this into reality.

Not all of us are born with God-given apparent talents. Some of us must find talents through hard work or relentless practice.

Let me tell you the story of a man who did just that.

Michael Jordan was born on February 17, 1963, in Brooklyn, New York, one of James and Deloris **Jordan's** five children. Jordan loved sports but failed to make his high school basketball team as a sophomore. He was at this point a failure. Did Jordan announce that he was no good at basketball? That some people were just "naturals"? That he could never be as good as the others? I can hedge a bet you didn't say yes.

No MJ, that glorious specimen, said – Just you wait and see.

He continued to practise and made the team the next year.

From there he went onto win 6 NBA Championships, earned a total of 14 MVP awards, was selected to 14 All-Star games, won 10 scoring titles, and is widely regarded as the best basketball player to ever step foot on the court.

But did you know he had a plan?

From the day he didn't make the basketball team he set the wheels in motion to devise a plan to become the best basketball player he could.

This plan began in Highschool as he worked on his technical ability to make up for his lack of physical stature. At the time he was 5ft 10 which by pro basketball accounts was the equivalent to Bilbo Baggins challenging Hagrid to a dunking contest.

After being selected as the 3rd pick in 1982 he quickly realised that he wasn't like the rest of his team. Whilst they were out drinking and sniffing cocaine in between games he was watching video tapes. Studying his opposition. Improving his craft.

You see it wasn't pure talent that got him where he wanted. It was a definitive plan. He planned his rise to be the best. He wasn't just born as the best basketball player alive he helped himself become it.

You see **improvement often comes before success**.

What few people realise are the hours he spent in the gym weightlifting, plyometrics, conditioning, technical improvement, tactics, teamwork.

Michael spent five years as a pro basketball player before he and his team earned their first championship in 1991.

He went on the achieve a record that is so impressive it is longer than most people's dissertation:

Rookie of the Year; Five-time NBA MVP; Six-time NBA champion; Six-time NBA Finals MVP; Ten-time All-NBA First Team; Nine-time NBA All-Defensive First Team; Defensive Player of the Year; 14-time NBA All-Star; Three-time NBA All-Star MVP; 50th Anniversary All-Time Team; Ten scoring titles — an NBA record and seven consecutive matching Wilt Chamberlain; Retired with the NBA's highest-scoring average of 30.1ppg; Hall of Fame inductee.

How is that for putting a plan into practice?

His greatest achievement was undoubtedly getting to star alongside Bugs Bunny & Daffy Duck as he saved the planet from the MonStars for which we will all be eternally grateful.

Getting The Girl

To this day I hold fond memories for Lola Bunny. My second favourite Rabbit-related animation after Jessica.

So how do we plan?

Now before you get flashbacks of GCSE English exam prep, the best thing about writing these plans is that can be as big or as small as you like with no need to remember exactly what was meant by " *"Nay, as they dare. I will bite my thumb at them, which is a disgrace to them if they bear it.* *bites his thumb" Come on what kind of a book would this be If I didn't quote Romeo & Juliet?

You may now be biting your thumb to me as you read that line and it brought back memories of the time" highlighter" referred to your scripts in class, not lines on a woman's face to make her more aesthetically pleasing.

How we plan is simple, it goes like this:

- The first step to planning is to clearly define your goals. Taking a few minutes to put your goals into writing. We give them life
- A goal must be a SMART goal. Meaning it must be Specific, Measurable, Attainable, Realistic, and have time to complete it. Make sure it ticks all of these.
- An Example – I will finish this book (specific) by the end of the month (measurable and attainable). The goal has a time constraint – a month and is realistic. This is a good goal (although the quicker you finish the quicker you can be attending pool parties with lots of really hot women, right?)
- Once you have defined your goal, it is time to list all the tasks needed to accomplish it. Ordering this and give an estimated time for completion.
- Next, it is useful to define the roles that you will take in fulfilling your goal as well as the roles of any others who will be assisting you. If you're getting fit do you need a PT? Will you be needing anyone's help to achieve your goal?
- Once you have determined your goal, the tasks required, the key players, and the tasks they will complete, it is finally time to start your scheduling. When scheduling it is important to plan a weekly schedule as well as a daily schedule. The weekly schedule is important for the overall success of the project, but it is the daily planning that will help you to track your progress and determine whether you are on schedule. You may set a daily task to

build confidence by saying hello to one stranger a day (although don't accept sweets or get into anyone's car).

- As the work starts, continually evaluate your performance to determine whether you are on track or need to adjust your schedule. This is where daily planning becomes so important.

- Finally, once you have successfully completed your task, review your planning process to determine how successful it was. This will help you by illustrating whether you have achieved an optimal planning process. This will help with future planning.

The use of plans makes life more manageable as we break it down into chunks. Using milestones helps you focus. Planning helps to make your dreams more attainable. Once a realistic plan is in place, you will be amazed at how achievable your dreams really can be.

Pinky: *"Gee **Brain**, what are we gonna do tonight?"* ***Brain***: *"The same thing we do every night, try to take over the world!*

Having a sense of purpose can go a long way to making you happier. A plan can help you establish your purpose. Once your plan is in place and you start putting it into action, you will no longer just "exist", you will instead "live purposefully." The rules for this can be used in all areas of your life from fitness goals to meeting women. Once you become good at regularly making plans and sticking to them you know that you are capable of achieving whatever you set your mind to.

A plan will make it easier to say "no" to things that are not as important to you. In other words, if an opportunity is not aligned with your plan, then it's not worth your time right now and you can feel free to say "no" to it without any hesitation.

"People think focus means saying yes to the thing you've got to focus on. But that's not what it means at all. It means saying no to the hundred other good ideas that there are. You have to pick carefully. I'm actually as proud of the things we haven't done as the things I have done. Innovation is saying no to 1,000 things."

Steve Jobs

A planned life will give you a sense of peace. You will no longer have to worry about whether you are making the correct decisions. Inner peace comes from knowing you are in control and have your shit together. Most of us hate chaos, being late makes us fret and anxious. Not having a sense of direction is a huge millennial problem we will later discuss but for now, know that having a plan helps ease this burden.

"Peace is a daily, a weekly, a monthly process, gradually changing opinions, slowly eroding old barriers, quietly building new structures."

John F. Kennedy

Having a plan will make you feel more powerful. It not only permits you to live your life according to how you want, but it also gives you the tools to do it.

"When one door of happiness closes, another opens, but often we look so long at the closed door that we do not see the one that has been opened for us."

Helen Keller

Finally, having a plan ensures that you will have no regrets when you get to the end. Because you have made the effort to plan your life to achieve the goals that you want to achieve, so long as you stick to your plan you can be confident that you will not be looking back.

"Accept everything about yourself – I mean everything, you are you and that is the beginning and the end – no apologies, no regrets."

Henry A. Kissinger

****

Decision: The Mastery of Procrastination

Procrastination and indecisiveness are major causes of failure. Men and women of great wealth, on the other hand, share the ability to reach decisions quickly and change their minds slowly. This chapter teaches you how *not* to be swayed by the opinions of others but instead to keep your own counsel (and that of your Master Mind group) so that you make firm, productive decisions that ensure your success.

This can be avoided by planning. Planning your life gives you control. If you create a plan then you get to make choices and decisions, rather than leaving things up to chance, or worse yet, letting others make decisions for you.

To avoid procrastination, it is important to identify and focus on your priorities when you create a plan because we all have multiple responsibilities and priorities in our lives.

I can make you one promise in life. You will not meet the girl of your dreams binging Netflix series.

AND as much as I like to watch those men make swimming pools out of sticks in the jungle clicking related video after related video on YouTube, it won't replace good quality sleep.

Stop the late nights. Go to bed son. It's the quickest way to meet the woman of your dreams.

Persistence: The Sustained Effort Necessary to Induce Faith

Most people will throw in the towel at the first sign of opposition. However, willpower, combined with desire, is necessary to ensure that one's objectives are reached. Hill provides four steps for cultivating the habit of persistence, your insurance against failure.

Quitters don't win and winners don't quit.

Nobody embodies this spirit more than Tom Brady. Tom Brady is widely regarded as the best quarterback to have ever lived.

However, it wasn't always that way. He wasn't even the starting QB in college, but he didn't let such a minor detail get him down. Brady played back up for two years before battling Drew Henson to become the no1.

Brady's life was one of numerous constant setbacks. He wasn't deemed better than Drew and yet he never gave up. He persisted. He became the team captain and the starter, but his struggles weren't over yet.

In America, they have a chance to impress professional clubs after college by attending something known as a combine. It's basically where players run a series of drills and skills to showcase their talents to scouts.

Getting The Girl

So, what did they have to say about Tom Brady?

Well:

-Poor build
--Skinny
--Lacks great physical stature and strength
--Lacks mobility and ability to avoid the rush
--Lacks a really strong arm
--Can't drive the ball downfield
--Does not throw a really tight spiral
--System-type player who can get exposed if forced to ad-lib
--Gets knocked down easily

Hardly a boy wonder.

When he went to the NFL draft, he was drafted with pick 199. Incredibly low. With 6 other QB's chosen before him. Brady was so embarrassed that he briefly left the family home during the sixth round and cried when recalling the experience for an interview 11 years later. Brady later said that when the Patriots notified him that he would be drafted, he was grateful he would not "have to be an insurance salesman".

It is safe to say nobody expected much of Brady as a pro footballer. Boy were they wrong.

Spurred on by wanted to achieve his goals on the first day of practice he walked over to Robert Kraft the owner and told him that he – the rookie 4th choice QB - would make the Patriots a success. Nobody believed him.

Since then Tom Brady has who led his teams to a record seven Super Bowl victories (2002, 2004, 2005, 2015, 2017, 2019, and 2021) and was named the game's Most Valuable Player (MVP) five times (2002, 2004, 2015, 2017, and 2021).

Even after winning 6 Super Bowls with The Patriots when he moved to Tampa Bay, they said he was finished at 42. He couldn't do it without his manager Bill Belichick.

He proved them wrong again. He led the Tampa Bay Buccaneers to the Super Bowl in 2021 and cemented his place as the best QB in the history of the game.

He never gave up.

Neither should you.

The Story of Tom Brady is quite remarkable and if you have time and want to see the man's journey then scan the QR code below I have handily created for you.

There are going to be times that you crash and burn when you talk to women. In fact, there are going to be times in life in general where things do not go right. It is not by these barometers that we measure ourselves but by the number of times we get back up.

As you go out and begin to explore the opportunity to talk to women, there will be some women who do not want to talk to you, it just isn't the right time. This is fine. It isn't personal and even if it was, it isn't a big deal.

We move on.

There are so many more women out there that would be lucky to meet you! Why are we denying them the opportunity by wallowing in self-pity?

We do not, because winners know that failure is only temporary, and success is just around the corner.

Power of the Master Mind: The Driving Force

Individuals work together to prove that the sum is greater than their parts. Through collective effort, you can bring people with different strengths and perspectives to coordinate their knowledge and efforts to attain a goal.

This principle of Hills is easily used when looking to increase your success with women.

Enter – **THE WINGMAN**.

The wingman or woman (a Wing woman is even better) acts as your "master mind". The person you share success and failure stories with. The person who gives you honest advice on where you went wrong and where you can be successful. You both bring your strengths to the equation to increase your probability of getting to the goal (was that two maths puns in the same sentence, I can keep adding these all day).

Having a great wingman can make things much easier but it isn't necessary. You alone have to put in the work to go through the Courtship Phases. Trust me when I say even the best Wingman can't help you seal the deal.

That's where you need to be your own Harvey Spector.

The best damn closer in the city.

The Mystery of Sex Transmutation

Sex transmutation is where you direct your sexual energy into more purposeful things. We know you think with your pants chief, just use that energy productively. A correlative to this principle is the importance of selecting a compatible partner.

We will discuss what makes a good partner in the chapter on relationships and we will also talk about women to avoid in this chapter.

Those toxic people can ruin any man's Inner Game.

Why have we spent all this time building up our minds to be strong and resilient if we are going to let a parasitic beast in to undo all the work from the inside?

Don't worry we won't. I will arm you will the things to look out for so you can spot a T-800 quicker than a German Shepherd or a kid named John Connor.

The Subconscious Mind: The Connecting Link

Hill describes the subconscious mind as the intermediary between the finite mind of man and Infinite Intelligence that enables humans to tap into the forces of the

Universal Mind. He emphasizes that it alone is the medium for translating mental impulses into their spiritual and physical equivalents.

Everything we have spoken about so far is about rewiring our subconscious mind. We are training ourselves to realise what Attraction Switches are being ticked by women. We are teaching ourselves what Attraction Switches we need to tick in women. Soon all the Courtship Process will be internalised, and you won't have to flick through a little book like Inspector Columbo.

Oh, and another thing, when you're doing it without thinking it becomes so much fun! You'll be pulling without even realising.

You see what the mind thinks the body telegraphs. Any woman can tell you about a man she knows is desperately on the prowl to pull, it oozes through their very pores.

The same as how dogs can sense fear, so can a woman when you approach.

That is why we have inner beliefs; this confidence will show in the way in which we talk.

If you don't have it yet, then we live by the rule of:

Fake It Until You Make It

We will tell ourselves we are good with women until we really believe it. Then we will say things with such conviction, the conviction alone will carry weight to our words.

Say it with your chest.

" You can tell by the way I use my walk I'm a woman's man , no time to talk "

Saturday Night Fever – The Bee Gees

The Brain: A Broadcasting and Receiving Station for Thought

Hill writes, "Through the medium of the ether, in a fashion similar to that employed by the radio broadcasting principle, every human brain is capable of picking up vibrations of thought which are being released by other brains." In this chapter, he explains the process by which the mind is stimulated by external vibrations and supplies a method for using emotions to increase the mind's receptivity to these sensory stimuli. I am talking about FUCKING DEMENTORS. Those people that suck the life right out of you.

Ever heard the expression "Mood Hoover"? This refers to those people who are CONSTANTLY DEPRESSING. Avoid these people. Like the plague.

Surround yourself with happy people. The psychological fact goes that you are the sum of the 5 people you spend the most time with.

Hang around with 5 miserable people and you'll be the sixth.

Such a fact is preached in the world-famous Robert Greene's book "The 48 Laws of Power". Robert Greene in his book gives laws from which a person can follow to obtain and keep power. Such a book is incredibly popular in prisons and amongst hip hop stars such as 50 Cent.

50 even went on to write a sequel the 50th law. Both books are a fantastic read and come highly recommended.

Robert in his book in Chapter 10 speaks of this. **Law #10: Infection: Avoid the Unhappy and the Unlucky:**

People who are perpetually miserable spread misery like an infection, and they'll drown you in it. Avoid these people like the plague. Conversely, if you associate with happy people, you'll share in the good fortune they attract and spread. Seek them out. Infection: Avoid the unhappy and the unlucky.

What does it mean to dodge infection, avoiding the unhappy and the unlucky? People who are hurt by circumstances beyond their control deserve sympathy and help. But others bring unhappiness on themselves and spread it to those around them by their destructive acts and influence on others. You can't change or improve them — they will change you by afflicting you with their problems.

People are highly susceptible to the emotions and pathologies of those they spend time with. Chronically miserable and unstable people have the greatest influence because of their intensity. Because they paint themselves as victims, it can take you a while to see that they cause their own problems. By the time you realize this, these infectors have sucked you in. Infection: Avoid the unhappy and the unlucky.

When your goal is power, those you associate with can make or break you. If you associate with infectors, you'll waste time extricating yourself, and others will lose respect for you due to guilt by association.

One of the most damaging types of infectors is the person who is perpetually dissatisfied and aggrieved.

Cassius, who conspired against Caesar, is an example of a miserable person. He couldn't stand anyone more talented and accomplished than him. His dissatisfaction and hatred of Caesar infected Brutus (who likely would have waited to ascend the throne). The result was one of the great tragedies of history.

The only way to fight this type of infection is by removing it, although often that remedy comes too late because, again, you've already been pulled into the person's web.

According to Law 10 of the 48 Laws of Power, the best way to protect yourself is by paying close attention to the people you surround yourself with, so you see any ominous signs. Start by considering their effects on others, rather than on who/what they blame for their problems. Avoid the unhappy and the unlucky.

Watch for these **characteristics of infectors** to avoid the unhappy and the unlucky:

- They bring misery to themselves and others.
- They exude discontent.
- They have tumultuous histories.
- They've left behind a trail of failed relationships.
- They've had unstable careers.
- They have a charisma that overwhelms people, especially their ability to reason.

Whatever you do, don't feel sorry for them — you'll entangle yourself in trying to help. While you're beside yourself with frustration, they'll carry on unchanged. Watch out for infection: Avoid the unhappy and the unlucky

At the other end of the spectrum, **some people attract happiness and spread it. Do everything you can to associate with these people**, so you share in the positive vibes and good fortune they attract.

Happiness and success aren't the only positive qualities you should seek out. Any positive quality of someone else — friendliness, charm, creativity, generosity, etc. — can infect you in a good way.

Although Talleyrand (Napoleon's Minister) was a conniver, he had other traits that made people want to be around him and they rubbed off on others: he was gracious, charming, and witty. Napoleon, who was a rough peasant, recognized this and kept Talleyrand around, hoping to absorb some of his charms.

You can do the same thing: **Strive to associate with people who have traits and qualities you lack.** If you're moody, hang out with cheerful people; if you're cheap, associate with generous people. If you have no luck with women, then hang around with people that do. You will pick up on things they do, the way they say things.

As Leonardo Di Vinci put it "good artists copy, great artists steal".

The Sixth Sense: The Door to the Temple of Wisdom

The Sixth Sense refers to the faculty of the subconscious also termed the Creative Imagination by which humans, through no effort of their own, receive communications from Infinite Intelligence. Hill calls this principle the "apex" of his Law of Success philosophy, for it can be comprehended and applied only after mastering the first twelve principles.

When you have finished the book, you will know all you need, to have women in your life. It is after this stage that you will begin to practice what you know. As you become better your mind will begin to develop your own strategies that will help in your pursuit. The reason being you will see things through your 6th sense and anticipate whether something will be a success. Whether that's a story you tell to show higher value or a joke you are waiting to drop. As you become better in social situations you can begin to see patterns emerge. Ways in which things play out. You can then predict (use your 6th sense) if these will help or hinder you in your life.

Just as a Cristiano Ronaldo can head a football into the goal in the pitch black (watch tested to the limit) as his body can anticipate where it goes based upon years of practice, so too can you begin to see if how your actions may affect before you do it.

Why put your hand in the fire if you know it's going to burn?

How to Outwit the Six Ghosts of Fear

To implement these thirteen success principles, you must prepare your mind to receive the philosophy. The first step to prime your psyche is to study, analyse, and understand the three enemies you'll have to defeat: indecision, doubt, and fear. This chapter outlines and explains the cure to the six basic fears that, although often hidden in the subconscious, hold humans back in their pursuit of riches: the fear of poverty, the fear of criticism, the fear of ill health, the fear of loss of love, the fear of old age and the fear of death.

Fear can be a powerful motivator and sometimes it can be necessary.

This chapter has been long but crucial as we have taken Hill's strategies to transform the mind. There is a reason his book is so popular.

Because it works.

The same methods that can be used to help you get rich can be used to give you an abundance of women in your life.

So far, we have gone over the Laws of Attraction and how to stimulate **Attraction Switches**. We have looked at the **Courtship Stages** and why the friendzone is so bad. Finally, in this chapter, we have looked to work on your **Inner Game** as without this belief in yourself nothing else will matter.

Like an astute canine, a woman can sense a man who has no conviction in what he says a mile off. So unless you want to be chased down the street like a postman that left the garden gate open, I suggest you take working on your mind seriously.

Ask any woman – **Confidence Is Key.**

It is not just for dating you should focus on strengthening the mind. In life, you will have many setbacks that will test you. By developing stronger mental resilience it will help you to cope with the crisis of mental health we seem to be suffering currently. You need coping mechanisms and ways to reset your mind when things get tough. Strength starts within.

Now on the topic of fear, there are some people you need to avoid in your dating life. You haven't spent all this time building up your mind to become undone now. We must mention the types of people to avoid just like the unlucky and the unhappy.

In his book, **The Art of Seduction** Robert Greene talks about the different types of seducers and how they present themselves. I must arm you with the knowledge of these so we can defend from them. In the chapter on relationships, I will explore this type of person and how they present themselves.

These are not the charming seducers that some aspire to be. These are not the Casanovas, the Cleopatras, the Steve McQueen's, the Hugh Heffner's of this world. These are the users.

The Voldemort's.

The Saruman's.

The Jaffar's of this world.

So, in our quest to turn you into a real Prince Aladdin let's not waste any wishes getting you out of a mess you should have never been in.

For now, Aladdin let us move on to the thing you only get one shot at.

That is making a first impression.

Getting The Girl

CHAPTER 4
First Impressions Count - What's yours?

"You never get a second chance to make a first impression"

Chapter 4 - First Impressions Count – What's yours?

"You never get a second chance to make a first impression."

Will Rogers

Well I knew exactly what he was talking about.

7 seconds.

That's it.

You have seven seconds to make a first impression.

The Harvard Study of Communications stated that it takes just seven seconds to make a first impression on another human being. Just *seven* seconds. These first impressions, which can be based upon anything from the shoes you are wearing to the tone of your voice.

Now I asked Gok Wan and the boys from Queer Eye if they were free to help with this chapter, but I am yet to hear back.

Don't worry I've got you.

The science behind it is pretty clear Whitney Johnson, the author of *Disrupt Yourself: Putting the Power of Disruptive Innovation to Work* tells us it straight "We make judgments in a nanosecond." Then once that impression is formed, it's "very, very hard to change it."

So, if we start strong boys we are onto a winner. "You get the benefit of the doubt," says Dorie Clark, the author of *Reinventing You: Define Your Brand, Imagine Your Future*.

Start strong, make a mistake – get forgiven.

Start slow out the blocks and we are playing catch up the whole race.

Be a Bolt, not a Bolton (relegated last year). Unless that's a Troy Bolton. Well, consider this chapter the start of something new.

What is the first thing you are going to get judged on?

How you look. Now don't panic if you weren't blessed like a Greek God remember that a woman's Attraction Switches are about a lot more than that. We can however stop you from looking like Theon Greyjoy.

This is where we are going to start Cinderella, call me your Fairy (very manly fairy) Godmother. Let's start your make-over.

One of the first things we need to talk about is your **hair.** Your hair, like your skin, is something you wear every day. You'd be amazed at the number of guys that have blown themselves out with a woman because they still have the same haircut they had when they were 12.

Now I couldn't possibly tell you the exact haircut to have as I haven't got a clue what you look like. I can tell you it won't have lines and patterns in your head though. Also, avoid the classic no 9 Ronaldo tuff.

I can direct you to the best way to decide and that comes down to your face shape.

We need to first work out your face shape before we can select the right types of haircuts.

I will now give you two ways to work out your face shape. Select the one that is easiest for you. One involves a tape measure (it's the only thing you need to measure to impress the lady's fellas) and the other requires a picture of yourself.

We work out your face shape as follows:

1. **Forehead:** Use a tape or a ruler to measure across your face from the top of one eyebrow arch to the top of the opposite arch.
2. **Cheekbones:** Now we need to measure across your cheekbones, starting and ending at the pointiest part below the outer corner of each eye.
3. **Jawline:** To Measure from the tip of your chin to below your ear at the point at which your jaw starts to angle upwards. Now for the quick maths, times this number by two to give us your jawline measurement.

4. **Face Length:** Measure from the centre of your hairline (providing you've got one) to the tip of your chin. If you do not have a hairline, where it would most likely exist were you to have one.

After doing this you need to write down which out of the four is the largest. Once you have this use the information below to categorise your face shape.

Don't worry if you are finding this difficult you can use the other method.

- **Oval Face shape:** Face length is greater than the width of the cheekbones, and forehead is greater than the jawline. The angle of the jaw is rounded rather than sharp.
- **Rectangle Face shape:** Face length is the greatest measurement. Forehead, cheekbones, and jawline are all roughly similar in size.
- **Triangular Face shape:** Jawline measures greater than cheekbones. These are then larger than the forehead.
- **Round Face shape:** Cheekbones and face length have a similar measurement. They are larger than the forehead and jawline, which also have a similar measurement. The angle of the jaw is soft and much less defined.
- **Heart Face shape:** Forehead measures greater than the cheekbones and jawline. The chin is pointed.
- **Square Face Shape:** All measurements are roughly similar. The angle of the jaw is sharp rather than rounded.
- **Diamond Face Shape:** Face length measures largest. Then, in descending order: cheekbones, forehead, and the smallest is jawline. The chin is pointed.

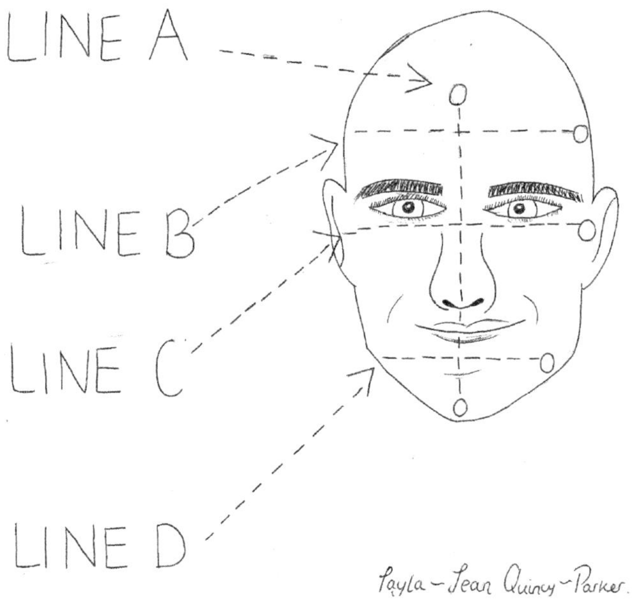

A good way to determine if you are struggling to do so in the mirror is to take a picture or find one of you looking straight on and print it off. Then borrow your sister's pencil case, whip out the ruler, and get to work. Use the dots to outline the edges of the face.

Face shape

Round-

- You have a Round shape face if LINE A is EQUAL to LINE C
- LINE B is EQUAL to LINE D
- Dimensions are the same as square, but the chin makes a half circle
- Celeb example – Leonardo Di Caprio

Getting The Girl

Square –

- You have a Square shape face if Line A is EQUAL to Line C
- Line B is EQUAL to Line D
- Celeb Example – Chris Evans (Captain America)

Oval –

- You have an Oval face shape if Line A is GREATER than Line C
- Line B is EQUAL to Line D
- Celeb Example - Jake Gyllenhaal

Diamond –

- You have a Diamond face shape if Line C is GREATER than Line D
- Line C is GREATER than Line B
- Celeb Example – Zayn Malik

Heart –

- You have a Heart face shape if Line B is GREATER than Line C
- Line B is GREATER than Line D
- Chin is a bit pointed
- Celeb Example – Joseph Gordon-Levitt

Triangle –

- You have a Triangle face shape if Line D is GREATER than Line A
- Line D is GREATER than Line C
- Celeb Example – Justin Timberlake

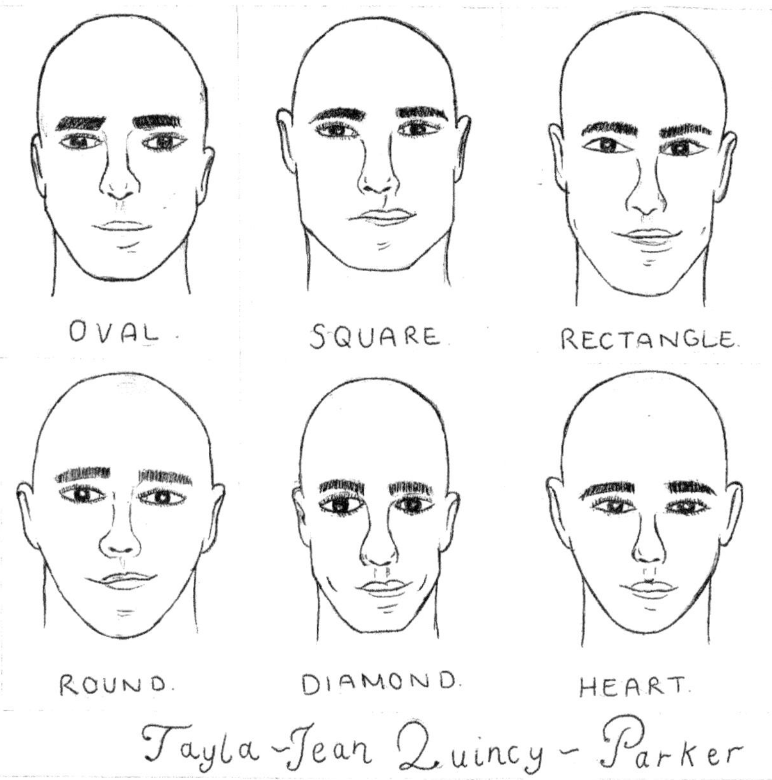

I am hoping you now know your face shape if not grab a friend you trust and ask them where you think you fit in.

Once you know your face shape it is easy to find a haircut that suits your face. A quick google of "haircuts that suit a heart-shaped face" will bring up lots of on-trend haircuts for this season. It is a great way to stay up to date and know what will and won't fit with your face. A good website I would recommend is FashionBeans.com it has lots of articles on style, hair, and grooming tips to keep you looking up to date.

Let's assume your little brother is playing COD online right now and he will throw a hissy fit if you use the internet so I will give a few suggestions as to what suits you.

Round Face Shape

A round face means we need to give it some shape. This loveable shape needs some edges.

- The key round faces are to add volume at the top without making your face wider
- Since round faces have little in the way of natural angles, you need to create the illusion of structure with your hair. So, if we cannot go wider, we must go up. (Just like the New York Skyline)
- A style with height on the top that's taken tight at the sides such as a pompadour or a flat top works well to add structure, as do front fringes
- Square corners in the high recession area of your hair will sharpen up any soft edges
- A full square beard will also help thin the chin area, giving the appearance of a more chiselled jaw. Beards can be the equivalent of makeup – they hide what you don't want to see
- **Examples – Side part, Pompadour, Undercut, slicked back, High-top, and tampered sides are all good haircuts for this face shape**

Square Face Shape

The square epitomises masculinity. Historically it was a god given that a square face meant you were stacking some serious testosterone. Chiselled like a Greek statue and features so sharp you would slice your finger.

- Versatile for long or short
- Classic, neat haircuts complement a square shape best—
- A close fade or a cut that has side partings and short layers
- As for facial hair a little stubble would help without hiding that good jawline
- **Examples – Caesar, Combover, Tight fade, Sweepback off face**

Oval Face Shape

The oval is a nice plain base. You can make it what you want. It is a good shape to have fun with and try new things.

- The way to make this face shape work well is to wear your hair off the forehead to create some volume and angles on top
- The most suitable style is a classic short back and sides and slightly longer on the top, with a side-swept parting

- Avoid a forward fringe. Forget when your mum uses to cut the hair with a mixing bowl kid. Too much heaviness on the forehead softens features and increases the roundness of the face
- **Examples – Buzzcuts, Quiffs, Crew Cuts, Mohawks**

Diamond Face Shape

A unique face shape that requires a special approach.

- We want to add width at the forehead and chin area
- A fringe can help to give texture
- It suits long styles where the hair can be tucked behind the ears
- If you take it too short, then your ears will look like Will Ferrell landed in time for Christmas and although in dungeons and dragons Elves can be rather sexy most women aren't looking for an elf to unwrap for Christmas
- A deep side parting works well
- A sweeping parting does also
- A small beard or 5 o clock shadow help narrow the chin
- **Examples – Grown out length, Medium hair pulled back behind ears, Long Afro (Bruno Mars), Dreadlocks, Ponytail**

Heart Face Shape

- If the cut is very tight this will maximise your narrow chin and width of the forehead and we don't want to that and end up looking like Megamind
- Instead, opt for a medium-length swept look.
- This face shape adores the Mid-length and long hairstyles
- Be sure to keep it well thinned out to allow movement
- As for facial hair, a beard will give fullness to the narrow chin
- **Examples – swept overhead, more hair is best, headband, long by shoulders**

Triangle Face Shape

- This requires the opposite of the heart face shape
- Aim for some volume to make this work
- Longer cuts up to nose-length work best, with full sides to give it depth

- **Examples – long hair down to the nose, mid fade with angular fringe, textured quiff**

Now as with all information you need to make this work for you. So, If you wear a suit for a living you may not be able to rock that Mohawk, the same applies if you work in construction and haven't got time for a side-parting to be slicked back every morning.

The information here is to give you some ideas of what naturally works best. You can take this information and make it work for you.

Your hair is very important.

A tip I would give is to grow out whatever you've currently got and then seek a trusted barber or salon (depending on the length) explain your desired goals and see if you can work together on a project. I feel developing a relationship with your hairdresser (non-sexual unless you REALLY want a free haircut) is crucial. Having a hairdresser that looks after your head in more ways than one can be fun but remember if you two fall out then you'll need to find someone new to manage your barnet. I know people that will cheat on their partner before their barber.

When I was in my teens, I had a quiff way before it was fashionable as I trusted my hairdresser who said it would suit. It did.

Then we decided to grow it. Now growing your hair can be an absolute pain but it is always worth it in the end. Regular trips to the hairdressers are essential. When you grow it, you don't just go Tom Hanks in Castaway on us. You need to make sure it grows the desired way. This is a key mistake I see amongst men growing hair. They often overlook that you may need a few style-stops along the way. Going from a buzz cut to a ponytail is not as easy as just avoiding the scissors for a few months. Along the way, you'll end up looking like the Pidgeon Lady from Home Alone if you're not careful.

I would recommend you go to the barbers or hairdressers **at least every 3 weeks.** I go every two as I like to look sharp.

You should wash **your hair about every 3 days** with separate shampoo and conditioner. We don't use all in one's boys. You may as well throw fairy liquid on it. I, particularly, wash mine every other day because of the build-up of the product.

Careful with over-washing or hair will become dry and you'll be looking like the straw man from the Wizard of Oz (that's a sure-fire way to be sent bags packed to home in Kansas).

Moroccan Oil is useful for dry hair and easily accessible. Regardless of what you've seen on Tik Tok do not be putting cooking oil in your hair unless you're planning on looking like a right turkey.

Bald and Balding

Jack that's great advice but I don't have any hair or not much is left. I know many a guy in this situation. Don't fret if your hairline is receding quicker than when you approach women on a night out.

Don't worry. Here are your options.

Try and keep the hair

1. You want to try and keep your hair then I would suggest starting Regaine spray also known as Midoxinil this helps slow down hair loss and stimulate growth. Regaine is a brand name and you can find alternatives online or at any Boots Chemist. Any alternative online Chemist will do as a prescription is easily done without a doctor's note needed.
2. Use Finasteride. Finasteride is an oral tablet taken to stop the conversion of DHT on the scalp which can cause balding. DHT can be caused by too much testosterone or a chemical imbalance. You can get this prescription free online or again at Boots Chemist if you're in the UK
3. Yes, using them both together will help and there are tons of scientific literature out there to support this. A quick google will explain all you need to know.
4. Get a modern One-Piece Hairpiece. Modern versions of hair wigs are fantastic and almost unrecognisable. Find a barber who provides them and get it fitted and cut into place. It is cheaper than a hair transplant but will need replacing. There is nothing wrong with these many women use extensions, weaves, and hairpieces. They

won't feel cheated or fooled they will simply come to accept this like wearing a hat. It is not a big deal

5. Get a hair transplant. Now hair transplants are not suitable for everyone and it isn't a miracle cure. The same cause of your hair loss can occur after a hair transplant. It is a more permanent fix. They are not as expensive as they once were and can cost around £3000 in the UK and can be cheaper done abroad.

Embrace it

1. Shave it all off boy. That's right all of it. No one needs those bits at the side. This says. World I do not need your approval and screams Alpha Male. Think of The Rock and Vin Diesel.
2. Make sure you do this regularly with a good clean razer. You can even buy tools to help you do it at home that come in a circular shape that you whizz around. It would cost a fortune if you went to the barbers every time.

The reason we began with hair is on your first impression it's one of the first things you'll be judged on. It's immediately in their eye line (not your dick pic, another reminder to stop sending these) and it allows them to conclude the type of person you are. Does it look like this man takes pride in himself? Does he appear to be socially savvy enough to know what suits him?

Now of course if you have a thing for Goth Women then you probably won't have a comb-over as it won't appeal to that selection of women, but such extremes need to be carefully weighed up. Unless you are trying to appeal to a very small selection of women then you want something versatile and can help you with the widest range. Regardless of if we all know Marilyn Manson has been killing it with the ladies for years.

Many men go wrong as they go in and ask for a haircut of a celeb or a friend in the hope it will make them look like them. There hairdressers, not miracle workers.

Some lucky men like David Beckham or Brad Pitt can pull off just about any haircut. Most of us cannot. We must find one that suits us. So, you are your very own Harvey Spector. Suits? Get it.

Skincare

John Wayne was to many a solid icon of rugged masculinity, individuality, and inner strength. Adored by men and women everywhere especially my Grandad, he epitomised what a man should be as the star of the Wild West Genre.

A giant of a man he starred in many Westerns, but it wasn't a cowboy film that put the bullet to his career. It was starring as the conqueror Genghis Khan in what is regarded as the worse films ever made. Now I am not here to discuss film choices but what I am here is to tell you about the impact of filming the film had on him, his family, and the crew.

You see the film was filmed (who'd of thought) in Snow Cannon. This was just downwind of where the USA tested 11 atomic bombs in 1953. Although assumed there was no harm to the public the tragedy after speaks otherwise. There were 220 people in the cast and crew. By 1981, 91 of them had been diagnosed with cancer and 46 had died from the disease.

John Wayne contracted cancer twice: in 1964, he was diagnosed with lung cancer and had his left lung removed, and in 1979 he contracted stomach cancer, which took his life. John Wayne has a skin cancer foundation named after him in memory of his son Michael who contracted the deadly disease whilst on the set during filming. Such a tragic end to many lives. Genghis Khan conquered a great man long before his time was up.

In paying homage to John Wayne, we must take looking after our skin seriously.

Scan the QR code for some words of wisdom.

Skincare regime

Gentleman the days of washing your face with the same flannel you use on your balls and leaving the house is dead.

Skincare – like oral hygiene- is something to get into your daily routine. I am going to explain some of the things you can do to help keep your skin in top shape.

At the most basic you must wash your face, use a good facial scrub, cleanse, tone, and moisturise.

This the very minimum to give you a fighting chance. I am now going to go through the different options available to you before coming back round to the previous in a little bit more detail.

Face Peels

For some men, the premise of dead skin doesn't strike a chord. They wouldn't even begin to know what exfoliation means let alone skin having multiple layers. Most men would consider a face peel as something almost entirely reserved for the Pink Ladies from Grease, but they would be wrong. There are many types of face peels available and the reason for using one can be varied.

A face peel is a procedure where a trained professional applies different strengths of an acid solution directly to the skin before then neutralising it. The results? It strips off that dead layer of the skin helping you look glowing. The best bit? It also removes dreaded acne scars.

You see for a lot of men that have been through puberty the face has borne the brunt. The skin is uneven, bumpy you may even suffer from the odd spot or you may be acne-prone (other solutions to this soon). In this case, consider a face peel as starting again and fresh.

Making your old tired canvas look new. I am also talking about wrinkles. It improves **skin** texture and tone and lessens the appearance of fine wrinkles. Now to some, this may seem extreme but if we are going to start talking about the skin then it's best to explain how we can make the biggest transformation off the bat.

As always consult a professional. Yes, it works. Trust me.

The cost of such a procedure starts at £100.

Botox

Yes, you read that right. Until we make the Philosophers Stone then we need to accept that time is one thing we will never be able to master. You are getting older every day. Which means you're probably looking older.

Most men get better with age. It's a known fact. You are probably much better looking in your twenties than in your teens. Almost certainly look more manly in your 30s than your 20's and when you hit 40 you get all those girls with daddy issues. You are a lucky sod.

However, getting there does not mean you need to look like poor, old Dot Cotton. There are things we can do, and Botox is one of them.

Now Botox is a brand name for a muscle relaxer other brands do the same, but it is most commonly known. Botox (Botulinum toxin) injections relax the **muscles** in your face to smooth out lines and wrinkles, such as crow's feet and frown lines.

After a time, like all muscles when not used, they begin to shrink which means over time the muscles that caused the lines will be weaker and this should help lessen how quickly wrinkles begin.

It is important to note that Botox is more preventative than restorative. It will not iron out as when the Botox fades, they will begin to show again, the good news for you is that the chemical peels will take away these layers of skin and remove the lines.

Having both done together is the best way to completely transform the skin. It is not a quick fix and can take a year or so of regular treatment of both, but the medical literature supports it will help eliminate wrinkles.

After your Botox injections after about two weeks, you'll see the effects set in and your areas will be noticeably less wrinkly (YIPEEE).

Now having covered the big two let's go back to the more daily routines.

Washing Your Face

Happiness is a habit, so is your skincare.

When I say washing your face, I am not referring to splashing some cold water and making a move. At the very least use a hot flannel to open the pores and place this against your face. After splashing with cold water to seal your pores.

If we want to do a proper job though then we are going to need a facial scrub. There are lots of these around, but I prefer the Nip Fab Glycolic Scrub. No10 facial scrub is another I have used that works great. Both exfoliate your skin. You can find them both online – Amazon – for less than £10.

Cleanser

Here would be a good time to use a cleanser on the skin. This is to clean dirt from the pores. There are lots of expensive brands out there, but I have found that they are all about the same. If you have sensitive skin, you may need to do some more research for your particular needs however a simple cleanser will set you back about £4.

Toner

Now I know when it comes to skincare, an elaborate regime isn't for everyone. But first impressions count right? We want to give you the best chance to make them give you the benefit of the doubt and cutting too many corners can cost you the glow you've always wanted.

Toner is made to minimize the appearance of pores, temporarily tighten skin, and naturally remove oil and dirt. It gets rid of impurities stuck in your pores after you wash your face. When added to your daily skincare routine and used regularly, it can have a major positive impact on the appearance and tightness of your pores (hello, aging **skin**).

Moisturiser

The best way to greet winter is with Vaseline and moisturiser.

The last one for our daily skin routine. Moisturise after cleaning your face. It is as simple as that. Moisturizing is an important step to maintain your skin's healthy cells and to protect them from irritation.

People who get this into their daily routine and begin to moisturize faithfully in their youth are much more likely to have beautiful complexions when they're older.

I use Bulldog Sensitive moisturiser. It is easily available online or in most supermarkets. It costs about £4.

Now we have covered all of the basics to keep you looking like you take care of yourself and to stop you aging before your time, but I will mention some extras you may choose to use.

Night pads / Night creams

Your skin is an investment, not an expense.

I use Nip Fabs glycolic acid night pads before bed. They help to remove dead cells from the surface of the skin leaving it fresher. **Glycolic** acid—my acid of choice—is the most popular ingredient in peel **pads** since it clears out pores, hydrates brighten, and smooths out the texture.

Sunbeds

Glowing skin is always in.

A controversial one to mention alongside skin but being as skin is the most affected it's important to place it here. As a personal choice, I use sunbeds once a week to maintain a tan and stay looking brown. I like the look and sunbeds when not overused can bring benefits that in my own opinion make them worth the risk. It is entirely your choice on this.

Some of the benefits are the increase of vitamin D, which can be used to help fight depression and release serotonin. Increased confidence, a better complexion.

The risks are well documented although the levels are conflicting.

It is therefore personal preference here.

And personally, I think most people look better with a tan.

****

Eyebrows

Your eyebrows introduce you before you speak.

Staying on the face we need to mention those slugs most of you have just above your eyes. The monobrow has never been in fashion. Eyebrows are one of the most important features of your face, so you should keep them looking their best. They help shape and frame your face. Therefore, making trimming and tidying part of your routine is a no-brainer.

You can do this yourself or visit a professional. If doing yourself then start by removing the weight if they join in the middle. You can remove weight with scissors and you're going to need to pluck or wax the middle. As you get older your eyebrows get that bushy, you'll be surprised Moses doesn't set them on fire and start talking to them.

Men often have a straighter eyebrows compared to a woman's curved or arched. It is important to note this. Unless you are going for the Boy George look. And do you really want to make me cry?

Now if you want to visit a professional you have two options: Waxing or Threading.

Threading kills. Trust me when I say there have been times, I have almost jumped out of the chair in pain. It does get a nice shape however and a true professional can give you shape to extenuate those eyes you want women to be gazing into.

Waxing is where I feel most comfortable. Hey, what can I say a few men don't mind women pouring hot wax all over their body in a dark room...

Waxing is less painful and still requires the desired effect.

Cost = about £8

Teeth

Good teeth are always in style.

There is a reason it is called a Hollywood smile. The research out there supports that having good teeth matters. In a survey taken by 1,047 nationally representative of all Americans, the results were conclusive.

The study showed the respondents images of people with varying tooth issues and asked to give their honest opinion about them.

They were not aware that they were comparing people with straight teeth to crooked teeth. Results of the study indicated Americans perceive people with straight teeth to have more desirable qualities than those with crooked teeth, including attributes such as being happy, surrounded by loved ones, and professionally successful.

- Almost one-third (29%) of Americans say the first aspect of someone's face they typically notice is his or her teeth.
- 24% say this is also the facial aspect that they remember the most after meeting someone.

So, Love at First Sight? Well, the chances are less if you have crooked teeth. When it comes to attracting the opposite sex on modern platforms such as dating sites, those with straight teeth are 57% to match and led to a date based on the picture.

What can we do? Quite a few things. Invisalign is just one brand that helps naturally straighten teeth using a brace. Another option is to get them completely redone with veneers. If those don't suit you have snap-on dentures, or you can book in with a dentist to see what they suggest.

Not only do your teeth straight making a difference but so does the colour.

White Teeth

In many cases, they just need a good clean from a dentist. This helps with surface stains to create a brighter, whiter smile.

Another option is to use a home whitening kit. Smile Direct Club does one and that starts at £80 which says it lasts for up to a year. This is an option.

You could also go see a dentist and get them done professionally including laser whitening and this is around £1500.

Of course, we can just stay regularly on top of our teeth with regular brushing and avoid products that may stain them but where's the fun in that aye!

Now one thing to take into consideration is that all this pruning and making ourselves look our bests also feeds into being successful for an attraction switch. People that look after themselves look as if they have their life together. They are in control.

All of these additions will make no difference if we can't trigger their attraction switches mind and I don't want to get you to get lost in the details. All of this does is give you some extra arrows to your bow.

It will NOT HINDER only HELP in our pursuits of a happy life with the opportunity to have women in there.

Mastering the next few chapters is of the utmost importance but making a good first impression enables you to show all the skills you are about to learn.

As you can see it is not being blessed with good looks but good grooming that will make the difference.

If you are lazy in your appearance what does that say about you? Are you going to be a provider?

In my grandparent's day, they would work construction then come home wash and put on a suit to go down the working men's club. They had pride in themselves and an air of respect came with it.

You need to take the same pride and care for yourself. Treat yourself like you are valuable otherwise why would anyone think any different?

Body hair

"In junior high P.E., I was way too shy to take a shower in front of the other kids. It was a horribly awkward time - body hair, odors... So, I'd go from my sweaty shirt back into my regular clothes and have to continue the day."
Will Ferrell

We are all born different and no one should feel conscious of their body hair. Some women enjoy a hairy man. Most modern women aren't too inclined, but it still comes down to personal preference.

Like with all the previous sections being well-groomed is the important thing here. If you are a naturally hairy man, then you want to make sure that you keep a few areas nice and clipped and leave the rest to do its natural thing. It is just impractical to keep waxing or shaving if your body naturally produces a lot of hair. THIS IS ABSOLUTELY FINE.

Back in the 70's Burt Reynolds made a career out of his hairy chest and the hairy chest thing does it for some women so fear not.

The areas you should keep well maintained are your nose and ear hair. Both are unsightly and should be trimmed often. There is no excuse for these to be overgrown.

Now if you are not an exceptionally hairy man then it's time, I started to give you some home truths.

Shave it off.

All of it except the legs and arms.

What purpose do you need hair on your belly and your chest for? A vest does the job.

Armpit hair. What is that about? Who are you proving you went through puberty to? Get rid. It causes unnecessary odour. It serves little purpose other than to collect all the sweat droplets you've got and nicely store them for you until you can get a shower. Have you any idea how many women have said "omg look at that man's sexy armpit hair, I hope he will come home with me!". Zero.

Also, as you get REALLY successful it will help you be aerodynamic when you are running away from all those women chasing you down the street.

If you must keep it and I see NO reason why then trim it to the smallest possible setting on your clippers. Women will thank you. Trust me.

Now we are on to one can be one of the biggest turn-offs for a woman when it comes to body hair and that is your pubic hair.

In my many years collecting survey feedback from women there is a resounding conclusion that they would not like sex to end up like a Bush Tucker Trial. Would you like to put your face down there on a woman that's had Alan Titchmarsh and the ground force team transforming it into a tropical paradise? So why on earth would she want to do the same for you.

Sweat. That's what you're going to do. That's then going to gather around your crown jewels, and you think the pink panther is going to want to steal those? Think again.

You may as well of put them in Fort Knox.

There is no need for pubic hair down there. Get rid. All of it.

Again, if for some weird nostalgic reason, you must "trim" then this must be the lowest setting known to man. Closely trimmed and neat. This may be where many of you start and that's fine, I know Mel Gibson was also quite attached to his Mullet in Lethal Weapon, it can be hard to let go. Trimmed is a great start and if some of you end there, then that's just fine. You must feel comfortable in your skin, that is the most important factor. Confidence is key.

"We Gonna See If He Still Got Some Magic In That Mike." – Rome – Magic Mike XL

Personally, if you dream of taking a woman to the clouds above then you raise your chances if you've got a shaven haven.

Baby powder is an excellent way to keep it smooth and acts to absorb moisture. After a while, your skin will get used to it and you can shave every day in the shower or bath to make sure you are always ready for battle.

Exfoliation helps with shaving rash so does regularly swapping the blade. Other options include laser hair removal or Veet Cream. You apply Veet and wash it off and the hair falls off. Be sure to follow instructions closely. Your skin will toughen as it comes accustom to the new procedure.

The expectation you have is for women to be carefully groomed and put together there so you must do the same. Practice what you preach. You want to make the experience as enticing as possible and pulling hairs out of their teeth is hardly appetising.

Manscaping is better than all the women escaping when they take off your boxers and are confronted by Cousin IT from The Adams Family.

If you must be a member of the Adams Family then be like Gomez Adam and Morticia Adams "You *don't just cross my mind, you live in it"*. This is the way you should want over women. You're not going to get there when they find out the reason, they called you Big Foot had more to do with your unusual amount of hair rather than the fact you had 12 inches at your disposal.

Body Composition

Arnold Schwarzenegger brought men's physiques into the mainstream in the late 70s and 80s. The Austrian Oak was a 7-time Mr. Olympia, who built up his popularity through his physique and an unforgettable appearance in the documentary *Pumping Iron*. His success stemmed from his ability to master his physique and led to a successful film career beginning with CONAN THE BARBARIAN. Mastering your body shows dedication and a powerful appearance is very attractive regardless of the blogs you've read that say Dad Bods are in. There only in your dreams because you want it to be real to make up for your lack of discipline.

Scan the QR code for a documentary on Pumping Iron for more information on Arnolds rise to the top.

I don't see many Dad Bod strippers getting booked nor did I see one in Magic Mike. That tells you all you need to know. If people aren't willing to pay for it then it's not in demand.

Like with everything we have covered so far in making a good first impression body shape plays a big role in how we can be perceived. We all have a natural body shape and a different metabolism. This is a known fact and cannot be controlled.

There are however many things that can be controlled.

If you are overweight, then we can start to tackle this. If you are skinny and want to build some muscle, then we can help there. If you're in good shape – fantastic let's keep it that way.

Body shape helps us with lots of things. It can tick the protector of a loved one switch if you look like you are fit and can protect yourself. It can tick the successful switch if it looks like you have worked hard to achieve something. Unlike things such as wealth that can be passed down or inherited your body is usually something, you must work hard for. It is all your own doing. We all know this that's why we make judgments based on people's body shape. Your body reflects the choices you make and the discipline you have.

Did you choose to sit at home eat KFC and watch late-night TV or did you have the discipline to run or go to the gym after work? Which one shows you would be a good partner.

Speaking of our boy Arnold in his book *The Encyclopaedia of Bodybuilding* Arnold talks of taking pictures of yourself from the front, side, and back. "This way, you can always check back to find out what kind of progress you have made" and he is right. The first thing we need to ditch is the scales. Weight is not the best measurement of progress. The mirror never lies, however.

The best start is therefore to take some good honest pictures of yourself or ask a trusted friend to do it for you. This is your base and whether we are hoping to lose fat or gain muscle this is our starting point.

Losing weight is extremely simple.

You need to be in a calorie deficit. That is it.

No fancy diets needed, no special tablets, no fat-burning drinks. Nothing.

You just need to burn more calories than you eat.

Calories are a measurement of energy and therefore the more calories the more energy is needed to burn it. When the calories are not burnt, we store them as fat or use them to build muscle. When we don't have calories, we begin to burn fat. Fat is your body's bank. So, some of you are a lot richer than you thought you were.

Here's how it works...

- **Calories In**
  This refers to all the calories you "take in" each day via the foods you eat and the drinks you drink. Fizzy drinks often contain calories we are not aware of.

- **Calories Out**
  This refers to all the calories you burn each day. This includes calories burned during traditional forms of exercise such as weight training or cardio. It also includes your normal daily activity such as when you stand or sit when you walk to the car or even brush your teeth. We then have all those weird little movements such as fidgeting with your feet you're your desk. Playing with your bear. Scrolling through this book on a tablet or flicking the pages. Finally, we must include those vital movements that we are not

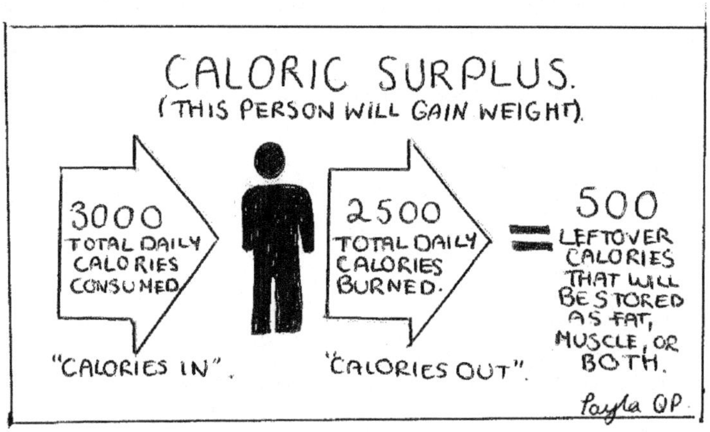

consciously aware of. Things such as your lungs pumping and your heart beating (your stomach rumbling).

When we want to gain weight, we then simply eat more calories than we burn. This then gives the body 2 storage options it can use the additional calories for **fat cells** and **muscle tissue**.

Therefore, a caloric surplus ***will always cause you to gain something.*** Either body fat, muscle mass, or a combination of both.

When we are training properly and eating just right the additional calories can be used for our benefit to building muscle. Most however do not use the additional calories and it just gets stored as fat.

Now the opposite occurs in a calorie deficit. When your body burns more calories than it consumes you are in a calorie deficit and it must get the calories from somewhere.

As it turns out, there are 2 fuel sources available (you were paying attention, earlier right?) within your body where leftover energy has been stored in preparation for this very scenario: **fat cells** and **muscle tissue**.

Therefore, **a caloric deficit *will always cause you to lose something***. Either body fat, muscle mass, or a combination of both.

Now for most of you out there when this is done correctly, we will burn fat. However, when people starve themselves and go on some of these extreme diets by cutting too many calories too quickly, we then can lose muscle which we want to avoid.

No magic pills. No extreme diet needed just a gradual reduction of calories below what you use to burn. As a famous Meerkat said – Simples.

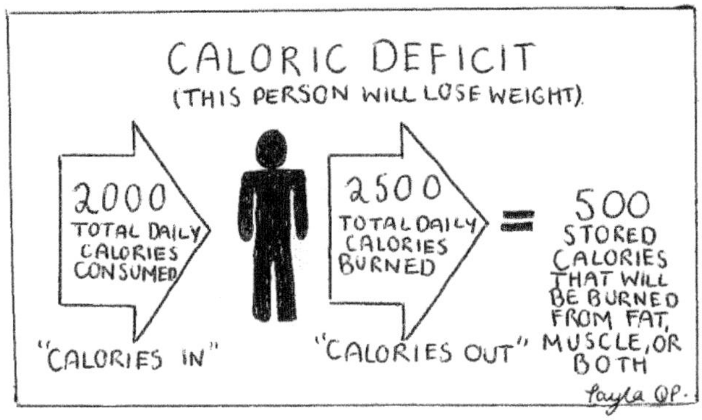

Now the final stage we can be in is known as **Caloric Maintenance**. This is where you are consuming as many calories as you burn so you stay roughly the same. It is very hard to be extremely accurate.

Once we know your Caloric Maintenance level then we can. Subtract or add **300 calories** to either **gain or lose** weight.

How we calculate this is by using good old maths. You can use a calculator or an online calculator to determine caloric maintenance levels.

The formula we use is the following:

- Convert your current weight into pounds
- take your current weight and multiply it by 13 if you do not exercise at all
- if you exercise a few times a week then multiply by 15
- if you exercise five or more days then multiply by18
- The number you'll be left with is a rough idea of how many calories you need to stay your current weight

Exercise can be anything from weight training, running, walking, cycling, boxing, etc

An example would be someone who weighs 200 pounds and does no exercise they would:

- 200 X 13 = 2600 calories

- Using this information for weight loss they would take away 300 so they would need 2300 calories a day to lose weight
- Using this information for weight gain they would add 300 calories so they would need 2900 calories to gain weight

A lot of other factors can play a role in your metabolic rates such as height, muscle mass, and intensity of training but the rough guide above is an excellent starting point and will work.

Do not drop the calories too quickly or you will lose muscle and your body will also enter starvation mode stopping yourself from progressing. Every time you feel you've hit a plateau you can adjust your calories down by 100 or up by 100. You can review weekly and continue until you reach your desired goal.

For example, if you weigh 165 pounds and exercise three days a week, then you would multiply 165 by 15 for a total of 2,475. That means your daily calorie intake—and how you will stay stuck at your current weight—is about 2,475 calories.

For professional advice, you can of course seek an online coach to help with nutrition, train plans, and accountability.

Sticking and keeping count however is a little bit trickier but again I can help. An app that helps you track your food that I use, and many others are very useful. It is called "**My Fitness Pal".** It is available on the app and Play Store. It allows you to keep a food diary. It is free to use. You can use the barcode scanner to scan everything you eat. It is extremely useful to keep track and stay on goal. You can also set your target calories and it will let you know whether you've got enough calories left for that ice cream or not!

Now we have covered how to add or lose weight I want to talk about the best way to dramatically change your body shape – Weight training.

Weight Training

Now Weightlifting isn't just about bulking up and building muscle mass. It actually has a host of benefits that include better posture, improved sleep, gaining density in bones, maintaining **weight** loss, boosting metabolism, lowering inflammation, and staving off chronic disease, to name but a few.

Now why it's true that you can't spot lose fat, weight training is like your cheat code. You see the more muscle you have the bigger your metabolic rate at a rate of rest. To put it simply the more calories you burn when you are sat on your arse playing the remake of Final Fantasy 7. More muscle needs more energy (Just imagine how many calories Barrett needs).

Now you could buy a copy of Men's Health or watch a YouTube video on a workout to do and that may get you some results but like the above, there is a much simpler way to make the infamous GAINS.

Put down the dumbbells and pull out your wallet. You are about to purchase a one-way ticket to Gainesville.

You need just two magic words to lift bigger weights and it's not "Wingardium *Leviosa".* Those two magical words are **Progressive Overload**.

The next section has been written after a conversation with Online training coach Karlton Griffiths. Karlton is the current PCA Classic Bodybuilding British Champion 2019. He offers online coaching, nutrition, and diet support. He is on Instagram should you wish to enquire into his services (reference the book and he will give you the best discount EVER).

The Progressive Overload principle states for a muscle to grow, strength to be gained, performance to increase, or for any similar improvement to occur, the human body must be forced to adapt to a tension that is above and beyond what it has previously experienced.

Simply meaning that you need to push yourself further than the last session to create adaptation. Remember we are after **Progress Not Perfection**.

So how do we keep track of if we are making progress?

How this can be achieved is by using a logbook.

A logbook records all your exercises and the way they are performed. You must track all your sessions, weights used for reps and sets. Any plain book will do where you can write out your sessions as you go through them. You can buy a logbook that already has a template from Amazon if you so wish.

It will look like this:

Exercise	Set 1	Set 2	Set 3
Bench Press	12 Reps	10 Reps	8 Reps
Notes on difficulty or any other feedback – injured this day – didn't eat, etc	Weight lifted – 50 KG	Weight Lifted – 60 KG	Weight Lifted – 70 KG

The purpose of this is so you can track where you need to improve week by week. We want to see where we were and plan where we need to go. We look to made small increments weekly in any number of ways.

It also helps if we begin to plateau. You may need to increase your food to get stronger. You may need to take a rest because of injury. The notes section is good for helping you remember why you performed the way you did on that day.

Execution

The most important thing when we execute any lifts is to ensure we use good technique. Form over everything. We can only push weight and reps with solid form and execution. There are many guides online on how to perform an exercise. If you are unsure of the correct technique, then a good YouTube channel to use is Athlean X who has lots of videos on different exercises and how to perform them correctly.

Working Sets

The sets in your plan are working sets only, warm-up/ feeder sets are not tracked in the program as that is person dependent. Warm-up sets should be lower reps to feel the weight, get comfortable with the movement but save energy for the main recorded sets.

For example: if you are on a flat bench and your 'loading set' weight is 100kg. You may warm up on 50kg for 10 reps, getting them used to the movement at a light weight. 70kg for 4/5 reps, 85/90kg for 2/3 reps. Then hit the loading set. We only need to record the sets that we class as "working" these are the sets we will use to measure progress.

Rep Ranges

The rep ranges are set for you to fail or be very close to falling within them.

For example, a set of 8-12 - I would expect you to fail before 12. Any more than that and the weight was too light. Any less than 8 the weight was too heavy.

Each rotation you should aim to improve the number of reps to maximise the range before improving the weight.

You will find that are two different rep ranges on most movements. The first set is a lower rep range, the 'loading set' is the heavier set. The lower rep range set 'back off set' will be reduced weight from the loading set.

We are basically doing our heaviest set first after being warm. Whilst we still have the energy, we want to start strong then come down the weights. After this, we reduce the weight as our muscles will be tired When we come down the weights, we will then do more reps to increase the difficulty.

An example –

Exercise	Set 1	Set 2	Set 3
Squat	8 reps	10 reps	12 reps
Notes – Eat well today	100 Kg	90 Kg	70 Kg

There are several ways to overload:

Heavier weight

Simply up the weight that is loaded.

More reps

Hit more reps inside the rep range. More time under tension.

Tempo
Controlling the tempo of the movement can make the set harder. Slowing the movement down on both parts of the movement will increase the tension on the muscle.

Less rest
By shortening the rest you will cause more metabolic stress to the muscle which will cause an adaptation.
One set, perform the exercise then drop the weight and repeat the exercise with little to no rest.

Drop Sets
One set, taken to multiple failure points within set rep ranges to cause as much muscle damage as possible. Hit the first set, rest for allocated time hit the second set, rest for the allocated time, and finally in the final set.

Rest-Pause Sets
1 Set, split into sets of 4 for 6 rounds. Using short rest periods. Aiming to pump blood into the muscle group.

Muscle Rounds
Controlling the eccentric (lengthening of the muscle) contraction, trying to slow this part of the movement down.

To summarise
Understandably this will probably something new to you, it is difficult to grasp at first but will quickly become second nature. The aim of this is to improve every week by some form of progressive overload. If we hit a plateau with the amount of weight, we can lift then we can do more reps. If we can't do more reps, we can have less rest or slow down how long it takes to do the lift. All of this is designed to push the muscles to react and make you stronger. As you become stronger muscles will grow and before you know it when you walk into a room Hulk Hogan's theme music will begin to play.

Go through the rotations, log all lifts, and beat it next time around, remember the form must be solid. Training should be enjoyable first and foremost.

For more videos on training and routines then Jeff Nippard has an excellent channel that looks at journal articles and the most up-to-date research that supports training methods. He details lots of different routines you could use and the correct way to perform exercises.

If you are still not too keen on using YouTube, then stick to your classic lifts. These are the foundation of any good bodybuilding programme. Stick to your big compound movements: Bench press, Squat, Deadlift, Military Press, Bent Over Row. Exercises that need a lot of muscle fibres will help you to grow quickly.

Again, as I mentioned there is lots of material out there for you to use it is just about choosing a programme applying the progressive overload principle and sticking to it.

In 12 months, you'll look like a new man – literally.

****

Clothes and Style

"Manners maketh the man"

Whilst manners or the way you behave may be a more accurate reflection of who you are as a person, the way you dress is often, how many people form a conclusion of who you are as a person.

You see not many women can distinguish the difference between a knight in shining armour or an idiot dressed in tinfoil. You are often assumed to be who you are based upon how you dress. The man in a Hi-Vis Jacket and a hard hat is presumed to be a man who works in construction. The same applies to a man in a suit – an assumption is made about this person.

Men in suits often have an air of power around them and none more so than one man. He has a slim build with a 3 inch long, thin vertical scar on his right cheek. He has blue-grey eyes with a "cruel" mouth. On top of his head, he has short, black hair a comma of which rests on his forehead. Physically he is described as being 6 ft in height and 168 lb in weight. Thirty-six years old with a Scottish father and a Swiss mother he is known worldwide for his sense of style. The effortless with which he carries himself. Orphaned at the age of 11 he then went on to be a commander in the British Navy.

His favourite drink is vodka martini.

By which I have no doubt you have concluded as to whom I am referring.

A man whose mere drink order speaks for itself.

Associated with luxury, Aston Martin Cars, fancy watches, tailor-fit suits.

I am of course referring to His Majesty's Secret Services finest – James Bond.

The air in which James Bond carries himself comes from the very fabrics in which his clothes are cut. He owns the space around him and everything that he does. He oozes Alpha Male and a gentleman who is in control. A man who is timeless in every sense, the ladies' man combined with the action man.

Taking pride in your clothes and your appearance shows control and ticks the alpha male switch.

Few could come up with a sound argument that James Bond is not masculine. He's tough. He's rugged. He's not just good at his job, he's good at it in a way that is undeniably testosterone pumped. He also is a huge hit with the ladies.

We aren't just referring to the tuxedo when we say that Bond is also perpetually sharp-dressed. His casual clothes are well thought out, well-cut, and sophisticated.

Now you don't need a Tom Ford suit to be 007. What you do need is to understand that clothes are to be functional as well as fashionable. A sign of maturity is making sure you are always prepared for any occasion. This is the modern-day equivalent of giving your jacket to a lady when walking home (you were smart enough to bring a jacket in the first place). By showing your clothes are well-thought-out, practical, and useful, you, in turn, show that you are these things. Yes, you are wearing gloves because your hands might get cold. Yes, you do have a scarf to protect your neck. You are an individual who is prepared for any eventuality.

A man who could react to situations – you know like those life-threatening, we need a protector of loved one moment? – to be equipped to deal with whatever may come.

This is the first thing you need to consider with clothes.

Functionality

What purpose do your clothes serve, are they up for the task? You see when you were 13 and you wore brand new white trainers to go exploring muddy fields with your friends you were naïve and knew no better. When you did it at 30 you were an idiot who should of worn wellies. One of the unconscious thoughts we think of when looking at other people's clothes is are, they dressed ***"appropriately"?*** Such a thought comes way before style or brands or anything else. Ask a woman who knows a man who has worn a vest and no top on a night out and she will tell you that the last thing she was thinking of was "what a nice vest". Or try wearing a shirt and tie to a Sunday League football game with your boots and see how many funny looks you get.

Now if James Bond can run, fall, and shoot in his jacket then the least we can expect is your clothes give you enough room to perform basic activities such as bending down. I am a huge fan of the skinny jeans myself (very guilty) but if you can't crouch or bend in them then maybe it's time for a different fit (actively test this theory by performing a few lunges to make sure they don't split).

A sign of a man is someone who can dress appropriately for the occasion with clothes that serve a purpose.

A true gentleman in Britain is never too far away from an umbrella that can fit himself and a lady. Such is how well thought out he plans his day.

You Define the Clothes, Do Not Let the Clothes Define You

Fashion comes and goes but style is eternal. In our pursuit of what to wear if we follow fashion trends, we are always behind the pack and racing to keep up. It is costly, time-consuming, and exhausting trying to follow and keep up with every new fashion trend.

So, stop.

Don't do it.

Style Vs Fashion has been a debate for a millennium but to be confident in your clothes and elude confidence, you must find a style that works for you. If you don't like wearing loafers and can't imagine trousers without socks, then great! Just don't do it.

You are a leader, not a follower.

An alpha male expresses himself through his clothes but is not defined by them. Being alpha is expressed in many ways. He does not become obsessed or insecure about his individual style or someone's style. He chooses what works for him and avoids the fashion trap. You must understand, fashion not only changes constantly – it's also not absolute.

Style is a way of dressing and carrying oneself that's both permanent and personal. It' shows you have a good understanding of the rules and context in which the clothes sit. It shows you appreciate history whilst knowing how colour and proportion come together.

When we think of style then it is when you are true to yourself. It is how you inject your personality into your clothes. It's in wearing a tie that makes your eyes bright, tilting your hat at a jaunty angle, or folding your pocket square in a devil-may-care sort of way.

Oscar Wilde put it best when he said, *"Fashion is a form of ugliness so intolerable that we have to alter it every six months."*

Fashion is what everyone else is doing and wearing at any given time. In other words, its trend is driven.

We are not sheep. We do not follow the crowd.

What can we do then Jack?

Many things we need to consider when thinking of our unique style. We will now consider the following things: body shape, height, age, profession, lifestyle and must-have pieces of clothing.

Body shape

There are a few types of body shapes men can fit into.

Your body may resemble one of the above shapes.

We have the **Rounded** where the body curves out in the middle starting at the neck and down past the waist. 26 % of the male population falls into this category. Celebrity example – Elton John & Boris Johnson (now wouldn't those pair make interesting dinner guests)

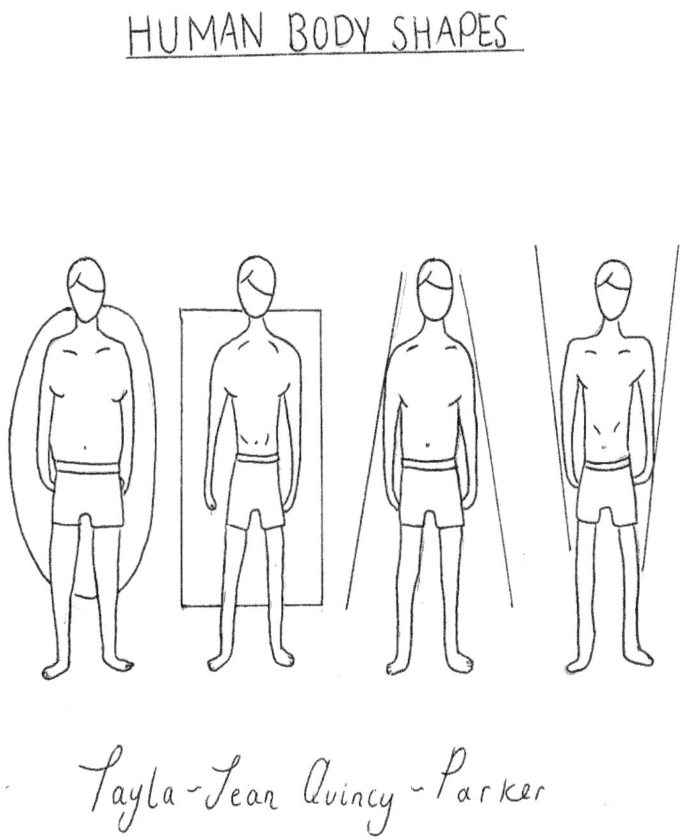

Some key trends for your body shape:

- You probably could have guessed the vertical stripes coming but what about pinstripe trousers or a shirt with pinstripes. Both have the desired effect.
- Make sure clothes are the right length. Visit a tailor to get clothes taken in. usually, when you go up in size there is a lot of excess material. Get this dealt with. A quick visit to a tailor can turn your clothes into a made-to-measure. The fit is almost the most important feature.

- Block colours are good here

We have the **Triangle** where your waist is larger than your shoulders.

This doesn't just mean your overweight. Your bone structure and how weight is distributed across your body can play a role. 14 % of the male population have this. Celebrity Example - David Walliams and Michael McIntyre.

Some key trends for your body shape:

- Vertical stripes will help give the impression your body shape pulls down. This doesn't mean everything needs to be stripy, they don't want to date a banana in Pyjamas, this is just an example of what goes with your body shape.
- Anything that broadens the chest so patterns or bright colours across the shoulders
- If you can find jumpers or sweatshirts that have darker colours around the bottom with lighter colours near the top this will also create the same illusion – again don't be dressing like a zebra crossing all the time this is just an example
- An overcoat that adds structure to your shape from the top is a great example of a jacket.

Rectangle

You probably resemble an NBA player. Tall and thin. Or you may be small in height but the same across. This is the most common with 40% of the male population falling into this category. The same size pretty much all the way. Celebrity example – David Beckham.

Some key trends for your body shape:

- Horizontal stripes going across your shoulders and chest will give the illusion you have more muscle than you do
- Anything to add some weight, so a cardigan or a jumper will beef you out a little bit

- Prints or colours across the shoulders draw the eyes' attention. We are trying to make you look more like Captain America after the serum than before.

Inverted Triangle

This is best known as the V taper in fitness circles. 5 % of the male population falls into this category. Usually for avid gym-goers. Celebrity example – Jason Statham.

Some key trends for your body shape:

- A mild V neck T-shirt (I don't rate this as who likes a cold upper chest) but they do suit this body shape.
- A size up and a slim fit shirt is a great combination. If you wear a slim fit in your size, then you'll look like it was sprayed on – not a good look. Yes, we know you go to the gym, no we do not need to see you where your muscles join through your clothes.
- I LOVE skinny-fit jeans but a slim fit is more than enough. If you wear too tight bottom clothing it makes it look like you skip leg day (when you defo don't right) The issue here is with a broad torso we want to try and take away and give you a more balanced image
- Trousers that have a pattern are good for this. Chinos with squarer fit or simple work trousers will make your BUTT pop like J-lo. Women love a good butt as well – trust me.
- Kinds of cotton that stretch are perfect. A cotton polo shirt will allow your shape to come through without looking try-hard.

Height

If you are a short gentleman, then you often feel as if taller women are out of your league. This is wrong. We can however look at ways you may look as if you are taller to help with your inner confidence.

You can buy inserts into your shoes that add a few inches of height. They are comfortable to wear and easy to add. They slip in and slip out. You can find many examples of these on Amazon.

Another one to remember is to get your trousers tailored. It is important to reduce excess material.

You will however save a fortune on trainers and shoes by being able to shop in the kid's section so there are some benefits aye.

At the other end of the spectrum, we may be so tall that we make the Big Show look small. In this case, do not crouch or begin to make yourself look smaller. Own it. Take up space.

It has never harmed Shaq being so tall and it won't to you either. You look imposing.

Again, tailoring is key here. Shopping for clothes that add layers stops it looking as if clothes drape off you. A suit or a blazer and shirt help break it up.

Age

Age is a big factor when thinking about what we wear. No one likes to see a middle-aged man in denim shorts and rolled-up sleeves on a T-shirt. Take this into consideration when dressing.

As a rule, the older you get the more smart and formal clothes to become. Hoodies get replaced with jumpers. T-shirts for polos and tracksuit bottoms for trousers. We want to look distinguished.

Many garments look equally great on both but do not be caught attempting to dress "young". You are a man who embraces father time, who grows old gracefully.

Dirty trainers are never acceptable at any age regardless if you're a student and your friends do it. Have respect for your clothes and look as if you are well put together.

Clothes should always be neatly pressed and wrinkle-free. If you had time to get ready, then you had time to get ready well.

Accessories play a role but do not be that person who has the dirty entrance wristbands from every festival they have been to still on their wrist. It may be a conversation piece, but it also shows you: live in the past, are starting your germ farm, and are so generic it is comical.

Profession

What you do for a job is going to have a large say over your wardrobe. If you wear a suit for a living you will no doubt have an array of suits to wear. These should always be dry-cleaned regularly. Shirts will be neatly ironed and cleaned. Ties will be well thought out and at least in a half-Winsor knot (you are not at school anymore). If you can do other knots then feel free to express yourself, I am just setting a minimum level of expectations. We do not want to look as if the suit is for our appearance at court and was hastily bought from Primark.

Not every man was fortunate enough to be taught how to do a tie. Not to worry young squire, we are self-made men and we can teach ourselves. Being able to do a tie is a very handy skill.

If you are unsure of how to do a half-Windsor knot, I have kindly got a diagram just for you. People make lots of judgments based on your tie. Yours will say you're here for business.

Shoes will be clean and polished to shine.

If you transport paperwork or a laptop you will carry a holdall, laptop bag (preferably leather), or a briefcase. You will not have a rucksack.

The coat should match the suit. We are making sure we look consistent in our choices. An example as such is an overcoat or a rain Mack. Not a parker jacket with a furry hood.

If you work in construction, you will no doubt have work clothes. These are fine.

If you work in an office with a smart casual vibe then this is your chance to show off your wide selection of clothing. You can mix it up between smart or casual.

Remember always dress for the job you want not the job you've got.

Lifestyle

This one is simple. If you spend a lot of time in the countryside at the weekends, then you'll want clothes that fit in there. Jumpers, wellies, big coats. Something Elmar Fudge would rock.

If you hang out at the skate park, then you'll need clothes that match.

You should have clothes that fit into your chosen hobbies. Whether this is the gym or swimming. It's important to have all the gear even if you have no idea what your doing – you'll at least look the part.

Must-have

Finally, our last section is on must-have clothing in everyman's wardrobe. These are the essential timeless pieces that will help you remain stylish no matter what the winds of fashion bring about.

These are versatile and should be a staple. Such items will allow you to effortlessly be ready for any occasion.

- A Black Leather Jacket – Since Marlon Brando, this bad boy has been versatile to go with a white T-Shirt or be worn with a shirt to make formal wear more casual.
- A Sweatshirt and Chino Jeans – this epitomises preppy. Paul Newman brought this one into the mainstream
- Dark Indigo Jeans – Comfortable to go with smart clothes or to be worn with trainers it is a must-have
- White trainers – able to go with a shirt, t-shirt or polo, it lets you look clean and fresh whilst making a situation less formal
- A Navy Blazer – such a blazer can be worn with jeans or trousers. It helps make a going out outfit or smart enough to be worn around the office
- A pair of black shoes – This again will be needed time and time again
- A black suit – not just worn to funerals. This is versatile to be worn for business or an office party. It is sleek and simple in its style.
- A Breton top – we've mentioned lines quite a lot in this chapter. Such a classic top suits a summer look. Looks great with some Stone Chinos.

- A roll neck jumper – it's an office party and Christmas look. It is smart, it shows you don't mind a bit of flamboyance in your life. It's that good they put it on the Milk Tray advert
- Military boots – great with jeans and good for dressing down
- Dessert boots- they go with jeans and great with a shirt or a T-shirt
- A nice clean watch – a man who doesn't need to keep the time has nowhere to be.

All of what we have discussed must be tailored to make work for you. I am merely offering suggestions and ideas based upon what I know works. This whole chapter is about ways you can boost your confidence and make a good first impression by knowing you have done everything in your power to make sure you come across as well presented.

You may not do it all at once and you may already have a style that you believe works for you but there is no harm in experimenting.

Knowing things such as your face and body shape can only aid you in making decisions moving forward.

We want you to be confident that when you approach a woman you feel as if you are looking your best. That's it. Not the best looking. We know that is nowhere near as important as we think it is! We do however need to look well-thought-out as if we are in control of our appearance and therefore our own life. That is attractive. That stimulates the attraction switches. We look successful if we can successfully choose clothes that make us look well put together, we appear powerful if we have muscles and go to the gym. We look like we make good choices if we choose hair that suits us or have clean teeth.

If we are lacking in any one area, then it is fine if we appear as if we have made the effort to work on our weaknesses. Who wouldn't want a man who is there for self-improvement?

Now spending longer getting ready than a woman is almost always a turn-off for many women and I am not suggesting you should do anything of the sort. I am however giving suggestions on ways you can put some thought into your appearance, so we get that benefit of the doubt when they weigh up in their mind if you are "a weirdo" or not.

Confidence is key.

We must look as if we own our own space.

A man that looks well kept, clean, and dressed well is going to get much better reception than a man who is the opposite.

Appearance won't help you seal the deal, but it will give you a nudge in helping enter negotiations in the first place.

The last thing to mention in this chapter, especially for older men is hormone replacement therapy. Such a thing is common in women especially going through menopause. Men do however produce less testosterone. A lot less.

This is one of the least talked about worries in society at present. **The reversal of men being men.**

Let me explain.

Penis sizes in men are shrinking.

In the last 40 years, Sperm Count in men has decreased by 50%.

Testosterone in men has been declining since 1982, a meta-analysis of 185 studies looking at over 48,000 men between the years 1973-2011 has found that male sperm concentration in males has decreased by over 52%. This worrying fact should send shivers down your spine.

With male's overall sperm count decreasing by 59% this is at the crisis point. If we were talking about female's oestrogen decreasing by such figures there would be a national outcry. However, we men are left to fend for yourselves.

The reasons for this are multi-faceted and there is no quick fix. Societal change, the role men are now being asked to play in society, the rise of the Beta-male, lifestyle choices, a growing obesity crisis will all play a role in the reduction of male hormones and quality semen production.

The reduction of the male here should also be a worry for women as well as men. If we look at sperm bank data from 1963 the average teaspoon of semen contained 99 million viable sperm by millimetre. By the time 2011 comes around this figure falls to only 49 million viable sperm per millimetre. The decrease in the sperm count and sperm quality means that male fertility issues contribute to 25 -33% of all fertility issues.

Meaning it gets much harder for women to get pregnant.

We need to up our games gentleman. Before we get replaced by the back section of Ann Summers for good.

Thankfully there are many ways to boost our natural testosterone production. Lifting heavy weights makes the body produce more testosterone. Ensuring we eat a well-balanced diet that includes lots of fats. I know what you learnt in primary school about avoiding fats, but they are wrong you need to put an emphasis on foods with high saturated fats like butter, coconut oil, eggs. There are also things you can't get just with diet this is where it's important to use supplements. The types of things you should be supplementing are Vitamin D3, fish oil, whey protein, and magnesium. Sleep plays a vital role in testosterone production, getting enough of it and deeper REM sleep helps with your testosterone. Playing competitive sports also helps raise this level.

Then we have my favourite way to boost testosterone naturally - Have more sex.

The more sex you have the more testosterone you produce.

As well as the natural ways to boost testosterone we can embrace modern medicine. Just like women do. If you had a poorly arm you would get it looked at by a professional. The same is true for your testosterone.

In the journal **A UK epidemic of testosterone prescribing, 2001-2010,** there has been a 90% increase in male prescribed testosterone replacement therapy. The good news is you don't even need to go to the NHS. Most private healthcare providers will also prescribe it.

I would recommend getting your blood works done online through a private company to see where your testosterone levels currently lie. A quick google search can show your nearest clinic or they can post it out to you, and you send it back. It cost about £80 – which is a steal to find out where you currently are. I have a feeling if your over 25 they'll be much lower than you thought. Thankfully you can get it rectified and put back into your teenage years! (whoop lots of random Boners)

The good news is the rise of low testosterone in men and these new Beta males mean far less competition for us.

We do our best to distance ourselves from these **beta males.** They live their lives seeking validation from others. Their very values and visions are that which were created by other people. They are the type that listens to mainstream media and girls' Instagram memes about how they should behave. They are the ones that ask women for advice on how to talk to women. That is like asking fish how to cast a fishing line. These men are lacking in self-reliance and do not have a strong sense of personal identity. They fall into patterns of neediness and approval-seeking behaviours. They are the men which do posts bashing other men for countless likes from other women. They record Tik Toks and often slate men. They think that a like on Facebook translate as an indicator of interest. It does not.

Beta males get friend-zoned. Beta males get walked over and ignored by women of value.

An alpha male is a man who is completely outcome independent, emotionally secure, and confident. He does not seek validation. Be the leader, not the follower.

Sometimes women are not even aware of a wolf in sheep's clothing. Matthew Hussey is a known authority to females on dating. Countless women watch his videos and go to his seminars. They feel as if he is there for them. To advise them on how men should be. Well, I am not saying he isn't. But did you know that Matthew Hussey used to be a Pick-Up Artist? Not just a Pick-Up artist he used to coach other men on how to pull women? Giving talks and one-to-one coaching on this before he found a new market to sell his wares. So the next time a woman sends you a Tik Tok or video about how men should behave, do a little digging and let her know exactly the kind of person the advice is coming from. Matthew Hussey probably helped more men get women into bed than those he has saved from getting in bed with the wrong guy.

To recap on what we have learnt so far-

- We know the theory behind attraction switches and that 70% of what makes a woman attracted to us is to do with these

Getting The Girl

- We know why we avoid the friendship zone and the different stages of the Courtship Process
- We know the importance of believing in ourselves and how we can work on our inner game. Confidence is key. We must believe it
- We have looked at all the ways to make a good first impression, how to dress, what haircuts we can have, and how to generally look after ourselves. We know that looking after ourselves shows we are not this needy male but a survivor that can bring value to women's lives

Now taking what we know we are going to look at how we can make social media work for us.

How can we use what we have learnt so far to convey that we are: a protector of loved ones, an alpha male, a successful risk-taker and pre-selected by other women?

We will show that we are confident.

We will show that we look after ourselves.

We will show them why they would be bloody lucky to have the opportunity to spend some time with us.

Jeez we are pretty great aren't we.

(if you don't believe it, neither will they)

Getting The Girl

CHAPTER 5
Social Media - Tinder, Facebook, Instagram

"Content is fire. Social media is gasoline" --- Jay Baer, Keynote speaker, emcee, author and enterpreneur

Chapter 5 – Facebook, Tinder, Instagram, Making Social Media Impressions

"You are the product. You feel something. That's what sells."

"Make it simple, but significant."

Don Draper

Mad Men burst onto our screens in 2007 lasting seven seasons until 2015. The premise of the show follows an advertising agency called Sterling Cooper located at Sixth Avenue. Mad Men was the nickname given to advertisers working on Maddison Avenue in NYC in the 1950s. Hence the name "Mad Men".

Don Draper is the creative director of Sterling Cooper. Don is looked upon as a creative marketing genius, and he is always figuring out creative ways to position different products to his audience.

He is also a huge hit with the ladies. That's because Don knows how to build a brand.

You are your own brand. Social media is simply a means by which to sell this brand to the world.

Social media is anything but social. It is contrived, it is edited, it is a highlight reel of the best things you want to portray to others.

Never forget – social media isn't real.

They aren't that happy, that important, or that successful.

The good thing is, you don't have to be either. Social media is a tool. So, let us wield it.

When using social media, we must realise we have different platforms for different things. We must use each platform differently but with a joint purpose. In marketing, we call this having brand alignment. You want to make sure the messaging is clear throughout.

It is no good saying you hate apples on Facebook and that you love apple pie on Instagram. You come across as disingenuous. People hate feeling lied to. This is why I wouldn't encourage you to tell any outright lies on social media. If found out it does great reputation destruction. I will encourage you to apply a filter to what you say. To not share each dying thought. To think before you speak. To be economical with the truth. To allow people to draw their own conclusions in part.

After all, you can't be held accountable because someone has jumped to some conclusion, can you?

Not your fault fucking Tigger read your tweets.

The art of social media management is therefore to try to tick as many attraction switches as possible through your use of your words, images, or collection of amazing memes.

Memes are excellent and people that can wield a meme show your ability to navigate acute social cues. You can become your very own Peter Kay with thought-provoking statements like

"Why does mineral water that 'has trickled through mountains for centuries have a 'use by' date?"

Or a classic Dad Joke like ***"My dad used to say, 'Always fight fire with fire', which is probably why he got thrown out of the fire brigade."***

Now you may not be a naturally funny person but by using other people's humour you associate yourself with the positive feelings people get when they read it. You become second-hand funny, as you choose the meme or the quote which then made someone laugh. Well done you.

Now before you start posting entire scripts of Kevin Hart's latest stand-up routine just know that such things are best used sparingly.

The Attraction Switches we want to tick through social media are:

1. Alpha male – leader of men
2. Successful Risk Taker
3. Protector of Loved Ones
4. Pre-selected by women

How we can convey these can be through words, pictures, or quotes. You have a wide range of choices.

That video of you getting egged by your mate. Hardly doing anything for you. Delete it.

One of you at a conference or giving a speech? This guy has something worth saying – Leader of men.

One of you at a boxing class? Protector of the loved one switch - he can protect himself and probably me.

One of you on holiday? - Successful risk-taker -that can afford a holiday.

And of course, you sat down surrounded by 3 beautiful women? Pre-selected by women - He is used to being with pretty women, so he must have value.

It is the subconscious mind that we trigger here.

Now I want to go over what the different platforms are for and how to use them.

Facebook

Mark Zuckerberg's creation has grown so big that the odds are your parents, grandparents, cousins, teacher, and the man who runs the local car wash are all on there. It has "buy and sell" groups, mother's groups, Jedi Council Appreciation society pages, and many more.

Facebook is for staying in touch with friends and people you know.

Facebook is not for dating.

Do not add random women on Facebook then slide in the DMs.

It is not its purpose. Do not try and make it that way.

On Facebook, you may share stories with friends, post old pictures, occasionally write a status on a topical issue.

If you want your social media to help enhance your dating life, then you will stay away from being controversial. You will not post too many topless selfies (guilty as charged) you will not enter the debate with people. You will not share fake news stories or your conspiracy theories. Leave that for a chat with your mates around a nice cosy fire in a tucked-away pub. Right the wrongs of the world in a safe space.

Remember anything published on Facebook can and will be used against you.

Facebook won't do much to help with dating, girls rarely find you on Facebook anymore to check out what you look like. They will use it to do a background check though. Does he post weird stuff? does he have a girlfriend? is his ex-girlfriend tagged in his pictures? – let's check her out. They can look at where you like to eat, the bad pictures friends tag you in, what your views are on most issues. Lots of things that can give a bad first impression.

So, as Don Draper puts it. Stay simple. Keep your Facebook simple and above all keep it private. Make sure you have the maximum-security settings on.

- Go to **Settings & Privacy** > **Settings** > **Privacy**. Under **Who Can See Your Posts**, change **Public** to **Friends**, or another option.
- To make your Friends list private, go to **Privacy** > **Who can see your friends list** and select **Friends** or **Only Me**.
- To make your profile private, go to your profile page and select **Edit Details**. Toggle off the information you want to keep private.

Another thing people will scan for is your friend list. You can make this private as well. Facebook makes your friends list public by default, which means everyone can see it, whether they're your friend or not. You can change your preferences from the Facebook settings or on your profile page.

- On the Settings and Privacy screen, select **Edit** next to **Who can see your friends list**.

Tinder

Tinder is a tricky app to navigate. Those pesky engineers are more meddling than the Scooby Gang. The whole thing is running off algorithms. There is a way you can be ghosted by the actual app and it all comes down to a **Personal Desirability Score.**

This score determines who sees you and who you see.

How does it work?

Every user gets given a PDS, to represent how much of a catch any person is. Users are then sorted into tiers based on their desirability score you then get presented with people approximately your level of attractiveness when you swipe.

It does this by using the mechanics of Chess Players (good old geek chic) with what's known as an ELO system. If people swipe right on you, your desirability score goes up, and it goes down if people instead give your profile a pass. If someone with a high score swipes right on you, that increases your score more than someone with lower ***"desirability".***

Another thing that affects who sees your profile is the ***"Visibility"*** of your profile. That being that the longer you're off the app the further to the back of the queue you go. Log in to be seen more.

Finally, its new introduction called ***"Type Match"*** where it hopes to match profiles where you share similar interests now plays a role alongside the ELO system.

Type match

Here it tries to group users into similar categories and show them to one another. It also uses Amazon's - **AWS image recognition.** This piece of software recognizes what is going on in an image and likely contributes to Tinder's **profiling efforts** by supplying information such as "This user likes people who are playing the violin in their photos".

The only way to help with this algorithm is to type case your profile to attract one particular type of girl.

Personal Desirability Score

Many factors contribute to this so I will outline these here for you. The first of which is How **Selective you are.** Equally swiping right to everyone and almost no one are penalized, though mass swiping right a lot more severely than being too picky. A right swipe quota of 30-70% seems to be the magic formula to help you get your Hermione.

If you reset your account, many times and get caught this can affect your score.

Swiping too much with TINDER GOLD. Swiping too often per day, or hour will trigger that you are a bot. This results in one of the dreaded ***Shadow bans***. It will also give you a very, very low score, rendering you nigh invisible.

The figure that triggers this is around **2'000 swipes per hour** in any direction will get your account "locked" for at least 12 hours of the app telling you to "Check back later for new people", potentially also carrying a permanent score punishment with it.

Changing your location too often as a Plus user can also lower your score.

Whether you actually send messages to most of your matches – this works with both sending and receiving.

Visibility

When you first download Tinder, you get a **New Boost.** This applies to both when you first have the app or when you travel to a new location. You will get shown to more users. Being active is the best way to boost how visible you are.

Now Tinder unlike in real-life rewards based on looks.

Knowing this you want to lead with the most attractive shot of your face. Body pics are great but if you lead with it then you will come across as try-hard. Your main profile picture is your most important so lead with your strongest. You want a waist-up headshot.

Avoid wearing a hat or glasses both will reduce your matches. Looking away from the camera is very popular amongst the most matched guys on tinder so steal this technique.

OKCupid did a study that showed that looking away from the camera and not smiling lead to the most matches.

Your second-best if you can't pull this off is a direct look in the camera with a smile (now I know that contradicts the last statement but it's one or the other).

Use a timer instead of a selfie for a better image. Leave the selfies to girls.

Now if you are going for a body shot it is best to be tasteful and artistic. Think playing on the beach or walking the dog on a hot day. This means ditching the gym or mirror topless pictures (damn it).

Now pics with dogs, girls LOVE. If you can borrow a dog – do it. It shows that sensitive side.

Who doesn't love a dog aye?

One of the most common photo techniques used among Tinder's elite 4 final bosses is taking photos with a low *aperture* setting.

A low aperture setting simply means that the focus of the photo (a person or a face) is very sharp and crisp while the background is blurred.

This is different from using a filter and aims to create aesthetically pleasing pictures.

Using a filter is another option, Instagram has filters you can use, Snapchat does and the iPhone itself has a few. Using apps to edit photos with filters is another option but be wary you do not edit your photos, so you become unrecognisable. Repix is but one app on the app store that allows you to edit your photos but many more can be found under the fun with filters section. Catfishing is never cool and will lead to you getting blown out at the first meet. Which is a waste of both of your time. We aren't here to convince them you look like something you don't. The purpose of a filter is to change lighting and colours to make things look more appealing. A nice sunset glow, for example, not dog ears and a sticky tongue. By making the environment look nice it helps to add to the whole feel of the photo. There is also the good old black and white to add some mystery. Dark and mysterious, looking like a 1930's sleuth detective (avoid the magnifying glass for full effect).

After all, we know the most important thing isn't how you look anyway. It's those pesky Attraction Switches and our ability to hold a conversation.

We also want to Improve poor quality photos or removing them altogether from your Tinder profile. It's an easy win to make you look more attractive and start getting more matches.

When selecting your photos use ones that are big enough to fit everything in. Ensure they are clear and crisp.

Remember how we want to tick the successful attraction switch? Well, you could have a picture of you throwing money off a cliff to emphasises your success (this isn't a good method) or you can display your high status by listing your occupation.

If you are a Royal Marine Commando, then I would want to make this known. Who doesn't want to announce to the world they are a trained killer? Steven Seagal has made a career picking up chicks off his ability to fight people on boats.

However, if you're a deep undercover operator like Solid Snake then probably best to leave that off your Tinder profile for fear of getting rumbled. Nobody wants to turn up to a date to get assassinated, do they?

The last thing you should consider is whether you want an image on there that allows people to strike up a conversation. Often this can be done in your bio but if you feel there is an image that people will just have to ask you about:

- Hanging off a bridge with one hand
- Surrounded by lots of Marvel Characters at a Comic-Con
- Balancing 5 plates on your nose
- Dancing with the Prime Minister
- Slam dunking on Elon Musk
- Playing the piano with Stevie Wonder on a hot air balloon
- Do you get the point? Anything to get them talking first is a good start

Now we are going to talk about attraction and how to build it in the next chapter, but I know you'll be asking **"What do I say for my opening line on Tinder?"**

You do not want to show too much interest, but you want to show confidence in your opening approach. Simplicity is key. You might want to paint the image of a story of the first time you meet or create a scenario where you see one another. This serves as a subsequent **Hook.**

Then once they take the bait.

You get to work demonstrating high value as we will discuss in the following chapters and building attraction.

Some examples of openers on tinder:

- When we go on our first date to the (insert coffee shop or restaurant) will you definitely be ordering (insert food or dessert) or will it depend on your mood on the day?
- Do you think we should take (insert food or drink) with us when we go to the museum or the statues might get jealous, I've seen Night at The Museum and Genghis Khan looks pretty scary?
- I was just thinking about which one of us would be better at leapfrogging over benches when we go to the (insert park) and then I thought well

> probably not me if I wear my summer dress again, so I will probably wear jeans, what do you think you'll wear so I know we won't clash?

None of the above messages comes across as beggy. You act as if you both going on a date is inevitable. You aren't wasting time with small talk. This is good old-fashioned Straight-Line-Selling as Jordan Belfort writes about in his book. You get to the purpose and you loop around until you get where you want to go.

Talk about the end goal early which is a date. The purpose of tinder is not to run the whole game here. It is to get the number – move away from tinder and go on a date.

If you don't want to get the number early, then go for Instagram if you are confident that it will enhance your chances based upon the values it demonstrates.

Waiting too long in Tinder World makes it possible you become just another "Tinder Boy" she will quickly lose interest in. No matter how exciting the conversation is you need to progress to the next stage and this is either getting the number, their Instagram, or going on a date.

A date is the best case, a number is next, and Instagram is the bare minimum.

Using other apps like Snapchat is possible but Instagram is for more serious contenders, we all know that Snapchat is where all the seedier conversations go down ...that just so happen to delete themselves...choose your battleground wisely...

Remember: you're both on Tinder because you want to meet people. You both matched which means you both find each other attractive. It's safe to assume that a date is what you're both there to talk about.

In your conversations you want to be conveying all the things we know women find attractive, you may talk about the time you stuck up for your little sister or how all the guys want to hang out with you at the weekend but you've decided to have a weekend to yourself (no-one tells you what to do) so you have some free time if she fancies a stroll.

You might talk about how you've had a great day solving a problem at work and your boss is extremely happy with you or that you have just closed a big deal (well done Harvey Spector). You will convey you're a high-status man.

You may even tell her how you are spending the weekend getting ice cream with this girl who asked to spend some time with you. This will probably strike a chord of jealousy that's so obvious you won't need a Sharingan to see it.

People love stories, we remember fairy-tale stories so vividly. Before the advent of books, we use to pass on tales by word-of-mouth through centuries. Stories are easy to remember and sit in the part of our brain that makes them have meaning. Many women wish their lives were stories so paint a picture with words and watch as your replies become that frequent your mates will think you're an extra in ER with the amount your phone pings (paging DR LOVE).

When conducting your stories and generally conversation be sure to use lots of "us" and "our" this builds a sense that you are in it together.

You can be a wordsmith or a blacksmith, one uses heavy metal objects to get women into bed and the other talks her into it. I know which one you should choose.

Make words your weapons and watch as women surrender before the might and legions of conversation you have at your disposal.

Instagram

The rapid rise of this social media giant gave the early adopters huge advantages when capturing target audiences. The rise of the influencer soon followed. Many a generation Z now aspires to go on a reality TV show then sell teeth whitening toothpaste to their followers on The Gram. Why wouldn't they? With users able to command 10k plus for a single post-it sure seems an easy way to make a living.

But Jack isn't this just basically a giant marketing channel then? You are correct. Excellent what I told you at the beginning with my boy Don. Everyone is selling something. Whether it's a product or themselves, Instagram is designed to sell things through pictures and captions.

It even has a little sales section just like Depop now.

Not very social for social media aye.

We can however use this to our advantage by embracing what social media is – a marketing tool. So, that's how we will treat it. A way to market ourselves.

Our purpose on social media is to convey that we are a person of value. We can do this in many ways and Instagram allows us to choose different tools to select to do so. On Instagram you can:

- **Post a picture -** This will be accompanied by a caption. The picture's purpose is to show people that follow you (or those that don't if you are in public) that you live an exciting life. You do things that make people believe you have value.
- This could be going on holiday (the usual) attending large events (concerts) taking nice pictures of scenarios (you appreciate finer things) you hang out with cool people (raises our social value) you look good (it is a picture after all).
- These are just a few examples of what you can do with pictures on Instagram, but the general rule is you want to post pictures that will increase your standing and make you look like a high-value male. Referring to the attraction switches any of these could be triggered here with a carefully constructed image choice.

- **Post a video –** This is also accompanied by a caption. A video allows you to show more than just a momentary glance, you can show you and your friends are having fun at a swimming pool or building a human pyramid with yourself at the top. You can also use time-lapse to speed up days or events showing more than one highlight in one single post.
- You can edit, chop and blend videos from different days.
- You can showcase a talent – showing a basketball throw, a penalty kick, building a birdhouse – the actual talent is irrelevant the action behind it shows you are a man of competence.
- You have many more options with videos, but they are watched less than a picture post

- **Create Reels –** Reels are like Tik Toks for Instagram. They are short videos where people show off voice-overs or dance moves to give a flavour. They can be good if you spotted something funny you wanted to share or have an exceptional talent in an area. They are in a different part of your Instagram profile away from your main page.

- **Post to Story –** Posting to the story should probably be your go-to. Here an image or video will last for around 24 hours. You do have the option to save these to something called your highlights. Highlights are a collection of your stories that you have chosen to save for people to watch later. They can be a mixture of what you are up to day to day, reminiscing on a moment, or even those really funny memes you've seen.

- **Finally,** Slide **in the DMs**- This is your opportunity to reply to someone's story or to pop up to them to start or continue a conversation. This is an approach method some use to talk to girls. When done correctly this is acceptable. We will go through how this should play out in a moment.

These are the options we have to us when using Instagram. A wide range at our disposal gentleman. Now before we do any of that we need to write a pretty epic bio to grab our reader in.

Bio

We want to optimise your profile to attract as many girls as possible. The impression we want to give is that you are a busy man, who does lots of fun things. Your honest and unreserved. You will give straight answers and you like to laugh. You, therefore, may want to add a quote about something you find important, mention your values or a thing which gives your identity meaning (such as being a vegan), talk about any interesting hobbies, and maybe what you do for work if you have a really interesting job which women will love.

An example

Gianfranco Casanova

- Full-time wind-up merchant, Part-time Real Estate Agent
- Scared of using the – in Bios
- Happiest when walking the dog or surfing, am yet to combine the two
- Family, Friends & Fun times is all I ask God for

I have kept the bio light-hearted, nothing deep, nothing political, nothing too controversial we don't want to close doors on ourselves before we have had a chance to speak. We also have several hooks should someone want to strike up a conversation with us. It's simple.

We show family is important – Attraction Switch

We show friends are important – Attraction Switch

We are busy and have interesting hobbies – Attraction Switch

Of course, we also mentioned dogs and who doesn't love dogs except for Mickey in Snatch who prefers DAGS, but we will let him off because he would probably knock us out with one punch.

Pictures

PICTURES! The whole reason the app was invented. Just like the guidance for TINDER earlier, most of the photo editing guidance will also apply here. Making your pictures pop with different focuses and backgrounds will help to make your profile more visually appealing.

Having pictures with a strong city break background or a monument not only shows that you are well-traveled but it also shows you understand how to take great photos. This is a skill. Now I am not saying it's time to invest in a selfie ring (but you know you want to) but I am saying that making sure your images are clear and crisp will make a big difference.

Pictures allow people to get a flavour of what type of person you are, if you like attending famous castle at the weekend then take a cool picture of you holding a sword in the armoury (only if you're allowed you don't want to go full-on Step-Brothers on me now Nighthawk) not only will it make a great photo but it's another opportunity to use as a conversation piece. They might share similar hobbies and want to talk about it or at the very least be like ***"WTF why have you got a sword in your hands !?"*** Which is far better than being totally off their radar.

Pictures with animals (please avoid animals that have been drugged or abused to take the images) show you have a caring side and maybe one day you can be admired as much as David Attenborough. Also, pictures of you and your friends having a laugh gives you social proof, it shows that you often have fun with people. You are in demand.

If you're a modern-day Greek God, then boy here is your chance to display your best features in a tasteful way. Pictures of you and your buddies on holiday with your tops off is a lot more socially acceptable than you in the gym but if you've got it kid then flaunt it. When she's faced with closing her eyes in the middle of the night and imaging her ex bearing over her with his beer belly hanging down as he sweats and grunts or she could imagine laying there gazing into your eyes rubbing her hands over your big wide shoulders when she's having some alone time, we can both conclude which one she would rather choose. Contrary to popular belief Dad Bods aren't in. Nobody wants to sleep with their Dad.

When you post a picture of you looking epic, you're actually laying a thirst trap. A thirst trap is an image or picture designed to get a response. From thirsty girls in this case. This works wonders when posted on a story. Stories are more private when people respond which means they are more open to slide in the DM's. Nobody else knows what they've said to you, unlike posting actual pictures. Lay the trap and watch as woman after woman replies to your story. What they reply is irrelevant cause what they are actually telegraphing is interest, **if they weren't interested, they wouldn't say anything.** It doesn't matter whether it's an emoji, a wow or an *"omg put it away"* you now have an opening and it's your job to carry the ball to the N-Zone and score that touchdown champ.

As mentioned previously in the book If you have a kick-ass job like a sky diving instructor or a rollercoaster tester then you want to post pictures of this. This is really cool. You want to show this off with a well-taken photo. If you are creative, you can make anything look good like cutting the grass on a hot Summer's day. With the right photo, you'll look just like the Diet Coke Advert gentleman.

Finally, we have the crème de resistance, pictures of you with other girls. Of course, you are used to being surrounded by other girls, they do it all the time. It is just what happens to you right? You can't help that girls like to be around you. Pre-selection is the most powerful Attraction Switch. Watch as they begin to compare themselves to the women you post.

You can do this any time you hang out with a friend that's a girl, or even when you're on a date, take the time to snap a quick pic. This works especially well on your story. A picture of you with a girl's hands in the background whilst out for food piques the mystic and lets others fill in the blanks.

You'd be amazed how well a photo of a dinner with a glass of wine and a girl's handbag in the background of the picture does. Girls won't be sure if you've got a girlfriend, you're on a date, or out with family. The not knowing drives the imagination wild. Women love to be detectives; they will plan the whole crime in their head for you, so you wouldn't even need to commit it.

Photos, where girls are touching you or leaning on you, are great cause they make it look like the girl wants you. The more girls in the picture the better, just make sure you are the only guy in the photo.

Remember with photos, lighting, filters, and angles are everything. Play around until you get a filter you like. Most people look better with some colour on their face or a nice sunset glow so here is a good place to start. Also, use the filters mentioned earlier in the Tinder section. Always take more photos than necessary and choose the best one. When taking photos of others, take about 10 +. DO this for any group of girls and they will love you, do so from different heights and walk closer and further away. They will love this! It's also an opportunity to strike up a conversation. Plus, once you take one good photo, they have a reason to come back and talk to you later *"hey can you take another photo of us please?"* ...Well if you insist ladies.

Don't be tempted to turn the camera around and take one of yourself, it is annoying and likely to come back to bite you. You will just piss them off. Act like you always get asked to take photos because girls are always talking to you, you've done this before right champ

Now there is another way to play Instagram which is high risk and high reward. This approach involves openly talking about dating girls and sleeping with girls with boyfriends. Now I know what your thinking – Jack are you insane- well maybe but it doesn't half pay dividends. What I am saying is what you convey in such a message is – not only do I attract single girls, but I am that irresistible girls in relationships can't help themselves! Even better if you are in a relationship and you want to talk to me – go ahead – I am receptive.

Some people will respond with how funny they think this is – there is your opening, some will pop up to tell you how bad these girls' behaviour is – there's your ***opening:***

"you would never do that would you *insert eyes emoji*"

And some will not be too impressed but that's why it's a high risk, high reward. There is a potential you can lose a lot of potential girls or upset ones you are currently talking to, so it comes down to personal preference. There is the slow and steady, build your brand and image or there is the Supreme pop-up shop approach – get it whilst you can cause if you don't someone else will.

You must find what works for you and your circumstances.

When you become confident in your game you will do things on socials that are for your amusement, this is cause you are confident in your ability to attract women and do not rely on " crutches" such as well-crafted images and witty captions. However, until you get to that stage you will want a social media presence that enhances your ability to make a good first impression. Having things to talk about in the DM's, posting interesting things on your story or memes that people find amusing are all opportunities to strike up a conversation without appearing weird or seedy.

The Early Bird May Get the Worm but The Second Mouse Gets the Cheese – Work smarter fellas.

****

Chasing a cat makes it hard to catch but lay down a bowl of milk and watch as it comes to you. When a woman pops up first it makes it much easier to establish rapport, you don't show interest, so you are on a level playing field. We will go over this in more detail in building attraction.

Followers

One thing which can set you apart from all the other men on Instagram is the number of followers you have. I know Jesus only needed 12 but you're not the messiah, just a very naughty boy. So, unless you're going to moonwalk over water at a pool party, we are going to need to give the impression that people care about what you get up to.

It's important to differentiate, they care what you are up to, you don't care what they are up to. This is the sign of the alpha. Therefore, where possible, you want more followers than you follow. This says – a lot more people care about my life than I care about theirs. *Remember leader of men?*

So, to give the impression, you are Maximus Decimus Meridius leader of The Armies of the North we want to crank up that follower count.

A quick way to do this is to select followers you can import from your phonebook and Facebook. Follow everyone you know and wait for them to follow you back. We are aiming for at least a 100 to make a start and for it to not look like you're a fake profile.

Go to your **Instagram** profile page by tapping your photo at the bottom right of your phone's screen. Tap the small person with a plus (and possibly a red number) at the top left. Tap the **Contacts** link. The next screen tells you that **Instagram** will find **people** you know, and you're given the option to **follow** them.

Eventually, over time you can begin to unfollow people that don't follow you back or those whose lives you are uninterested in, but it is a quick fix to gain followers.

Another lesson we learnt in Defence Against the Dark Arts by Gilderoy Lockhart (the great pretender) is you can purchase Instagram followers. Many sites sell followers if you want a quick fix. Remember these will not be active accounts, they won't interact with your pictures, they won't like them or comment. You also must have an account that's set to public. If you are on private, then it doesn't work. It comes down to personal preference again, but legitimate followers will always look better but hey if you can pass other achievements off as your own like Professor Lockhart then why not aye?

Instagram is luckily not very intrusive, and people are quite happy to accept strangers, but this doesn't mean we run around following every girl who looks good in lycra shorts.

A better way to use this to your advantage is to maximise following people when at parties or gatherings. It's quite cool to say *"hey you seem cool what's your insta we should follow each other"* with alcohol in the mix most people will be receptive and once they've followed you are not very likely to unfollow. It's a good way to build up your following and sets up an opportunity to reconnect at a later date. It's especially useful if you take a group photo or a picture with many people in it and you say – *hey what's your insta I'll tag you* – or – if they take a picture ask them to follow you so you can follow them back and see it. Such a throw-away comment doesn't show interest and gives you a potential conversation starter at a later date.

Where lots of guys go wrong is as soon as they get a girl's Instagram they slide in the DM's. You haven't given time to build attraction and it looks desperate. Act like you've done this before, and you were in no hurry to talk to her. Even if you said you would. You are a busy guy, you're probably already talking to lots of women, she needs to wait her turn, right?

Then when you do pop up, you're sure she's been following your life and you've been showing off your attraction switches. How do you know this? Cause thankfully Instagram shows you who's been watching your stories. This makes it easier to find who has been watching you than hiring Liam Neeson to track them down. You never know she could think she needs to work hard to win you over cause after all the dating pictures you've posted she already thinks your Taken champ.

Now as for the best times to post to grow your followers well that comes down to simple data science:

- Best times: **Wednesday at 11 a.m. and Friday from 10 a.m.–11 a.m.**
- Best day: **Wednesday**
- Worst day: **Sunday**

This is one of the joys of stories, they can be checked at any time and binged watched. Instagram Stories that appear at the start of your feed is from accounts that you engage with the most, whether that's through likes, comments, story views, reactions, or DMs.

You should be posted to your story a lot more than an actual post. When someone regularly watches your story, it boosts your profile and helps push you up the algorithm.

So, by posting to Instagram Stories more often, you have a better chance of reaching viewers as they browse their daily stories — and the more views you gain, the better your ranking will be.

Stories are a good way for people to keep up to date with what you are doing. It's a good place to show off how exciting your life is, how many women you spend time with, how you can find joy in simple things -like the sunset – or even just that you actually get out of the house. No matter what you are trying to convey stories are great. They can be used more often, display more things, anything really good can be saved and the rest just gets deleted.

Think of posts more like the shop front. They stay there more permanently. They need to be more carefully selected. They show your core values.

Stories are like an ad campaign. The ad may change depending on the message.

It's especially helpful to use stories if the person following you follows a lot of quotes or meme accounts. These can quickly often flood the person's home page, so they don't see your posts unless they physically go on your profile. People will often do this when they first follow or if they are interested in you. Other than that, they'll just look at each post or story as it comes.

Now whilst we are on who sees what it all comes down to good old-fashioned data. Instagram just like Tinder has an algorithm to determine who sees your actual posts. It has moved away from the chronological way it used to show them. Knowing how this works may help you, increase followers, boost potential likes, and show your posts to the right people. It also decides what it shows you.

Have you ever wondered why it shows you accounts you don't follow?

Well, it does this based upon your historically liked posts. It guesses that because you liked something previous, you'll do it again.

Therefore, what you see in your Instagram feed is a combination of all of your Instagram behaviours. The accounts you interact with the most, the people you are tagged in photos with, and of course, the type of posts that you like and comment on.

So, if you want to show up on people's feeds more often, what's the best way?

The best way is to encourage them to engage with the posts you put out there. Give them a reason or incentive to do something about what you have just posted. Think of something especially funny or thought-provoking if you are struggling to kick start a flurry of likes organically. You can always delete the post at a later date.

What this then does is gets your followers to engage with your posts. They dish out a load of likes and comments. Instagram sees this and moves you up the rankings, so they see your posts next time. You repeat and gradually more people see your actual posts.

As you can see this is more much complex than just stories. But it doesn't mean it's impossible, it just takes a little bit of work to think about the type of things people often comment or like.

This is where good old thirst traps, funny pictures, and group photos come into play. It encourages people to like and comment.

As I have mentioned Instagram's algorithm reacts best to comments, likes, reshares, and views for videos. This is the game you are playing, how many people can I show my advert to?

Keep this in mind when planning your content and captions.

This is of course if you want to raise your followings and make your profile seem more active.

That comes down to personal preference, for some people Instagram is just a landing page to show you exist. If you prefer to play the game in real life than in the virtual world then don't worry too much about chasing that blue tick champ in the making, social media is not necessary to be successful with women, it is just another tool you can use to make a good first impression.

If you have no game in real life, no amount of likes on an Instagram post will save you.

Sliding in the DM's

The best way to slide into the DM's champ is by replying to stories. It's less intrusive, gives you something to talk about, and doesn't convey the interest that a direct DM would.

Bottom line: context matters. Think to yourself, "If I got this message, would I want to respond?" If the message is too vague, random, or rude, the answer is no.

One thing to take into careful consideration is whether this person is in a relationship. If they are and they've given you no signal that is opening to that sort of response, then I would leave it. Especially if you are starting on your journey to being irresistible to women - stick to the single girls. A quick glance at their profile should give you this information. If you are unsure, then shoot your shot Hawkeye, the worse she comes back with is *"I have a boyfriend"* and you just apologise if anyone has been upset and you wish them a good day. This avoids conflict and reduces the chance of her calling you a creep to all her friends and potentially ruining your chances there.

Trust me, girls talk.

However, if all you've done is a reply to her at the park *saying "where's this? It looks nice there"* then there's nothing at all to be ashamed of and you can hold your head up high knowing your message was tasteful and didn't convey that much interest. If she wants to be a bitch about it then that's her problem.

If she doesn't respond, then don't message again. You've tried and if she wanted to respond she would have. The more times you message, and she ignores you – the less perceived value you have.

If she comes back with one-word responses like "Yeppp" or "Lol" those are subtle signs to leave her alone. We can read social dynamics – we would rather move our energy onto other women.

It just means you haven't built enough attraction yet, trust me when I say, if you do build enough attraction, you'll see the signals – she will start to reply to your stories, like your posts, or even slide in your DM's.

If she does respond to your message then lookout for exclamation points, emojis, and smiley face's in her responses. These are signs that you're in the clear to keep the conversation moving

The first thing any girl will do after you have just slid in the DM's is checks your profile. That is why you must have cleaned it up and done all the mentioned above. You have a range of posts that convey you are a high-value male.

Now you've got the conversation following, you're going to run some stories that we will talk about later which show you are a high-value male. Remember the goal of this is to move away from Instagram to date or to get the number.

We don't want to get caught spending weeks in the DM's. A week is more than enough time to run some stories, build attraction and then ask for the number or to meet up.

Just be straight if she's not keen- **honey I'm not looking for a pen pal.**

A good way to do this is to be subtle, here are some examples:

- I am going out to see my friends Friday but if you don't have any plans drop me a text on 07******* and we can see if we can grab a coffee
- I'm out in ***** this weekend, if you are about we can catch up see who can sink the most jager bombs, unless you're scared of course?
- Any nice parks near you? I fancy a walk this weekend somewhere different, I may even let you accompany me if you can behave
- As much as I am enjoying our back to forth, I'm going, to be honest – we need to move this to WhatsApp cause it is encrypted and I'm sure they are on to me after the last bank robbery

The tone is casual and non-committal, if she says no that's cool you can keep the conversation flowing, run some more stories try and build more attraction then try again. If you get the knockback twice then I would call it a day and move onto someone who will appreciate your time.

THINGS NOT TO DO IN THE DM's

There are always some unwritten rules to avoid. These are:

- Don't compliment her, you'll come across as a creep. You are also showing too much interest – the same goes for flame and love heart emojis.
- There used to be a thing where you waited double the time they did to reply, it's better to stay with the natural rhythm, reply when you can but don't look eager
- Avoid sending pictures of yourself on DM's, she knows what you look like. Pictures of your day, food, etc however give things to talk about.
- NO DICK PICS. EVER.

To summarise, Instagram is a tool in which you can use to make a first impression. You can do this by your posts which tell a story about your life. Cleverly chosen pictures and videos can flick Attraction Switches and show that you are a high-value male. You can use many different tools but the easiest one to use is Instagram stories. Replying to other people's Instagram stories is the best way to slide in the DM's. The goal when sliding into DM's is to set up a date or get their number.

Facebook is the social media best used to stay in touch with friends and family, it is not a place to approach women.

Tinder is a dating site specifically designed to meet women. The aim here is to get them off tinder to something else such as Instagram or getting their number.

Social media can be used to start The Courtship Process, or it can be in the middle of it when they are checking you out, to see how comfortable they are. You do not need social media to be successful with women. It is just another option you can possibly use to make a good first impression. You can have a further reach with socials to make an impression with people than you can in the physical world as you are limited to the number of places you can be in.

Social media will never replace conversations in real life, and it cannot be a crutch to rely upon. It can however when used properly, seek to aid you in your pursuit of a life that is rich in the opportunities to talk to lots of women.

Getting The Girl

Social media is nothing more than a marketing tool.

Sex sells.

As Jeff Bezos said, ***"it's hard to find things that won't sell online"***.

CHAPTER 6

Opening Pitch - Hook a Duck

"When we are selling our ideas, the audience must first buy us"
Peter Coughter, The Art ofthe Pitch: Persuasion and Presentation Skills that Win Business

Chapter 6 – Opening Pitch – What to say

You see in order to know what to say we must first speak of attraction. We must understand the basics of Attraction before a single thing comes out of our mouth. You see all of the Chapters in the book build on top of one another like the foundations of a house but sometimes in order to lay one brick, you must know what is coming next. So, before you say a single thing let me explain attraction then we will go into exactly what to say in your opening pitch champ.

Attraction is not logical. Attraction is not a choice. Ask any woman who moans about always fancying bad boys or lads that are mean to her. She will go on and on about why she can never find a nice guy. The answer is simple – probably because you're not attracted to them in the first place.

Attraction is not logical. Never has been and never will be. You see what girls should like logically is not what they emotionally respond to. That's because girls don't choose to be attracted to a guy. They can't help it; it's exactly why they are not attracted to the kind of guy she's been told she should date.

No, a woman experiences attraction when a guy displays certain qualities. The same Attraction Switches we have been talking about since the 1st Chapter. These are hard-wired into her brain. She can't help it, she doesn't want to feel attraction, she just feels it.

So, our job is to look at how we build this attraction and keep it.

If you can make a girl feel attraction to you, the rest of the game gets a whole lot easier.

We need to first understand that men are women are so vastly different in the way we think it is no wonder the book ***"Men are from Mars; Women are from Venus"*** (Gray 1992) has sold 15 million copies. It was also the highest-ranked work of non-fiction in the 1990s where it spent 121 weeks on the best sellers list.

The book is a great read and delves deep into the psychology of men and women. It has many great things to take away and for us to consider. Such as:

1. Women want men to listen to them while men desire solutions to problems.

2. Men are motivated when they feel useful, women are inspired when they feel loved.
3. Women and men communicate differently and assign separate meanings to the same words.
4. Most importantly women are emotional, and men are logical

It is this fourth point that is so crucial to understanding attraction. You see men seek logic and reason to aid them in their decision-making process. Women on the other hand are motivated by emotions then backward rationalise why they behaved in the way in which they did.

To put it simply, you cannot present a logical argument as to why a woman should be with you. No matter how good your use of entrance affects on your PowerPoint presentation kid.

You must stimulate her emotions. Once you've done that instead of her giving you every reason, she shouldn't sleep with you, she'll tell you every reason she should.

What to say

When you see a woman, you like you have 3 seconds to initiate contact. The purpose of this rule is we take nerves out of the equation. When you start to over-think a situation, you begin to think of all the things that can go wrong. You get yourself caught in an endless mind-loop or how you're going to crash and burn and thinking about what to say.

Saying something is better than saying nothing.

Often, a guy will see a girl he is attracted to but will hesitate and delay going over to talk to her for fear, shyness, or nervousness. The 3-second rule is designed, therefore, to get you to respond to seeing an attractive girl *before* the onset of an indulgence in negative thought patterns.

The feeling of approaching may be tough, but it is nothing compared to the feeling of a missed opportunity. As you get more confident and approach more girls it will make sense why you strike up a conversation as soon as you can. You then get into your rhythm and your flow.

The wait is like creeping up a steep cliff before you begin the rollercoaster. You make It seem worse than It is. Better to just shoot your shot, Clint Eastwood.

When you first talk to a woman or a group of women you use something called an **Opener.**

Now the reason I say a group of women is that beautiful women are rarely found alone. Especially at nightclubs and bars. Therefore, we are going to go over how to talk to groups of women as well as women by themselves. One of the reasons women congregate in groups is for safety. Safety from all the idiots that wander over and ask if she wants a drink. Women aren't stupid they know that's not what you are really asking. Therefore, women have learned to stick together like King Leonidas and his men.

We can meet women anywhere –

- University
- Bars & Nightclubs
- Work conventions
- Sports Events
- Concerts & Gigs
- Work
- Supermarkets
- Hobbies
- Walking down the street

We can meet women anywhere. One thing you will become calibrated to the more times you speak to women is their proximity. Think about it like this – a woman can stand anywhere she wants but she just so happens to be stood near you? That be itself may not be an Indicator of Interest but combine that with eye contact and a smile and boy she's lighting up the runway for you to strike up a conversation.

Trust me when I say if a woman does not want to be near you, she won't be. In fact, you may have seen a woman literally run away from a creepy guy in a bar or swap places with her friends. Proximity is important and something we should be aware of. By itself however, doesn't mean she's attracted but it does mean you've got an opportunity to say something so let's make it count.

Openers

Openers do exactly what they say on the tin. They have long replaced the cheesy chat-up lines that women expect. They are designed to give you something to say to get into a conversation with a woman. They are not to make up the bulk of the conversation.

There are two types of openers**. Direct and indirect**.

Direct is when you straight out walk up to a girl and say something like:

Guy = "Did you know you can tell a woman is happy by where her feet are placed?

Girl = "No ..."

Guy "Yeah you see if her feet are placed behind your head, she's usually having a good time, depending on the guy of course"

Now as you can imagine such a line displays immense confidence. If said with a cheeky smile and a "gotcha there" tone, then it's possible you can get away with it.

An example of other **direct openers**:

- You look like someone I'd like to meet.
- Are you confident enough to accept a sincere compliment? Good, so am I, you go first.
- You are so hot tonight, I want to get to know all your darkest secrets, tell me one thing your mother doesn't know about you
- I'm not sure if you're into this stuff but I noticed you have a cool energy, so I had to come over and see what's the deal with you, so what IS the deal with you?
- Have we already slept together, and I didn't call you back because I can't get over the evil look you keep giving me, I bet you can't even remember my name, can you? Do I need to introduce myself again?
- Pft, it's mad how much you remind me of my next girlfriend. And you are?

These just a few examples of how a direct opener works. They are easy to come up with yourself, but this is the shotgun approach. Not the sniper. This is best reserved for when you're feeling highly confident and in a good flow. If you use one of these when you've already got a woman on your arm and these will work a charm. When using a direct opener, it's important to be able to laugh at yourself. Such a line cannot be taken too seriously. A mischievous smile goes a long way.

People that don't smile don't get laid.

Humour has unzipped more dresses than you'll ever realise.

For some women, they'll love the direct approach but for most, you convey too much interest and the thrill is in the chase boys. She already knows she has you.

That's why an indirect opener is where you have something to say to them that doesn't show you are interested in her sexually.

An **indirect opener** is designed to not convey interest. It serves to start the dialogue. The reason it works so well is that the woman is not instantly on the defence. It doesn't appear like you are hitting on her. This is especially important if the person you are talking to has a boyfriend. The last thing you want to do is blow your chances before you know where every stand. Let's say even if she was open to cheat and she's there with her boyfriend's sister. She almost certainly isn't going to even entertain such conversation when she is there. However, conversing about something that seems normal gives you the opportunity to later pull her away from the group and see if she is flirtatious. It's a marathon, not a sprint and you don't want to fall at the first hurdle.

An Indirect opener is therefore your optimum move when opening a group of girls. The idea is to start a conversation without showing any interest to the girl, "I am here to talk/ ask you something, that's all", this is the "Safe" way of opening, she would most likely won't reject you simply asking her a question unless she is having a really bad day (it happens don't take it personally).

An example of some **indirect openers**:

One that works well if you're not a "conventionally" good-looking person and your target is quite good-looking, or you perceive her to be higher on the ranking system, is to use humour to draw attention to this detail. It is best used when one on one, for example - standing in line at a bar.

- You walk up to a girl with a serious look in your eyes and say the following... (Shake your head in a disappointing way) "Hey, let me tell you something about good-looking people... we're not well-liked."

After a moment subsides, you smile, and like that the humour should click. Now she is laughing with you and you are sharing an inside joke. Not a bad way to strike up a conversation.

Humour is a great way to strike up a conversation. Another example of humour is to play off the fact women hate wearing the same clothes as each other. It shows good social cues that you can recognise this and draw attention to it. You walk past a woman, do a half-turn, look her up and down and say

- "You know, I almost wore that EXACT SAME THING tonight. That would have been SO embarrassing."

If delivered right we should be getting a laugh about now, if not then you walk on with nothing lost. Anyone watching will probably laugh at the fact she didn't laugh. What you are conveying is that women of beauty do not bother you. You must be familiar with being around pretty women because when you see them you just have fun with them. You don't get nervous. You laugh and tease.

True alpha-males don't worry about being around girls. They take to it like a duck to water. Women can spot this. When you feel or look at ease around women, then they relax. They don't feel as if there is some nervous energy and your about to break out a sales pitch into why they should give you their number.

You can always start a conversation then go enjoy your night and pick it up later. If you made her laugh now then feel as if you want to go elsewhere, you say something like " you can have that one for free but the next one will cost you" then you turn and walk away without looking back. The fact you never look back will drive her wild. She will probably stare at the back of your head thinking "what the hell just happened?" or at least, ow he was nice, so glad he wasn't a weirdo.

Getting The Girl

A very common indirect opener is to ask for a female opinion on something. Most females are happy to give an opinion and you aren't conveying interest here. This is known as an **Opinion Opener**. Another thing to be aware of is females and their intuition. Women often try to find the true meaning behind your words. We can use this to our advantage.

When you talk about "a friend" women assume you're on about yourself. Every woman believes she is a decedent of Jessica Fletcher and Inspector Morse. They all consider themselves great detectives. Ask a female how many murder documentaries they watch, and they can probably tell you how to get away with murder in more ways than you'd be comfortable hearing. So, we play on this knowledge using this to our own advantage in the way in which speak. By knowing that women believe they can see through things in some of the things we say things that leave room for them to jump to their own conclusions.

For example:

- You approach a group of females and say, "ladies I'm after a female opinion on something, I need to shop for a friend so Victoria's Secret or Agent Provocateur?"
- It will do several things, firstly they will assume the "friend" is a girl you are seeing – did we just tick Pre-Selection? Yes, we did boy.
- Secondly, they will all have an opinion on lingerie, women LOVE lingerie
- Third, neither brand is cheap this shows you can afford it – successful switch
- Fourth, you show you have good knowledge and excellent taste
- Fifth, it is easy to follow up this conversation with something like -hmm why?

If a girl is interested in, you then she will begin to show signs. It will look as if she is investing in the conversation and she will ask something like "Friend! Yeah Right!" or "So who's this friend then !?"

They are only asking so they can find out if you are single.

This then gives you two choices on the follow-up here.

You can play coy – "now, now, I can't reveal all my secrets, you wouldn't want me telling people if I was buying you lacey underwear, would you?" – Sparking a little jealousy and giving the impression that you are taken. This will plant a seed in her head. Women love a challenge.

Or you can tick another attraction switch – Protector of loved ones – with a*: " well I am actually buying it for my friend who's going on a date with this guy she has been seeing (add extra info if you like) and it's the third date and we know what that means right girls?*

Well, my friend has been out of the dating game for a while so I said I would make sure she had something nice for him to unwrap. She can't be rocking up like Bridget Jones, can she?

This will spark a debate. Trust me.

They may talk about many things such as:

- How long do you wait to sleep with a guy?
- What you should or shouldn't wear
- If it matters
- What this guy is like
- What she is like
- How do you two know each other
- Where are they going

Lots of things. You can even use this to your advantage by asking them follow up questions like:

- Where do you think is a good 3rd date place?
- What about a first date?
- Do you believe in the 3rd date rule?
- You could even tell a story about a good or bad third date you went on.

You see the possibilities really do begin to open once you strike up a conversation. The hardest part is often just having the courage to say something in the first place.

The next stage after this is to roll into your DHV stories, we will get to that in a minute but let me give you some other openers you can use.

I want you to inject your personality into what you ask, the conversations flow better if you can relate to real scenarios but if you can't then go for good old – Fake It Till You Make It.

You can easily create your own opinion openers. All you do is make a list of things you could ask a woman to get her opinion on, which are interesting enough for her to reply. If you're not sure if they will work, then test them. These can be easily tested on friends or colleagues. You can gauge their response and see which ones work well. Which ones get lots of feedback or a big *" ooo good question"* which ones get single word answers, or which are totally boring and worthy of the scrapheap. The key for a great opinion opener is to ask her something that can help you to lead the conversation somewhere else.

A good example would be *"Can I get your opinion on something, if your ex-friends' sister accidentally sends you a nude, should you tell him, or should you respond to her?"*

After they give their answer you can follow it up with *" does it make a difference if she is really hot ?"* or *" what about if I tell you she tried to sleep with me when she last broke up with her boyfriend ?"* or *" what if I tell you he is my ex-mate cause he tried to message my ex-girlfriend after we broke up ?".*

All of these take the conversation in different ways and will get different responses. The words you have used also carefully show Pre-selection as you are wanted by other girls, you don't take nonsense from your ex-friend and you aren't driven by just sexual desires as you are carefully considering it. Girls also love to give advice. They will offer tons of advice on this. This can nicely be transitioned to – *so now iv shared an embarrassing story tell me, someone, you shouldn't have slept with/ about the worse nude you've got.*

Then you're into a conversation. Well done champ. That's all an opener is for, to open a conversation and give you something to say. The reason people use pre-rehearsed lines is as they often find themselves in a situation where they don't know what to say. When you have something already scripted this removes this worry and fear. You know what you are going to say because you have a few of them written down or memorised.

As you get better at talking to women you will move away from having to use anything written as you will know what types of things work or do not work. However, until then, assume the role of an actor and learn your lines boy.

The opinion opener is great as it is pretty low risk, but we have other options in our arsenal.

A Genuine Compliment Opener can also work well. This is where a guy offers a sincere and specific compliment to the person he is about to talk to. The big difference here is it singles in on one person whereby an opinion opener can be said to an entire group. A genuine compliment opener must be said with confidence and a nice slow tone. It is said thoughtfully, not rushed, and looks well thought out. An example of this would be:

- Walking past a lady, or positioned behind, turn head , make eye contact, and say *" I like those spaghetti heels your wearing, where are they from I know a girl who would love them, are they hard to put on, or did you do it all by yourself like a big girl ?"*
- This is a playful compliment, it has a tease in there which throws her off a little, gives her something to bite on if she wants – *yes, I did it all myself*
- The mention of – I know a girl who would love them – immediately makes them think you've either got a girlfriend or you are seeing someone. Pre-selection.
- It also puts them at ease as they think you're talking about the shoes not trying to hit on them with a cheap compliment
- Spaghetti heels show you are a rounded person with good fashion knowledge- you are competent, this is an attractive quality – if you are unsure what they look like a quick google search will give you an idea

This only works if the compliment is genuine and specific. It can be about many things, a girl's nails, dress, or make-up. Knowledge is powerful. Showing your informed-on things is attractive

I cannot begin to describe the number of times I have got into a conversation with a woman about make-up only to recommend she try the Urban Decay Setting Spray for them to be amazed at my knowledge. They will often say something like *"how on earth do you know that?"* Then with a cheeky smile, you can say something like *"it's not my first rodeo"* or *"well nobody wants to wake up with make-up on their sheets, do they?".*

You see how I am implying that I am used to being around women, this is the reason as to why I am so informed. Appearing dumb may work for Joey Essex but he is a unique case, it also helps that he is ridiculously good-looking and fabulously wealthy. He makes it seem endearing, but it shouldn't be your go to move.

The science also supports what I have said on humour and intelligence. Written in 2013 Greengross and Miller brought together these findings in their book - **Mating Intelligence Unleashed: The Role of the Mind in Sex, Dating, and Love.** In the book, they draw on all current and cutting age psychological data and research as they present the process of what they call Mating Intelligence. Within this, they conclude that Human mating draws on a range of mental skills and attributes--from the creative use of pick-up lines to display certain characteristics (haven't I been telling you this since Chapter 1) and goes far beyond just physical looks.

When looking at humour and intelligence, for example, Gil Greengross and Geoffrey Miller found in a sample of 400 university students that **general intelligence and verbal intelligence** both predicted **humour production ability** for example the ability to write writing captions for cartoons. , **which in turn predicted the lifetime number of sexual partners (a proxy of reproductive success).** Being able to be funny helps get you laid, who would have thought?

To be funny though we usually must be smart enough to say a joke, the best way is to just try them and see what works and doesn't work. If your fortunate to have a Dad, Uncle or close friend who is always telling tons of jokes, then listen out for the ones that get the most laughs, then simply steal them. It works. Girls won't care if it is original or not.

Going back to the study the numbers tell the full story. Men that were described as "funny" "received phone numbers from 42.9% of the female participants and were refused 57.1% of the time. In comparison, men in the "not funny" group were refused 84.6% of the time and were only accepted 15.4% of the time. You haven't got to be Rain Man to see the impact that made. Just imagine how much better they would have been if they were funny AND read this book?

Now back to the make-up.

It is then easy to transition the conversation to – *well do you always take your makeup off after a night out?* Then you can follow up with something cheekier like " *even on all them one night stands ?"* women will of course deny ever having had a one night stand or say something lie " *I don't do that*" at which stage you would reply *" of course you don't ..*" then move onto another topic. She will feel as if you are judging her. This will make her want to work a little harder to now win your approval.

You see women have an anti-slut defence. They do not want to feel like one nor be accused of being one. It would bode well to also never say a woman is. They value how selective they are around choosing their mates. Now there is nothing wrong with making fun of their ex's that's fair game and usually work very well but you do not say that you think a woman is easy. This is the easiest way for her to reject you.

Treat them with a degree of respect in this regard unless you want them to explode like something out of a looney tunes cartoon.

This reputation protection is important to them. It is also why women use reputation destruction as their means of operation when trying to hurt someone. They will discredit them, using rumours and gossip to try to ruin their reputation. You will have seen it when they break up with a guy or in office politics. They prefer the indirect approach of attack. Working to undermine the person by spreading gossip and lies.

Be aware of this when talking to women. Their version of events that they share with others will most certainly be tailored and cropped to suit their obscure version of the truth.

Remember there are always 3 sides to every story. Yours. Mine. And the Truth.

We know that women often believe other women. It's part of that Girl Code thing we missed at school. We can use this to our advantage with what is known as **An Introduction Opener**. An introduction opener works really well if you are already mixing with a group that is talking to your group. It also works well if you are stood next to a group of girls and they have been there a while. The final occasion it works well is if you see a woman at the bar who's ordering a lot of drinks and you offer to carry them over to her friends.

In all cases, you are simply going to get one female to introduce you to another or a group of. This is done very simply by asking the person like *"Your friends look really cool, I want to meet them, can you introduce me?"* if the energy and the vibe are right, most girls will happily be obliged. If you come across as genuine you can easily meet lots of women, this way. You see women trust other women, so when a woman introduces you then you already have social value. You aren't that creepy guy who has walked across the bar staring at them. You have been introduced by someone she already knows.

You must remember this is just an opener. It gets you into the conversation. Having something to say after is also important otherwise you will exchange names and then the conversation will die. Also, it is not an interview, don't start asking lots of questions like:

- Where are you from?
- What do you do for work?
- Come here often (I was nearly sick writing this)?
- So, where you going tonight?

All you are showing is that you are the same as every other loser that's tried to talk to her tonight. You aren't that guy. You are a man of value. Instead, you are going to have some interesting and cool stories to talk to her about. You are going to bring value to her night and to the conversation.

By the time you are finished she's going to be delighted you spoke to her. Well done you champ.

The last type of opener you can use is an **Observational Opener**. The good thing about an observational opener is that you don't have to memorise or rehearse any lines. That's because you are simply going to be commenting on something you have observed. Something in real-time, right now. You come across as a statement that gives them an opportunity to reply. An example would be:

- *"You look like trouble"* this will almost always be responded with a why do you think that or a why? then it's up to you to justify your reason – an easy one would be, you know why your trouble, what I really wanna know is why you're here, what mischief have you got planned for tonight?

- Another one might be – *"you look like a Libra"* she will then probably hit you back with a what made you say this? or no I am a Capricorn etc. This then gives you an option to justify your answer or even better get her to prove it. I don't believe you, prove it. At this stage, she will probably show you her social media or drivers' licence. Well done you, you now have her name or her socials if you decide to find her at a later date, depending on how the conversation goes.

This is a range of strategies you can use to "open" a conversation. It will be fun to play around with a few to find one that works for you. It's great to add your personality into them, make them your own. Originality works great. It's also best if you speak on topics you know as it allows you to **Frame Control** and leads the conversation how you like.

When you are opening a conversation **YOU NEVER OFFER TO BUY A GIRL A DRINK.** You are not a walking ATM. This shows you must buy her attention. Are you looking for a prostitute? Because as much as I LOVE Pretty Woman, you aren't going to get your own Julia Roberts by throwing cash at the situation. Sure, she may spend some time with you but is she interested in you or that big thing in your pocket – your wallet.

You promote what you permit. If you start by buying her things, then where would this relationship go anyway? You may as well set up a standing order there and then. This is a fool's game. An alpha male never has to buy a woman a thing in order to be attractive to her. Save the spending money for when you are dating.

It has no place here. Most women will happily accept the drink from you then drop you like a bad habit with any number of excuses. Maybe what you're actually conveying is she is going to need a drink to listen to your boring conversation? Perhaps you can offer to buy her some paracetamol as well before you give her a headache? Come on. Does this sound like an alpha male, leader of men moves to you? Nope. Didn't think so.

When you offer to buy a drink you also do two things. Firstly, you convey too much interest, and this usually works against you. Secondly, you are treating it as a negotiation, I buy you drink = you talk to me. Girls are also great at reading between the lines remember. She will also think that you think that buying her a drink means she is going to sleep with you. It doesn't. It didn't and it won't.

If she asks you to buy her a drink, then she is hustling you. You simply tell her *"I don't buy drinks in this place"* or *"I'm not in the buying drinks game I'm afraid doll"*. If she chooses to leave, then you haven't lost anything and kept your dignity.

If she is genuinely interested, you can say something like *"have you forgot your purse tonight?" Here let's make a deal, you buy us some shots and I'll buy us some drinks*. Now, this is a fair offer and any woman interested will take it up. After all, shots are cheaper than drinks so she has a good deal out of it.

It also means you are both **equally investing** in the situation. This is far better than you trying to win your approval. As a wise man once told me **"you can't buy your friendship".**

****

We must remember we are talking about the initial attraction period. Paying for things when dating and further down the line is fine and, in some cases, comes across like a real gentleman. It won't however help us when we are trying to build attraction with a female. Being successful may be attractive but you don't have to spend money on them to prove it.

Now it isn't just what we say when we open but also how we say it. You see in a place like a bar or a nightclub there will be two kinds of guys. Those that look like they are having a good time and smiling, enjoying the night. Then we have those who stand in the corner, leaning against a wall trying to look cool or act tough.

Trying to be cool, ain't cool bro.

You see these men are signalling that they are scared to interact, and they find safety in numbers. The back is seen as a vulnerable area to the human body. They are guarding this. They are looking scared. You know what? they probably are. Approaching women can be quite terrifying at times but it doesn't have to be. They are trying to cover their nerves with safety in numbers.

They will also safely in their numbers watch as you go around collecting numbers.

The game is played by being sociable and smiling. This is the mindset you need. Look as if you are having a good time and people will naturally want to be involved. To do this you want to be slightly above the energy level of the people you are talking to. You are going to raise the group and inject some energy in. You know those friends who when you are around you can't stop laughing and things very quickly get excitable? Well, this is a good reference point. You want to look as if spending time with you is fun. I have a guy I use to work with called Jack (scary I know) and every time I see him, we crack into the same old jokes and have the best of times. What then happens is the eyes in the room seem to magnetise in our direction. Girls and guys a like start looking over with that fear of missing out. When you are in this state it is easy for you to strike up a conversation. We could be a mid joke and I can point at a girl and say some obscure quote from Anchor man and Jack, and I will laugh. This then invites conversation. The girl will come over like what the hell is going on and the next thing we know we are all having a laugh. Now I am not saying you need to have a person like this but think about this mind-state. Be in a playful mood. Playful people laugh, joke, and tease. This is how you should be when thinking to start your openers. Everyone likes fun. Don't take life too seriously, after all, none of us get out of it alive.

We must also consider where you are approaching women. The dancefloor is not a good place, it is noisy and hard to communicate. Also, women are on the dancefloor to dance. Don't be that guy whispering in her ear as you try to get her to Dutty Wine. Instead, choose areas like the smoking area (you don't have to smoke – you can say you are there for fresh air) the bar when waiting for a drink is a great place to strike up a conversation, the queue as your waiting to enter a venue or any other place that is not at night is a great suggestion. This is why talking to women at work or the park or on a University campus works so well. It is not noisy like at night-time. You cannot be confined to just talking to women at night. As mentioned previously, beautiful women can be found anywhere. Use this to your advantage.

It never hurts to have a good relationship with the venue staff if you are a regular there. This is easily done, be polite and courteous. ALWAYS befriend the doormen. This will work wonders for you in the future. You never know when being friends with the doorman will work to your advantage when trying to get into a venue. The way to do this is easy:

- When leaving the venue try to say goodbye to the doormen. They will remember this. Especially if you say thank you and shake their hands (not possible during COVID or any other pandemics).
- Offer to buy them a water or an energy drink when on shift. This is an easy way to get into the good books.
- If you see something happen, they should know about then let them know

Having a doorman on your side is a wonderful thing. It will look cool to a girl if you take her to a place and you don't have to queue up. It looks great if they just know your name.

When you get good at it, you may even get in for free or you can help get girls in the venue by leveraging your relationship with the doorman. The most doorman will happily let you in if they think you are going to return the favour later. Food and drinks go a long way if a doorman is working a long shift. Don't try and bribe them. Most will feel insulted and aren't allowed to take cash. They aren't going to risk their job for it. Also, you want to befriend them. Friends don't pay friends.

Simply walking by and asking if they want anything when you come by later may be the difference between you getting in or getting cold.

Another tip for having a better night out in general regardless of whether you are aiming to speak to women is to get your names on the guestlist. Such a small detail of pre-planning can help with queue-jumping, cheaper entry, and even be the difference between being told a venue is full or you are allowed in. For extra points always put a plus 2, then if you arrive at a venue with any ladies you have met, they can get in under your name. You have already begun to add value to their lives and it's only been a few hours.

How you say it

Communication has **three parts**: the sender, the message, and the recipient. The sender 'encodes' the message, usually in a mixture of words and non-verbal **communication**. It is transmitted in some way (for example, in speech or writing), and the recipient 'decodes' it.

The magic number for how we communicate is **7, 38, 55.**

That being 7% of the Spoken Word, 38% of the Tone, and 55% of the Body Language we use makes up our ability to communicate.

Therefore, if we want to be effective when approaching women and create attraction, we must be aware of how we use all 3 together.

We have already spoken of **what** we can say having looked at the range of different openers available to us. Now we must think about **how** we say it. When speaking the expressions on our faces must match our words. If you are telling a joke but not smiling, then people will instantly see these do not match up and makes it appear as if you are untrustworthy. The same applies to if you were smiling whilst telling a sad story, people would think you are some sort of monster who has no empathy.

Therefore, we must make sure our facial expressions match what we are saying. Raised eyebrows when surprised and a pursing of the lips when contemplating a question can add power to our communication to make us seem genuine and sincere.

As for your body position, we don't want to be directly facing the woman or the group of women on approach. I have kindly got a diagram to show you the optimal body positions when initiating a conversation. The important thing here is to raise your chances of being able to start a conversation.

We don't want to face them with your body, only your head needs to be turned to strike up a conversation. The position of your feet can be a give-away. Are your feet pointing towards them or away from them? Do you like you are seeking their approval or just having a conversation, but you could leave at any moment? We want to give the impression we are a man of high value and therefore one of the best ways to start a conversation can be when walking by a girl or group of girls. As you go past you can stop, turn your head, and give them your opening line. If you feel as if they are buying into the conversation, then you can gradually turn more of your body to join them. If they do not, then you simply walk away and to any bystanders, it just looks like a throwaway comment and doesn't lower your value the same way as it would if you went charging in then got rejected.

When you are engaging in conversation after you have given your opening line and moving onto your stories you want to continue to give the impression that you may leave at any time. This does two things:

- You look non-threatening as they don't think they are stuck with you all night (OMG WHY CAN'T WE GET RID OF THIS GUY)
- You give the impression that you have somewhere else to be – you have value – they must give you a reason to stay in the conversation – they can chase you

The best way to combine this is by slightly shifting your weight to your back leg on occasion and making the space between you and the group of girls larger, then when the conversation picks up you can go back to standing still. Standing still is important as nervous people fidget. We don't want to fidget. We want to appear as if we are in control of our bodies.

We can also combine the body language of leaving with a **False Time Constraint.** False Time Constraints are wonderful and best used after an opener just before your first story. You literally tell the girl or group of girls that you are going to leave soon. Such a great line takes the pressure out of the situation and demonstrates you are not looking for value from them. You are just going to have a conversation and leave (we, of course, know this may not be the case but how many girls do you think would let you talk to them if you said *" Hi I'm here to try and pull you all night "*).

A False Time Constraint looks like this:

- I need to get back to my friends but let me just tell you this quickly ...
- I really must leave in a minute, but have you noticed ...
- I'll be quick because I know (insert girl's name) is looking for me, so let me tell you about the time ...

You can see how such a phrase relaxes the conversation. Then if you can see they aren't feeling it, you can walk away knowing that you told them you were going to leave anyway.

You can also use a False Time Constraint just when you know the conversation is starting to flow well. This will generate a loss-aversion moment in the female's mind/minds, and they will ask you to stay. Now, who is doing the chasing champ?

When you are settled into a conversation with a lady or a group of ladies it's important, we appear relaxed. One of the best ways to do this is to lean back. When we lean back, we look relaxed. When we are speaking, especially in a loud environment, do not be tempted to **Peck.**

Pecking is the thing hens do when they collect grain and walk around. They pop their head in then pop it back out. Guys do this all the time, pecking their head in to hear what a woman has to say then pecking it out. Who do you think has the most social value, a man leaning into a girl or a man with a woman leaning into him? You guessed it. It's the man that's relaxed letting the women come to him. If an environment is especially noisy and you feel as if the person/people you are talking to are invested in the conversation you can suggest moving to somewhere quiet.

Tone

The final aspect of communication we must master is the tone in which we deliver our messages. The tone is best when varied. We want to aim to not come across as boring and monotone in our delivery *"Bueller.... Bueller.... Bueller...."*. Instead, we want to vary our communication to keep them interested. When getting near a good point of the story you can make your voice go high then follow with a sudden drop and almost a whisper. Building up the suspense. A deep voice is universally attractive to women but if you don't have a naturally deep voice then you can practice speaking from your diaphragm. This helps to lower your tone. If you have a particularly difficult accent or speech impediment, then look into getting voice coaching from a professional. There are lots of actors and actresses that offer this service. It will also allow you to practice routines and materials with them whilst getting feedback on delivery. In the modern age, this can be done over Skype, Zoom, or Facetime so accessing help is much easier. You then have someone to help go through what you want to say and how you want to say it. You want to be expressive in your voice, emphasising the correct points in a story. Many people don't use pauses as effectively as they can. Pausing builds suspense and allows people to digest information. Avoid saying "erm" a lot. This is equivalent to a mind fart. You are better replacing your erm with a pause. It makes you sound more in control and as if the words you speak naturally flow better.

When speaking use, a tone that carries and is loud enough to be heard. Loud voice & plenty of pausing and it will be almost as enjoyable listening to you as it is listening to Stephen Fry.

Now we have covered what to say when opening a conversation and we have covered how to say it. I have gone over how quick to say it (4 seconds), I am now going to explain when to say it.

The simple answer is – as soon as you enter a place.

That's right, as soon as you enter somewhere, start a conversation. You see conversation flows naturally. When you are in a talkative mood you can easily bounce around talking to different people. You would have seen these people before at parties or events that seem to know everyone! They don't really but they love talking to people, so they get to meet them. When you are starting this is going to be difficult but over time you will get used to talking to different people and this will become natural.

You also demonstrate something called **Social Proof.** Social Proof is a term that means you have perceived value because others are valuing you. Kind of like pre-selection. You see that **Social proof** is the concept that people will follow the actions of the masses. We see this all the time on social media with influencers. Where people follow the actions of individuals they admire.

Now although the rise in social media has allowed us to see this principle in action more clearly social proof itself isn't new. There have been a variety of studies conducted on the topic that shows people are more likely to conform to the group decision. The most infamous example is the **Solomon Asch conformity experiment** that took place in 1951.

Asch was a psychologist who set out to test the theory that people are likely to conform to the choice of the majority, even if the decision is clearly wrong.

Surely people wouldn't do something they think is wrong just to fit in right...

In his experiment, Asch gathered college students to participate in a line judgement task. Each group was shown images of lines that were then labelled like the ones below:

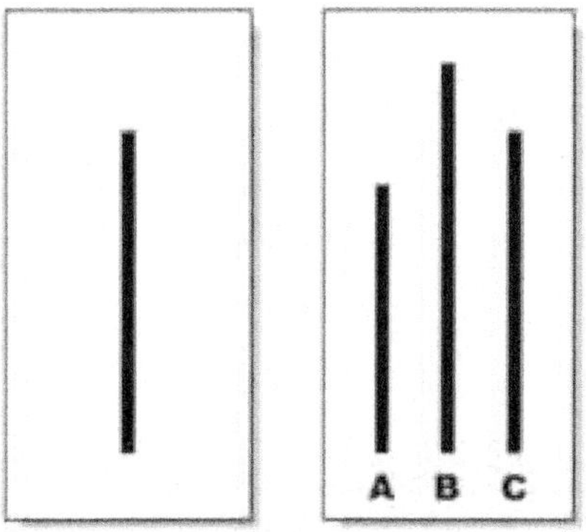

They had to answer which line - A, B or C was the same as the line by itself on the left. Both images were presented next to each other for careful and easy comparison. To test his theory Asch divided participants into groups of eight.

However, only one of the people in each group was being tested. The other seven (the control variable) agreed beforehand what their answers would be, which the real participant did not.

Each person had to state which line was most like the target line. The correct answer was always obvious, and the real participant went last each time. There was a total of 18 trials, and the control variables were told to give wrong answers in 12 of them. During those 12 tests, 75% of the unknowing participants conformed and gave the wrong answer at least once.

In the other six trials when the control group gave the right answer, the unknowing participant gave the wrong answer less than 1% of the time.

When Asch asked the unknowing participants why they conformed, he found that people follow social proof for one of two reasons:

1. They want to fit in with the group.
2. They believe the group is better informed than they are.

You now see how we can use social proof to our advantage. Once others in a venue start talking to you, it then becomes acceptable for them too. If others laugh at your jokes it encourages them to laugh at your jokes. Social Proof is a powerful tool if wielded correctly.

We, therefore, demonstrate social proof by having fun and a laugh with our friends. In any situation, there are those observing and those being observed. To be observed you must look as if you are having a good time.

Walking around a venue before finally plucking up the courage to talk to someone demonstrates low social proof. Everyone has seen you scoping out the entire venue before you have finally settled on a group to approach. This is a rookie error. Women can sense it a mile off, compare this to a guy who enters a venue, saying hi to lots of people, gets a few hugs off girls, goes to the bar, and is known by the bar tender – his social proof is through the roof.

Now when you are talking to girls in other settings such as work, the street, etc the same rules apply but are viewed differently. Your social proof at work might be directly related to your job role. In a position of power but are well-liked by your colleagues and those beneath you? Great social proof. Hated by everyone because you act like Genghis Khan and a warlord in a war-torn state then don't be surprised if you struggle to build attraction.

Now there is one last thing to cover on approaching women in a venue. That is, we know venues are not just full of women (we can dream) there will also be other guys in there. This is not an issue and something that shouldn't concern you in the slightest. It doesn't matter how many men are in the venue because my name isn't Macaulay Culkin and **I never go home alone.**

One thing an alpha male does not concern himself with is other men. The only competition is in the mirror. Men that come on a night out and hang around in a large group of men usually go home with men. Now I am not saying this is an issue, but I am sure if you wanted to go home with a man you probably would have chosen a different book. You see, what I am saying is that in order to attract women you are going to have to spend your time with the women. There are going to be occasions when other men are there talking to women or come in and interrupt you. This isn't an issue. You see, you just treat men like ugly women. The same stories you tell them will work on them. When a guy tries to barge into your conversation, you address him head-on. Now I am not saying you must confront him but if you back down then you don't look like a strong male and this is going to lower your value.

My mate G.V use to be a master of an Alpha-male approach to other men on a night out. He would do this thing where he would greet the guys by tapping them on the chest and slowly pushing them away at the same time. He would be *like "Hey buddy, you cool?"* Smile. Place his hand on their chest, tap it, push them back then enter the set of people. Then start with whatever line he had chosen. As you imagine this was one hell of an entrance. The confidence and the bravado immediately got the girls' attention. Then if the guy wanted to re-join he would do this thing where he would hug them with one arm but squeeze them really tight so they would get smaller and it would make himself look bigger and he would say something like *" woo, woo calm down I'm not here to steal your girls they just want to talk to me, you can wait your turn".* Now it helped that G.V at the time was into the gym so he had the impression of a guy that could look after himself (self-improvement and first impression remember?) but it also showed that he was a leader of men. This was very attractive at the time. You see the important thing to do is to deal with the man head-on. By approaching and addressing the issue it shows you are confident. Now you don't have to do this physically like G.V, in fact in most cases I would say it is better to do it verbally. If you have some well-prepared lines and a sharp tongue you can do way more damage with those than your fists.

You can say something like *"Look what the cat dragged in and you came empty-handed, look girls he has turned up without shots!"* This does 3 things:

- It says I do not consider you to better than me and I am not impressed by your appearance
- It puts the other guy on the back foot because you are suggesting he is coming and not bringing value
- He then must justify not bringing shots (why on earth would he at this stage) this then means he will spend time trying to prove himself to the girls or even worse he goes and gets some shots. If he does that you look like the

alpha and you can even add a line like *"see girls, I told you he would get us some shots, cheers kid"*
- To most guys unless they have a solid game this will blow them out the water, they are playing catch up from the get-go

You see all am trying to do is with my words convey that this guy isn't impressing me, and he is coming into "our" conversation. You can do this in many ways by your words or your actions. You could say something *like "Well before we were rudely interrupted where were we girls?"*. This creates an Us Vs Him dynamic and it makes it very difficult for him to come in and take over the conversation. Women do this all the time.

They have a wonderfully simple line that can be devastating to a guy's chances. Women often use this tried and tested chunk of kryptonite *"Do we know you?"* or *"Does anyone know this guy?"*

Ouch. That hurts.

We know it hurts because what it is really saying is:

- You are an outsider
- You are not wanted
- Go away

We have a special term for these women. You have no doubt met them throughout your life. They are in some cases the preliminary to the final boss. We are, of course, talking about the **Mother Hens**.

Mother Hens

Mother hens differ from normal girl-mates as they go beyond the normal protection that females offer to make sure the guy, she is talking to isn't a weirdo. These are the super-protective, will do anything to stop them forming any kind of sexual relations with any man type.

Unfortunately, this is like going on a bear hunt. You can't go over it, you can't go under it, you're just going to have to go through it. You need to address this gigantic Snorlax-blocking-the-road of a Cockblock in order to move forward on your adventure.

The Mother Hen is often the least attractive one within any given friendship group. It's a difficult situation as we know women are ranked based on the attraction switches, we spoke of earlier. This means that women who are not viewed by men as conventionally good-looking can often fall into this role. The stereotype of them always being ugly and fat is not true. Women can develop a negative reaction to men if they are never approached and feel as if their friends get all the attention. This can present itself in many ways with them often saying things such as *"can't we just have a night without boys tonight* "or they will ridicule their friend with *"omg can you just not talk to a boy for a change".* Understanding why they behave this way is important, they feel left out. One of the best ways to help combat this is to spend time talking to the friend and making them feel involved. If you win over the friend, then that gives you a clear run at the final boss. Think of them like the pre-cursor to M.Bison or Akuma.

With all Mother Hens, you want to introduce yourself and pay them a genuine compliment acknowledging they are a good friend. This will disarm them and give you a chance to show them you deserve to talk to their friends. Where most people flop is, they don't deal with the Mother hen, and then later she drags away the girl they were talking to. Best to deal with the bomb that's ticking first.

We also have the Mother Hen who believes she is morally superior. She thinks she is the Florence Nightengale of Nightclubs, the Mother Teresa of Bars, The Joan of Arc of Kebab shops. She is too holy for all this foolery. She will try to make others follow her strict virtues. She has probably been with her boyfriend forever and therefore thinks every relationship should be like hers. She will tell her girlfriends how they should behave and how every relationship should start as hers did. The best way to deal with this type is to ask her about her relationship and boyfriend. Show an interest in her life and find out the things she thinks a boy should be. Then all you do is repeat those back to her to get her to agree. Once she has told you the important values you can show you agree and demonstrate them in the stories you tell. Does she think it's important to meet the parents? Great! So, do you, remember that time you took a bottle of wine (that you knew was the favourite of the mother) to the girl s house parents' house of the person you were seeing? Yeah me either, but she doesn't know it's not true. You are trying to convince her you are a Knight in shining armour not a Knob in tin foil.

We must also accept that some people can just be having a bad day. It happens to the best of us. If you were having a bad day and wanted to spend some time with your friends would you want a stranger coming over to mess things up? Probably not. Here empathy is your best tool. Find out what's bothering her, explain that you're not here to mess things up and you're just looking to make new friends. Maybe you can help each other, you can listen to her problem and she can introduce you to her friends. This makes her feel valuable and lets her blow off some steam.

If you have an epic wingman, he may even be prepared to take one for the team and entertain her whilst you move onto the girl you want to talk to.

We can also use a direct approach ourselves when dealing with a Mother Hen that puts her in the spotlight and highlights to her friends her mean behaviour. You can say things like:

- Are you always this grumpy or just when Snow White is in town?
- Are you flirting with me?
- Was it a late night?

Be careful when using this as it may make the Mother Hen worse but for some drawing attention to their behaviour will make them back off. They will see how silly they are being and correct it.

The Mother hen could also be going through her "Men are Trash" or "All Men Are FuckBoys" phase. She has probably just been ditched, came out of a relationship, or had a bad experience with a guy. We know there are guys out there that give us true a gentleman a bad name, right? So, we don't take it personally.

The last time you saw a woman take down this many men her name was Jill Valentine and she was blowing heads off trying to escape from the Nemesis. She is just venting out her frustration and you're the chosen target tonight. In this case, no amount of convincing from you is going to help, in fact, you talk to her then bouncing on to her friend is going to make her feel even worse. Not much will fix a broken heart other than a distraction. Unless you have a wingman to scoop in and entertain then it's probably best to wait until the lady you want to talk to isn't with her or move onto someone else. You can't win them all champ.

Now to recap on what we have gone over so far:

- We have looked at what women are attracted to – The Attraction Switches
- Why we don't want to be in the friendzone
- How we can believe in what we are going to say and have inner confidence
- We have then looked at how we can make a good first impression through self-improvement
- We have now looked at how we approach women and what we can say first to them
- We know how to say it and how we can handle other guys and girls

We are now going to look at how we can build attraction after this initial conversation and an obstacle you may be hit with called the **Bitch Shield**.

****

Bitch Shield

The **Bitch Shield** is a screening tool employed by women to weed out weak men. It is a Darwinistic tool designed to ensure she doesn't waste her time talking to men of low value.

The thing is people use shields when they need protection. It's a tool used for defence. When we don't have to defend ourselves, no shields are necessary. In an ideal world, guys would want to create a safe environment when they are trying to make a good first impression; one that wouldn't require a shield at all. This is our aim with an Indirect opener and a False Time Constraint.

The Bitch Shield, therefore, is a reaction to men's behaviour over time. It is a learned coping mechanism for women to use in their day-to-day life. It doesn't just apply on a night out but can be used in all manner of settings.

You see women have been approached thousands of times in their lifetime, sometimes directly and other times discreetly. They have learned to learn that men usually only talk to them when they want something (shame on us, aye). They have found out that when being nice to a guy and sociable these guys end up thinking they are in with her or don't leave her alone. They follow her around like Minions and Dr. Gru. So, in response, they have developed the Bitch Shield.

Understanding the Bitch Shield means to also understand the role men have made in its creation. By understanding what has triggered it will help us understand the solutions.

Now a Bitch Shield can present itself in many ways:

- A fake ring
- A real ring
- "I have a boyfriend"
- "I am not interested "
- Insulting you
- Not giving you eye contact
- Giving you indicators of disinterest, such as turning away from you
- Not laughing at jokes
- Starting to dance or pull friends toward the dancefloor
- Positioning themselves in hard to talk places, swapping places with friends when dancing or sitting down, etc

Now women do not have to talk to you, and it is their choice if they don't want to. This is fine there are many women out there that do want to talk to you. However, some may want to talk to you but are undecided so instead of finding out they will throw up a Bitch Shield to weed out the weak men.

Women use these horrible, aggressive bitch shields for three reasons. They put them on at different times for different reasons.

The first reason is that she is having a bad day. In this case, you are going to be the target for Medusas snakes here so watch out unless you want to be turned into stone Perseus. Don't worry this doesn't mean the game is hopeless, it can be possible to turn a bad day around. Now when you do this it is also a very powerful position you find yourself in as she now knows your someone who can move her emotionally.

I can give you countless examples of times when working in town a girl would fall out with a boyfriend or would be getting upset, shouting, screaming, and sometimes even fighting because there in a bad mood. In these situations, if you can crack through the initial test then they will happily open and tell you what is bothering them. They will find joy in having someone to confide in and if you can begin to make them laugh will form a connection with you. They will see you as someone that brings value. You can help them.

The second reason a girl may project their Bitch Shield is a direct result of clingy men. You see when women are nice to guys these weak men then spend the rest of the night following them around like a lost puppy. This gives women the **"Ick".** This is that weird feeling where they think a guy is a creep and want to be as far away from him as possible. It is why they have developed a coping mechanism for when this happens like saying *"I am just going to the toilet, wait here"* and never coming back. Now experienced women know this feeling, so before allowing it to get there they will throw up their Bitch Shield to scare off these weak men to save themselves having to run away from them all night. Can you really blame them? Wouldn't you do the same if you had an annoying girl -who you didn't find attractive- following you around all night? Luckily, we are aware of women feeling trapped and that's the reason we use the **False Time Constraint**. When we use this, we are saying – don't worry we aren't like those other guys – we give them a sense of relief and allow them to let their guard down, this gives us a chance for them to get to know us.

The last reason that women use the Bitch Shield is when a woman is of high value, she will use this as a **Shit Test**. That is to literally see if you can get over the first hurdle. Can you imagine what it must be like for a woman who is constantly hit on? Think of it as a recruitment company, you are going to have your filter questions. First, they must pass the screening questions (like the ones on Indeed) even before they can submit their CV. Then you will go and check relevant experience. Then you will check qualifications. Then make a shortlist. Then do a phone interview. Then first interview face to face before finally the second face-to-face interview and finally deciding from the candidates.

A high-value woman is going to get lots of applicants. Especially if the candidates all think they have got a shot. I will explain later how 7s and 8s get more attention than 9 and 10s for this very reason. People only take the shots they think they've got a chance with.

Now from a woman's perspective is it so bad to include a Shit Test and use the Bitch Shield? No of course it isn't, it is just part of their sorting process because they know a true Alpha-Male, one that ticks the attraction switches, will not be deterred by such a test. They are probably used to overcoming obstacles all the time. They will of course not be put off by a few comments at the start of a conversation, will they? They understand sales and realise that all this means is they haven't built their value high enough yet.

A strong woman wants a strong man.

Now the Bitch Shield can be separated further into two types. The defensive – she turns her back, says go away, and refuses to engage in conversation. This is the most difficult to deal with as you don't have anything to work with. When this happens, our energy Is probably best spent elsewhere. I would make a graceful exit and find somewhere else who is interested in a riveting conversation.

The second type is on the attack. She is coming for you now boy. She is trying to put you down. Especially if they have friends around them. She will say mean things and try and make you jump through her hoops.

Remember it's a Bitch Shield **it does not mean she is a Bitch**.

Luckily for you, I am now about to arm you with Excalibur. Skywalkers Lightsaber. The Keyblade. Soul Edge. The Buster Sword. Frostmourne. The Master Sword. Basically, the biggest, best most ultimate sword you can think of. Got it? Good.

Settle down, class is in session. We **are going to learn how to destroy Bitch Shields**.

1. We do not react to what she says. Treat the comments like they are coming from a child. You would not be emotionally stimulated by childish comments from your niece or nephew or a stranger on the street. You are not going to be hurt by them. If you react emotionally then she has won. She is in the driving seat. Amateurs go on the offense and get aggressive. This shows weakness. She can

control your buttons. You would not make a good partner for her. You are weak.

2. Approve her actions. This sounds counter-productive but think about it. When you approve what she says you take some of the sting out of it. A comment like *"Come on you can do better than that, what else you got?"* This shows you don't mind obstacles and you are almost unconsciously showing her obstacles don't mean anything. Like when a child is being mean, and you show the comments aren't affecting you they lose their effect. You can follow it up with something like *"I love when a woman isn't shy"*. You see only an alpha male would react in this way. He would not fear a little challenge and wouldn't be affected by any comments. As they say, **a Lion does not lose sleep on the opinion of Sheep.** You are showing that a stranger's opinion of you will not shake your self-worth. This is very attractive. You are demonstrating to the woman that regardless of what adversity you know how you are and most likely where you want to go. By giving your approval you steal her power.
3. Interrupt her flow and break her frame. We do this by interrupting her pattern of speech and behaviour. We are throwing her off as we are not reacting the way she expects a man to react. We need to shift her perception of you as quickly as possible. We want to disprove her theory that we are not good enough for her. We will not allow her to humiliate us and send us on our way with our tail between her legs. The best way to do this is to respond with something that is so out-there it interrupts her brain pattern. Darren Brown has done numerous works on this and he explains it like this- when getting mugged and a mugger asks for your phone or keys or objects ask the mugger a question that is removed from the situation to disarm them. Such as What's the colour of the front door in the house you grew up in? Such an off-topic question makes the brain freeze as it isn't expected, and this throws off what the mugger was doing. This may give you the time you need to escape, call for help or throw the mugger so off completely they decide to call it off. This is because we have patterns and logical steps to

things in our minds. When it gets interrupted, we become disturbed and unsure of what course of action to take.

Have you ever been interrupted in the middle of a task with a phone call or somebody comes in and after you take a minute to *remember "what was I doing again?"* The same principle applies here. We interrupt the flow of the brain and break the pattern. Throwing a curveball to throw them off.

An example of how we can do this is in the following script:

Guy: *Quick question, I need a female opinion on where would be a good place to go for food on a Sunday that is NOT in town?*

Girl: *Why should I care.*

Guy: The Carebears were ok I suppose but I preferred Barney you know the big purple dinosaur? (she will no doubt nod her head – she is starting to react to you now) I think he was a lot more fun but I've kind of grew out of it now.

Girl: (thinking wtf is this guy on – we are interrupting the brain pattern) erm where the hell is that from?

Guy: I can tell you're a strong woman, everyone else is so boring. Listen I got to get back to my friends but before I do, I know a girl who would love your shoes/dress/bag could you just tell me where you get it from?

Girl: ASOS / Online / Amazon etc

And bingo, we have gone from a very hostile conversation to having her answer one of our questions. This leaves it open for you to run a story or ask something else. The more she talks the more she is buying into the conversation.

Now the above is just an example I have written and the actual conversation may flow very different but the important thing is to interrupt the pattern, break the flow, make them pause or think, not react to their mean words, approve their actions then go on with your next hook question (hook meaning something that requires a response or investment).

Deliberately mishearing or playing off one word in a sentence is showing you are being playful and not taking her comments to heart. Just like you would with a child. Remember there is power in not reacting. We want to be playful but not condescending. I used to play football with a lad called Rando (not his real name, he has asked me to change it to this specifically to avoid the heat from his current girlfriend) on a Sunday morning. He was great at this. He would tease and be playful with women when we were out and was never phased by anything they said. Once you are in this mindset you realise how being playful can be fun.

To summarise in this chapter, we have explored how we can open a set of people. A set can be one person or many. We know have different tactics and strategies we can use to engage in the initial conversation. We are aware of the importance of congruence (how our bodies must mimic what we are saying). We understand that women may make it difficult for us and that's alright as we know when to walk away and when we need to show them, we are worthy individuals. You know have a range of different ways to open a conversation and can invent your own that follow the same pattern. It's important to put your own spin and authenticity into them but if you are struggling you are welcome to use my examples. The hardest part is often just getting going. Once you are over this initial fear of this **approach anxiety** you will realise just how fun it can be to talk to people. You will develop threads and patterns of speech that you know work well and avoid ones you know will not help you.

When you start out do not be concerned with success. It is fine to fail, what we are trying to do is improve our skill levels. When you begin to internalise these thoughts and actions you will see how effortlessly it flows out of you. Like someone who has practiced martial arts for years, your reflexes will become honed and you will instantly know what to say and how to say it.

Remember you are a wonderful person. Some people are going to be so happy you had the confidence to strike up a conversation. When you are fun, playful, and bring value to a conversation people want to be around you.

This can be addictive. Talking to people is great fun regardless of if it goes anyway. Enjoy the conversations and now feel well-armed that you know you have something up your sleeve to start a conversation within 3 seconds of course.

A good show that shows you exactly what it is like to approach women was called - Keys to the VIP. It was a live show with no actors where men who considered themselves to be good with women went into a nightclub and competed against one another. This wasn't reality TV it was a one-off competition judged by a panel of pick-up experts.

The best of which to come on the show was Cajun. Cajun was a professional.

Scan the QR code to see Cajun in action

CHAPTER 7

Attraction - How to build it and keep it

"Attraction is not a choice"

Chapter 7 - Attraction – How To Build It And Keep It

We covered attraction at the start of the last chapter, so I want to jump straight into it with much ado (love Shakespeare).

I am now going to talk about the ways we can build attraction. I will equip you with further tools to use once you've made your **opening pitch**. What to say after you've made contact and where we take it from there to build attraction through a range of different methods.

We are going to go through all the different ways we can demonstrate the **Attraction Switches.** Think of the previous and the subsequent chapters like toolboxes. You get out each toolbox for the relevant part of the job. Sometimes you need to go back and get a different tool that's fine. The important thing is you were equipped with the right tools in the first place then it's up to you as to how you decide to use them.

The key to building attraction lies in the ability to maintain and hold a good conversation. You see people that you consider naturally good with women are great conversationalists and they are so used to talking to people they are not fazed by such interactions.

Salespeople especially have this skill, to strike up a conversation with just about anyone. Now Jordan Belfort, the famous Wolf Of Wall Street has a great sales book called the Art of Straight Line Selling and in there he has two key principles that we can apply to conversations.

The first is understanding the 3 straight lines. In it, he says that in order to make a sale, people must be high up on a straight-line scale from 1-10 to buy what you are selling.

With a 0 being no chance of buying and a 10 meaning it's a certainty. There are 3 different areas Jordan says someone must be confident in before they make a purchase: The product, The company, and you the salesman.

Now in this case the product, the company, and the person selling it are all the same. It is you. You are the product you are asking them to buy into.

Now natural salespeople have a way of controlling the frame in a conversation and taking it the way in which they know will better their chances of completing a sale. However, what Jordan teaches in his book is the use of scripts. That is , scripted things to read to the people you are potentially trying to sell to. Now scripts aren't essential to helping your success with women, but they are useful. After all, not everyone is comfortable making things up on the spot so why wouldn't these people want an idea of what to say beforehand?

In the film, Jordan teaches his salespeople a script to help them when pitching stocks & shares in companies. Now we won't have a word-for-word script as we know that normal human interaction doesn't work like this. We need to be able to go with the natural ebbs and flows. We can however have an idea of a few stories we may tell that we know they will like and will show us in a, particularly good light. These are known as our DHV stories.

Now using stories is always best if they are authentic. It is easy to go back through your life and think of a few things you have done that have shown you in a good light. If you can't think right now, then use this minute to reflect. Think of a time where any of the following happened:

- You took a risk and it paid off
- You were successful in something
- You helped another person
- You made a decision that people followed
- You spent time with women
- You have been funny
- You have won something
- You spent time learning something new ad stuck to it
- You improved in some way

Any of the above can easily form the basis for a good DHV story. You see the purpose of a DHV story is to just tell them in a non-bragging way that you are a great guy. That's it. We are hoping to trigger their attraction switches by telling stories.

You see humans are fascinated by stories.

"We are, as a species, addicted to story. Even when the body goes to sleep, the mind stays up all night, telling itself stories." — Jonathan Gottschall, The Storytelling Animal: How Stories Make Us Human.

Go in any setting from school to marketing boardrooms and see the power stories can have. Need I say it – The John Lewis Christmas Advert?

Scientifically this works because when we hear a story that resonates with us, our levels of a hormone called *oxytocin* increase.

Oxytocin is a "feel good" hormone very similar to how serotonin makes us happy. It works by boosting our feelings of things like trust, compassion, and empathy. Why wouldn't we want the person we are talking to to trust us and empathise?

A neuroscientist at Princeton University looked into this in their 2010 study entitled "Speaker–listener neural coupling underlies successful communication" and published the following findings:

In agreement with previous work, the story evoked highly reliable activity in many brain areas across all listeners."

"Communication is a shared activity resulting in a transfer of information across brains. The findings are shown here indicate that during successful communication, speakers' and listeners' brains exhibit joint, temporally coupled, response patterns."

This is telling us that the storyteller and the person hearing the story have the same brain responses. They become joined for a short time. When you hear a story told well you experience it the same as the person telling it. This is a powerful tool you can use in your conversations. This is why DHV stories work so well they play on the natural love of stories with female's affinities to "get to the real meaning" which allows them to infer good characteristics about you without you labelling them. Remember what we said earlier we must stimulate the emotional before the logical.

You see we can't just tell a woman we are a leader of men or protector of loved ones. That would look weird and come across as boasting. Remember how in the last chapter I spoke of women wanting to read into things? Well, we play on this by telling stories and letting women unpick the meaning behind them. To do this we use something known as **Demonstration of Higher Value Stories** or **DHVs** for short.

DHV Stories

DHV is any action or story that increases the perceived value of a person in the eyes of the people he is talking to.

I'll give you an example:

Guy: You remind me of my sister you're a little bit goofy aren't you

Girl: Ahem excuse me I'm not goofy!

Guy: It's fine, my sister is already bumping into things, this one time she phoned me cause she got her foot stuck at the bowling alley, you'll never guess what I did

Girl: What did you do?

Guy: I rocked up to the bowling alley with a chainsaw in my hand and waved it around saying well if someone doesn't get her foot out of there in 10 mins I'm cutting straight through it, I've seen enough horror movies to know how this ends!

Girl: No way you didn't!?

Guy: Pft all I'm saying is within 10 minutes she had her foot out and we were driving back home with two free slush puppies and whenever I go bowling there, I always get the best lanes now. I can't leave my sister hanging right

Girl: Omg that's crazy!

It's then up to you where you take this story you could ask them if they like bowling, slush puppies, where do they like to go on dates, what's their relationship like with their family any number of things but one thing it doesn't do is come across like an interview.

Now a lot of girls will know it's not a true story but it is still funny if you can say it with the right expression and we convey we are a protector of our loved ones and we don't mind going that extra mile for people we care about.

Such a conversational thread also encourages them to open about situations without you having to ask. The whole point of the story is to stimulate emotion but also show you are a good person. That's it. This is all you are doing in a DHV story. We are breaking up the boring question-answer pattern and throwing something new into the works. Now we must remember this is just a tool and just repeating story after story won't build attraction itself but if we add stories into our conversation then along the way we will build attraction.

We are adding attraction spikes within our conversations. We are making ourselves seem more valuable. Women enjoy when men have things to say beyond one-word answers. If she says she enjoys swimming and asks if you do you can tell her about this time you went swimming with your ex-girlfriend as you had to teach her to tread water before she starred in a film. Now, most people will be *like "omg, cool what film?"* Here I would recommend using humour rather than lying, say something like *"ow she was in Jaws, she played it so well you would never believe she was the Shark".* Then you wait for the smile and move on. It is about being playful and having a laugh with your stories. Having something to say is powerful. If you are happy to speak from your head, then great but if you prefer to plan out the things you might want to talk about then there is no harm in this. You must choose what works best for you. For most people in the beginning they would like to have some sort of plan of what to say. The good thing with humour is they will still hear you talking about being with girls or being a leader of men and attribute this to you even though they know it is a joke.

Now demonstrates of high value or DHV's do not have to just be in stories. In fact, they can often be best done in person. Holding the door open for a woman, sharing an umbrella, offering a coat or jacket, moving them out of the way of a bar brawl (putting them behind you and out of harm's way) all these demonstrate higher value. If you are a manager at work and you take a work call and speak to your staff with respect but it's clear you have a sense of authority this can be attractive (don't be one of those bosses from Horrible Bosses).

When having conversations, we must know how to structure the conversation. We want to move away from – Question – Answer – Question towards a more -Question – Answer – Statement.

I'll give you an example

Question – What do you like to do?

Answer – I like to go out drinking

Question – What do you like to drink?

This turns into an interview and is boring for both sides of the equation. Instead, you want to follow a Question – Answer – Statement, this shows you have something to offer.

Question – What do you like to do?

Answer – I like to go out drinking

Statement – See I had a feeling you were an alcoholic, you're just like Becky from work

Her – I am not an alcoholic! I just like a drink .... Etc

Or another example

Statement – See I knew a friend that really liked red wine that was quite old. I think you probably have a particular drink you're into as well

Her – yes actually I like Gin etc ...

Another example

Statement – I gave up drinking to stop women taking advantage of me, I know your game

Her – what game?

You see how we are showing we have something to stay whilst also extending the conversation along. It is more interesting and can be playful or insightful.

If she says she's into star signs, then you guess her star sign or say you believe in them (if you do) and what star sign you are. You see this structure allows the conversation to progress and doesn't become boring. It is also easy to fit your DHV stories in here as well.

DHVs

Now DHV's can also be shown rather than told. They are in your actions and the things you do. Have you ever worked at a local pub where the fat, old and bald manager managed to sleep with all the fit young barmaids?

It certainly isn't because he is a high-value male, but it can be because the girls are attracted to leadership. The fact that the bar owner or the manager was telling other people what to do and bossing them around would have made the female employees unconsciously feel that he was a high-quality person to mate with.

Now, it might seem that it was the all-encompassing grand title of manager that made him attractive, but that would be inaccurate: it was how having the title made him behave- This was what that made him attractive.

A manager or bar owner has power and makes decisions. This is attractive.

Luckily for you, you don't need to own a bar or be a manager to show you're a leader.

The simplest way to accomplish this is to call the shots.

When you are talking to or spending time with a girl you must make decisions. If you met her in the day, then you can tell her to join you for some coffee. If you met her at night, then you can ask her to join you in the smoking area outside for a breath of fresh air.

The more she sees you making decisions and calling the shots. The more the girl will realize that you have high value as a leader.

The thing you don't do is ask for permission. Alpha males don't ask they are decisive. *"Would you like to join me for a cup of coffee, perhaps?"* Is much less attractive than, *"Let's go get a cup of coffee."* You don't need to be domineering but do make sure to be decisive in your leading.

****
*

Another way to DHV can be through your use of games or observation tools. Playing games alludes to this playful side of you I have been speaking about and the mood you can be in when talking to people. Now taking inspiration from Del Boy the following is a game you play when on a night out which helps display value.

Getting The Girl

The game is simple and called the 5-question game. It's always good to attach a forfeit such as a drink or if you are well into conversation maybe a kiss.

Guy: let's play a game I know it's dead fun

Girl: What game?

Guy: It's very simple, you'll get it easy. If you win, I'll (insert). If I win, you (insert)

Girl: Okay, how do we play?

Guy: It's simple It's called the 5 questions game. I'm going to ask you 5 questions and all you need to do is to tell me a lie for each answer. Easy right?

Girl: Ok I can do that

Guy: Ok. So, do you want me to start with a practise question, or are we good to go?

Girl: No let's start.

Guy: Right, so what's your name?

Girl: John (or any lie). If a girl will does tell you their real name here, giving you a great chance to give a playful comment about them being rubbish

Guy: See I told you it was easy. Now, where do you come from?

Girl: Moscow (some lie)

Guy: What bar/club are we in right now?

Girl: Guys Bar (any lie).

Guy: This is where your acting comes into play. You simply pause, look down for a minute, and stroke your chin or something similarly distracting. After a short moment, change your tone of voice and ask, "how many questions was that"?

Girl: If she answers 3 you win (most people will lose here). However, if she correctly lies to you and says a different number you proceed onto the 5th question.

Guy: Here you need to be taken and back and appear somewhat shocked. Say wow, I don't believe it, you really got me. Have you played this game before?

Girl: No, I've never played it.

Guy: Excellent. I'll have a Redbull thanks for playing.

Girl: You GOT ME!

This is a great little routine you can use that's fun and interactive. It is just a longer version of the Del Boy "I bet I can make you turn your hands over without touching them". Feel free to use that classic as well.

Another game that's great to play on a first date or when you are both really having fun is to guess who is on a first date and who is sleeping together. This works best in restaurants where people usually sit as couples. It can be a good time to talk about other people and share jokes (remember to keep it respectful and not be cruel this isn't attractive).

You see being playful is an attractive trait. If you can make a conversation interesting by talking about a range of things, she will enjoy your time. **Storytelling and humour** are the best tools for this.

One other way in which you can make your conversations more meaningful is to sit down and make a list of 10 things you think are very important in a woman beyond her physical appearance. For example, you may want to be with a woman who is close to her family. Knowing this you then have an aim for something to find out during a conversation. This can be through direct questions or by making statements off the back of your stories to find out. You could tell a story about your family and see what her relationship is like with hers. You could ask her "family *is important to me, what's your relationship like with yours?".* You are both demonstrating value with this question and finding out the information you wanted.

When we DHV in person we do it by our fashion choices, our body language, the tone of our voice, the way we command the room, how we interact with other men, how we hold our heads, by having social status, by being funny, confident, them seeing we tick the attraction switches, not needing to be liked, taking calculated risks, being funny, having a thick skin, showing intelligence all of these things can be done in person. People see these first-hand.

Body language plays a crucial role as discussed previously.

Getting The Girl

Social psychologist Amy Cuddy of Harvard Business School is studying how we evaluate people we meet. Cuddy is known for her research on power posing, e. This research suggests that if you strike a strong pose—where you take up as much space as possible—your levels of testosterone rise, while cortisol levels drop. The result: If you do it for two minutes before going into a job interview or other public performance, you will have more confidence and perform better. When you are out be sure to take up space. Such a study goes onto highlight what confident men do. When a man is confident and feeling powerful they begin to take up space and make themselves bigger. They own the room. Whether this is spreading out on a chair with their arms wide open or physically stood with their feet apart or shoulders back. DHV's that are non-verbal are just as powerful. Do you look as if you are seeking validation from someone by your body language or they are seeking validation from you? Think more closely about how you stand next time you are talking to a woman and what message this is projecting.

We can display high value by the many choices we make. As explained in the Chapter on first impressions, the clothes you wear or the car you drive can speak for you. For some people, it says this man is a successful risk-taker he is of high status. This is very common amongst younger females who associate named brands of clothes and things such as fancy cars or watches to be status definers. As women age, they look for other status definers such as being a business owner, having a high-status job, or a nice house. In all situation's women are looking for hints that you are a high-value male.

If you want branded clothes but can't afford the shop prices, try apps like Depop to find them second hand at a much-discounted rate. The woman you're talking to has no idea whether they were bought new or not.

If you can develop a side hustle that you can pass off as your business idea you appear like a man who is successful and not afraid to try new things to make his way in life. There are lots of side hustles you can do.

Here are **10 Passive Income Ideas**:

- Sell on Amazon – sell products through Amazon to generate additional cash
- Rent out a room – Air BnB, spare room
- Create a gaming app

- Buy a Vending Machine- Put this in a high footfall location or ask permission of shops and generate the income
- Invest in Dividend Paying Stocks – Put your money into stocks that pay you're a regular income, this can be done through a Stocks and Shares ISA to have tax-free earnings. Companies such as Fidelity & Hargreaves Lansdowne offer these
- Grow a YouTube Channel
- Invest in Rental Properties – Renting out a property to a single tenant or to multiple tenants through an HMO (House with Multiple Occupancies) is a great way to earn money with little effort required on your behalf. You can even outsource this to an agent who does the hard part for you
- Peer to Peer Lending – with something like the lending club you can lend money to people and charge them interest which they pay you back over time.
- Affiliate Marketing – You sell a product in affiliate marketing; you earn a commission by promoting a product. The product you promote online should be something you know about and that you believe is high quality. You can use a commission platform like the Commission Factory, RewareStyle, or ShareASale. You could also sign up as an Amazon affiliate.
- Start an ATM business – did you know you can buy ATMS and rent them out? That is those £1.25 per transaction charge people pay. Although we may be moving cashless one thing you will see is with the closure of so many retail banks leaves a gap in the market for someone to capitalise on offering the service of dispensing cash.

These are just a few examples of Passive Income Streams you can use to generate extra cash and it shows the value within yourself, that you are willing to try new things. You can also learn some highly sought-after skills. These can then be traded for a salary or project work later. It also shows you like to learn and be prepared for the future. All of these are DHV's.

10 **High-Income Skills to Learn**:

- Cyber Security
- Copywriter
- Content Creation

- Digital Marketing
- Email Marketing
- Lead Generation
- Online tutoring
- Public Speaking
- Podcasting
- Sales Closing

Here are some more examples of ways you can better yourself. Remember self-improvement is a huge DHV but more importantly, you need to grow as an individual. We want to always be striving for better in life. This means being open to learning new skills. Now a lot of courses can be taken on apps such as Coursera, Khan Academy, Skillshare, or many Universities that offer free courses for you to study.

It is always good to have something to talk about when speaking about your own development. This can be a new book your reading or a course your studying, not only will it help you improve as a person, but it also says to the person you are speaking – I like to move forward in life.

You see DHV's can be many things in life, from how we stand to what we study. Building attraction is simply demonstrating we are of high value. We do this by the many tools outlined which convey DHV's. This can be done using stories (easier), in person by our actions or by someone else telling them how great you are. You have a wealth of tools for you to choose from. Arm yourself wisely young squire. Choose the tool that best suits your personality and begin to incorporate others. This will help you to display value as you will have a range of weapons to choose from when on the hunt. The good thing about learning these different techniques is they are transferable in all areas of life from sales to asking your boss for a promotion. If you have a range of ways to tell them, you are worth it other than being direct then this can only help you in life. Once you become familiar with the different ways you can display value it's just up to you to choose the ones that work best for you. Using tools is part of our DNA and ancestry. We as Hunter-Gathers have used tools for millenniums. The early Stone Age (also known as the Lower Paleolithic) saw the development of the first stone tools by Homo habilis, one of the earliest members of the human family. These were stone cores with flakes removed from them to create a sharpened edge that could be used for cutting, chopping, or scraping.

The next leap forward in tool technology occurred when early humans began striking flakes off longer rock cores to shape them into thinner, less rounded implements, including a new kind of tool called a handaxe. We were not settled on having just one tool to hunt. We went on the prowl for more innovative ways to help us catch prey. We didn't get Bow and Arrows until about 50,000 years ago. We, humans, are very clever at finding ways to make hunting easier, from spears to laying traps.

Disqualifiers & Disinterest

Showing disinterest in a woman is one of the most powerful aphrodisiacs you can use. When you convey or say, *"I don't want you"* she goes *"Why not?".* The exact opposite applies when you convey too much interest too soon. She goes *"I can have him when I want him and now, I don't want him*". As they say, gentleman, the thrill is in the chase and they weren't lying. When you convey disinterest, it allows you to talk for much longer and allows the group of women to relax. They aren't thinking – Omg this guy is desperate to read me the Karma Sutra – they are instead able to enjoy the conversation and when you repeatedly use disqualifiers or show disinterest, they begin to wonder why you aren't interested in them in the first place. When this happens, they instead try to show value to you. You see people like to be liked. They want to feel loved and attractive. When they don't get this from you, they then feel as if they perhaps haven't shown you all their attractive qualities, so they begin to qualify themselves to you. This is what I mentioned earlier instead of chasing the cat, put a bowl of milk down and watch as the cat comes to you.

Disqualifiers work in multiple ways: they buy you more time in the group, they help to build sexual tension later, it shows you aren't trying to win her over or impress her which it turns builds attraction.

When thinking of your own disqualifiers it is best to have a few on hand that works in any given situation, you don't want them to be too specific so they can be used when needed.

The key is to say something that isn't personal, you would never talk about weight for someone who is overweight, and as a rule, don't comment on things people can't easily change such as birthmarks. We aren't trying to be mean here.

We are trying to use our playful manner to say things with a tongue-in-cheek approach. The Irish word for this is having the Craic. This is what we are aiming to do. A mild remark that just shows that the other person isn't that impressive.

An example:

Guy*: **Jeez you can dress her up, but you can't take her anywhere***

This can be deployed at any time especially if a girl is starting to be loud or mean to you. They are best said with a smirk on your face or slightly breaking into a smile, so they and the group know you are saying it with an element of humour. Such a remark will disarm the person you are talking to. It is always a good idea to use these on the girl you would like to eventually talk to one on one if you're in a group. The person you are aiming for. You want to use disqualifiers on her to make her work a little harder for your validation.

Women will tell you numerous times they have been attracted to the "Bad Boy". This "Bad Boy" usually treated her a little mean and acted as if he didn't care whether she liked him or not. We can take the psychology away from them by using disqualifiers ourselves. Disqualifying a woman allows you to show her that you aren't like all the other guys who are just attracted to her for her looks. It lets her work for your attraction.

Here is an example of disqualifiers you can use to disarm a woman and begin to make her work a little harder for your attention:

- *Your quite weird aren't you* ...Fun – the important bit here is the delay in the use of Fun
- *You remind me of my girlfriend* – Later on when she mentions your girlfriend you can say something like, well what I meant to say is it's crazy how much you remind me of my next girlfriend or you can say – silly me I keep doing that ever since she died when she asks you what she died of you can smile, nod and say something cheeky like " well it involved me her the bedroom

and a cucumber so we will save the story for another time" she will understand this is a joke and it shows a good social calibration

- *OH, SORRY I couldn't serve you better, your highness…*- This works well if she is interrupting you or getting loud, you use this to scold her.
- *You're not cool enough to hand out with me* – disqualifies her as a suitor, she will no doubt ask why then you can follow it up with - Ok tell me what's special about you I'm interested
- *you are too young/old for me – an* easy one to use and very effective
- *Get your phone out and write - Note to self: Do not date this girl-* then say sorry just had to write something down quickly, make sure she can see over your shoulder as you write
- *You're so nice, way too nice for me, I would walk all over you* – Remember not to break stride when saying this and continue into the conversation with the group or story you are telling.
- *Ask for her name and then say – You are like in the top 3 (insert name) I have met tonight. Follow it up with a comment about her height and then say you like girls that are taller/smaller* the others were taller or smaller depending on their height
- *Where is her off button? IT–* A great line for someone who is very talkative or interrupts you. Remember it should be delivered then quickly moved on from.

These are just a few examples of ways you can show Disinterest by your words. It is best if you can find a few that fit naturally into your manner of speaking. Just like with DHV's Disinterest can be shown by your actions as well as your words.

The most common way to do this is at the beginning of the interaction here you ignore the woman you find attractive and spend more time speaking with her friends. This shows you are disinterested. This is the most common and effective way to run a conversation. **You start by showing the least attention to the person you are attracted to.**

Remember we are always trying to embody the alpha-male attributes and look at ticking those attraction switches. An alpha male would not get blown away by a woman because she is attractive. He is used to attractive women. There is no reason he talks to her more just because she is attractive. He is not easily impressed.

A way he can signal this is by not being too agreeable. Disagreeing with a woman's opinion on a topic of conversation says you have your own mind. This highly attractive trait (especially if you can articulate your opinion well) says to her and her friends you won't bow down to her just because she's got a pretty face. You need to be more than just attractive to change my mind.

Letting a woman know that there is just something about her that you're not keen on, in fact, there is something about her that stops you from dating her. Such as "You're a Liverpool fan? I never date people who support Liverpool … (any sports club or club they belong to works for this)". Remember the key is in the execution and ending it with a cheeky smile.

****

Teasing

Moving on from using direct disqualifiers like the ones above, sometimes we want to combine the words we say to come across as teasing. Teasing a woman with a playful joke like saying "You don't get out, much do you?" invites conversation and helps to set up sexual chemistry for later. The important thing when teasing is to smile. We don't want them to take comments too seriously or to heart else, it will appear as if you are just being mean for no reason.

Teasing comes with risks but without risk comes to no reward. Only confident guys tease and have fun with attractive women. This is because they are not aiming to please them and are not seeking validation. It is a great way to make you stand out positively and heightens attraction.

When teasing look for a thread that is the opposite of the woman you are talking to. If the girl you are talking to for example wears little make-up, you can comment on how you wonder how she will look after she went swimming. You bet she looks completely different.

Another one to use is when a woman is dressed nice and clearly made a lot of effort to come out that night or wherever you've met her you can tease her by asking if she was getting ready in a hurry or if she has come straight from the office. The teasing is best done in the tone of the delivery and with good facial expressions.

Teasing works best when it is observational. It's very hard to script these so this is where your natural observation skills should come into play. If she is on her phone or checks, her phone you can say something like *"jeez is your Only Fans account really booming at this time? YOU can tell the punters to wait whilst you have a real conversation"* Now I am assuming she doesn't actually have an only fans account otherwise it may turn into a very different conversation (you lucky boy) but you are looking for her to laugh or act offended and get the humour in it.

When teasing you can aim to portray her to be highly sexualised if you make sexual innuendo. Say you say, I bet you like bananas and she acts offended or gives you a look as if you are making it sexual you can say *" Woah get your mind out the gutter and pack undressing me with your eyes".* We want to look spontaneous and cool when we use a tease.

Another way we can show disinterest is to under-react to what she says. When she is making jokes or trying to dominate the conversation, your expressions can be slightly under the rest of the group. We are then saying – you aren't impressing us that much. Girls use this all the time. You are only turning it around on them.

You can break eye contact and begin to stare into the space behind her or turn your head. This gives her the impression she is "losing your attention". This is a great non-verbal **Indicator of Disinterest**.

An **Indicator of Disinterest** is anything that conveys to them that you are not interested in. Many of the things we have talking about can be an IOD.

We give an IOD when a woman gives us an IOD. We don't reward her for showing us she isn't interested.

It goes like this:

Guy: IOD > Girl: IOI > Guy IOI

Guy: IOI > Girl: IOD > Guy IOD

Girl: IOD > Guy: IOD. Girl: IOI

Girl: IOI > Guy: IOI

As illustrated above we don't reward their indicators of disinterest. We are not the ones seeking their approval. We give them the same energy they give us. If they show us, they are interested we may return it with a little interest ourselves. If they show, they are disinterested we show the same. Remember **a Lion does not care about the opinion of sheep.**

We are not seeking their approval. This builds attraction.

IOIs

Now **Indicators of Interest.** This is how we know when we are winning. When a woman is starting to become interested in us, she will do certain things. In fact, before you even talk, she will display IOI's if she wants you to talk to her. These are little signs, like big flags saying COME TALK TO ME. You see most women don't do the approaching. Instead, they throw out subtle IOI's, sometimes unconsciously to attract men to talk to them. They lure them in.

So, you ask, Jack what are these magical signs to know when a woman is interested?

Well luckily for you. I have the answers.

Luckily for you, there is a wealth of knowledge to be found on how women indicate they are interested in you. Thankfully, you have me, who has pulled it all together in one place.

There is a wide array of research that has looked at how Women use nonverbal strategies to signal sexual interest (see Moore, 1985; Perper, 1985; Walsh & Hewitt, 1985).

The researchers concluded that women would offer a wide range of non-verbal behaviours that express their interest in men.

You see, when a woman walks into a bar with her friends, she will begin to look around the room to see the lay of the land. This very normal behaviour shifts slightly is she sees someone she finds attractive. At this stage, her gaze lingers. This is the brain quickly computing whether she believes he will make a good mate. Women are hardwired to do this regardless of culture. Meaning this isn't learned. This is just one of the Indicators of Interest that all women are born with. Gaze, therefore, is a key part of when women signal interest. If she is looking in your direction then there is a reason, either you've got ketchup on your chin or she fancies you as some sort of tasty snack.

The woman would then maintain an extended gaze at the man until he notices her, she smiles, then she breaks the gaze, returns the gaze again, smiles, and again breaks the gaze. The good old – "I'm *shy, come talk to me Fred Flintstone make my Bedrock"*

"The eyes chico they never lie" Tony Montana

Now Bolmont (2014) **in Love is in the gaze: An eye-tracking study of love and desire** goes into lots of detail about the role the eye and how people position themselves to see people they find attractive is cross-cultural and applies universally. This journal article published in psychology looks at how you can tell when a woman is interested. Now you don't have to read it because in a short while I'm going to give you a handy list of points that tell you when she's interested. I am too good to you, aren't I?

"Dr. Wilson: What exactly did Cuddy tell you?
Dr. House: Nothing that your body language isn't telling me right now." *–House the TV Series*

A woman interested in a man will want to look her best. In doing so she will play with her hair or fix her dress. Her body language will also change. Perper T (1985) in his book **Sex Signals** documents the weird ways we change when we are around people, we find attractive. Dr. Perper's ideas are based on more than 900 hours of scientific observations made wherever men and women meet -- in singles bars, restaurants, parties, or even train stations.

It isn't just their eyes that give them away either often women will adopt an open body posture (e.g., arms away from the body), or they shift their body, so they are oriented her body to face him. Such behaviour is documented in the journal article **Giving men the come-on: Effect of eye contact and smiling in a bar environment** Walsh, D. G., & Hewitt, J. (1985).

These are also cross-cultural universal signals before you think they are conditioned or learnt later on. Such things such as an eyebrow flash combined with a smile was a common signal in a range of cultural backgrounds, from the Balinese to Papuans, French, and Wakiu Indians (Eibl-Eibesfeldt, 1971).

"The most important thing in communication is hearing what isn't said." –Peter F. Drucker

Body language can work both ways. It's equally important to know when women aren't interested. That's why we talk about IOIs (indicators of Interest) we need a few of them to be really sure. We don't want to see one thing and go all guns blazing like a Battle Royale on Fortnite. You see women have an equally impressive array of nonverbal shut-down behaviour's; they will lean away, cross their arms over their chest to shut them off, avoid making eye contact, Even goes as far as to play with their fingernails to say – listen this dirt under here is more impressive then you right now. This is the exact opposite of saying they are interested (Moore, 1998).

These are so effective that Moore & Butler in their book **Predictive aspects of nonverbal courtship behaviour** (1989) can predict the outcomes of interactions based just on their non-verbal signals alone. Trained people can do this to a scary high degree of accuracy.

You see we make non-verbal signals without even knowing it. Women do this just as much as men. That's why it pays to pay attention.

When you walk into a room, at work, at University, or at a bar women are usually present. When they notice you, they can do one of two things. They can signal they aren't interested. They can signal that they are.

You see women behave differently when they are single or open to being approached. The first thing women do when they are on the lookout is to sit, stand or dance in an area where they have a good view of the door. This way they can look at who's coming in and way up their options. Women love to look from a distance. The second-place they like to stand is an area where lots of guys must walk past. The bar or near the toilets. You see when women don't want to be approached, they do the complete opposite. They will hide away in the corner or they will go to the middle of the dance floor far away from where they can be bothered.

A great giveaway for if a woman is interested is the position of her feet. (I'm not talking about them being behind your head) Women and men subconsciously point their feet in a way that's easiest to move. You see it comes back from being hard-wired into our brains to face the direction we quickly want to go to. If a woman's feet are pointed in your direction, then there is a strong chance she wants you to make a conversation.

Another giveaway is when a woman plays with her hair. If she looks in, your direction and starts fluffing up her hair or playing with it then she is attempting to make sure she looks her best. Why would she want to look her best for you if you weren't attractive? Some science supports women get hotter when seeing someone they find attractive, so they often scratch the area behind their ear or on their neck. This is due to the blood rushing to these areas quickly. It also may cause them to turn redder and flush in the face. We must realise that often these are subconscious. They may not realise that by flicking their hair they spread their pheromones in the air, literally attempting to snare men with their own chemicals.

All of this is supported in numerous journal articles such as Abrahams (1994**) Perceiving flirtatious communication: An exploration of the perceptual dimensions underlying judgments of flirtatiousness**. Hugill (2012) **Women's Body Movements Are a Potential Cue to Ovulation. Personality and Individual Differences.** Lastly, Patience (2001) **Does Women's Hair Signal Reproductive Potential?**

Proximity is another important one, they can stand anywhere in the bar or on the dancefloor, but they have chosen to stand near you. Now check the space around and if you feel as if they have made a choice to stand here then that's an IOI, if the venue is just crowded then you can't safely say it is. You see women will stand near guys they want to talk to them. Especially if you're in a high-energy group. They will want to join in the fun.

"I wanted it to be you. I wanted it to be your badly" You've Got Mail

Check a person's body position when walking past you. Especially in crowded places. If they cross your path with their body open facing you directly this is a sign, they are attracted to you. If they cross with their back to you this is an IOD.

I'm also just a girl, standing in front of a boy, asking him to love her." Notting Hill

Look out for women on their phones. If they are on their phones and not having fun in a group, then clearly, they are here for another purpose. Look out for this.

Women may also over-express with loud laughs or seems to act a bit silly. This is to draw attention from guys that are nearby.

Look out for eye contact and smiles. Women may also walk past you a lot to allow you to talk to them. If they are passing by you or your group and giving you a smile and eye contact, now is a good chance to start with your opening pitch. Sometimes if the IOI's are so strong all you need is a simple "Hello" as your opening Pitch to be able to speak to the group. However, to be safe go with something indirect like we mentioned earlier.

"You had me at hello." Jerry Maguire

Girls might expose more skin while you are around. A woman sits up straight to emphasis her breasts and crosses her legs or ankles to show them to her best advantage. She may tilt her head and hips to expose her neck. When girls expose their necks, it is their way of feminizing themselves and making themselves more vulnerable to create that polarity.

"No, I like you very much. Just as you are." Bridget Jones Diary

We need to be hearing what their words ARE NOT saying.

Now when you are in a conversation you want to be looking out for indicators of interest to let you know it is going well. Lucky for you I have pulled together an entire list of things to look out for. So, if there's ever a section you'll want a photocopier for it's probably now.

The following is a list of some IOIs' you may get when talking to a woman:

- Her body is facing you, regardless of other people being around her. If her feet are pointed right at you, despite other options, that's a big IOI
- She touches you when you are talking (even as little as a hand on your arm). This is a very big IOI. She may do this after you tell a joke saying how funny you are.
- She makes her self-look prettier – smooths, curls or plays with her hair, adjusting her dress, re-applying lipstick or Chapstick, fiddling with her bag

- She doesn't break eye contact
- When she does break eye contact, she looks down as if shy- very good indicator she wants you to go talk to her
- She pushes her body up against you, even leaning on A girl knows when she "accidentally" brushes her breasts against you when walking past you. She doesn't do it with just any man
- Her body language to you is open (shoulder's back, arms uncrossed).
- She begins to change her energy – improves her posture, maybe pushes her breasts out
- She begins to peck. Seems to be leaning in
- She ACCIDENTALLY shows off more skin - her dress slips a little off her shoulder or she shows you her legs
- She begins to stroke or comfort herself. It can look like she is, sliding a hand along her own neck or collarbone. (This is a very powerful one. It tells you something about where her mind is – she wants you to be caressing her).
- She mirrors you. She copy's your expression or words.,
- She re-initiates conversations when you stop talking
- She giggles especially at your bad jokes
- She tries to get rapport and build comfort with you she seeks your validation
- Her eyes wander towards you ever minute
- she makes a big thing of tossing her hair to make sure you are paying attention tosses her hair
- She holds eye contact from across the room
- When she joins her friends, she comes in laughing at something you have said

- She asks you for a lighter, what the time is, what time it closes, where the toilers are or anything to strike up a conversation
- While you're talking to her group, she is particularly talkative in an attempt to grab your attention and put the spotlight on her
- When she starts to ask you question such as your name or your age (you will of course make her guess because we are playful right)
- Disagreeing but laughing at the same time
- She gives you and uses nicknames for you

- She asks if you have a girlfriend
- She mentions your girlfriend without you saying you have one – she is fishing for information here
- When she must go to the bathroom, she comes back to you
- She avoids mentioning her boyfriend, this is also known as plausible deniability. If you don't know then that's better for her
- When the topic of things you like comes up she shares the same interest and tells you she likes it. She may also ask for help. "Can you teach me to cook?"
- After telling a joke or making a fool of herself she looks at you to see your reaction
- In order to not be obvious, she continually looks at you from the side
- When she thinks you are valuable, she will begin to introduce you to her friends, maybe leading you by the arm.
- She begins to invest in you finically this can be from buying you a drink to buying you food. She is saying we are at least equal. A big one is she will try and call you out on your behaviour saying you are a womaniser or some sort of player. She is looking for justification here for her own feelings and wants you to give her a reason to like her. It also says – I know you attract a lot of women
- When she is leaving she tries to say goodbye. She wants to tell you she is leaving; this is a good time to grab her number
- When you are leaving on your way out, she asks you where you are going, you can either grab her number or invite her along with you
- When you call, text, or message her she responds

Now I know that's a lot to look for so maybe it's a good idea to bookmark the last few pages to read back. Even better borrow a girl's hair grip after you finish the book and you start surrounding yourself with beautiful women. Those pesky hair grips get everywhere and it's about time they went to some practical use.

One thing we must be actively conscious of is that an IOI by itself does not mean she is interested I'm afraid George Clooney. When looking for an IOI, one alone is not enough to be sure but if you start getting a few then you know you are doing something right. This tells you how you are doing in the conversation.

"It was a million tiny little things that, when you added them all up, they meant we were supposed to be together ... and I knew it. I knew it the very first time I touched her. It was like coming home. .. only to no home I'd ever known ... I was just taking her hand to help her out of a car and I knew. It was like ... magic." ~ Sleepless in Seattle

Also, remember to show a degree of tact. Sometimes a woman can do things subconsciously that she isn't aware of. This is her body telling her that you are a man of value. You are pointing it out and saying – see you are attracted to me you played with your hair! Will make you come across as a stranger character than Gollum from The Lord of the rings. Keep these secret signals to yourself. When you become experts at spotting the signals it is like time slows, you see things at a different pace. You begin to see as you win over a woman by the more IOI's she gives you. This power will leave you feeling like Dr. Strange but it is important to remember, as, with all things, you may interpret signals incorrectly. This is why we look for multiple IOI's to make sure.

"They say when you meet the love of your life, time stops, and that's true." ~ Big Fish

When you become socially attuned you will notice these the more interactions you have.

Finally, we have a few Unconscious IOIs that she does without noticing:

- When her friends go (to the bathroom or bar or dancing) but she stays to talk with you
- if you move, she follows you or waits for you
- She doesn't flinch or pull back if you happen to get too close, she is comfortable

"If you're a bird, I'm a bird." The Notebook

The biggest IOIs to look for are when you stop talking or the conversation pauses, she wants to continue to talk and keep the conversation going. She seems to laugh at your jokes more than is necessary. You're not that funny, trust me.

The IOI's are like the gold rings on sonic, the more you collect the better you are doing. If this was Grand Theft Auto, it's like learning the weapon cheat. It will give you an unfair advantage over all the over guys. Well it may not be fair that you know how to tell when a woman likes you. But hey is that your problem? It sure isn't. It's not your fault that you were smart enough to take time to learn what makes women tick.

"You have bewitched me, body and soul, and I love… I love… I love you." ~ Pride & Prejudice

Cat and Mouse theory

The final thing we use to build attraction is the Cat and Mouse theory. This is where we combine what we know about being playful and knowing how to build attraction, how to look out for IOIs, when to give them IODs and we put it all together in a little game like our boys Tom & Jerry.

Now I know how much you want to be a pussycat but, in this instance, we are the mice. We know that women like the chase. When they think they've got you like our boy Tom you slip out from their fingers. It's the combination of sweet & sour, hot & cold, and Ying & Yang.

We dangle what they could have just in front of them, then as they think they've got you- pull away. Now we aren't doing this to be mean, we are doing this knowing that if a woman thinks she has conquered you too quickly she will grow bored and seek a new challenge. We know that if she *"can't quite pin you down"* this will drive up the sexual tension and make her desire for you grow larger.

"Choose me. Marry me. Let me make you happy." My Best Friend's Wedding

If you have never seen Tom & Jerry, I will give you a brief synopsis. ***Tom and Jerry*** are an American animated media franchise and series of comedy short films. Tom is the cat. Jerry is the mouse. In the show, Tom tries to capture Jerry. Jerry is very smart and not only doesn't get caught be makes Tom jump through certain "hoops" or controls his actions. From making him run into rakes or walls to literally jumping through flaming hoops. Jerry is one step ahead of Tom and not easily fooled. Although Tom is doing the chasing Jerry is in control.

You need to be Jerry.

You are not going to jump through their hoops, but you are going to get them to jump through yours.

Now when girls are trying to exert their influence she may try and see if she can get you to jump through her hoops. She may ask you to hold her bag or her drink. In this case I would say *"I'm into mergers and acquisitions not the holding game bub"* and refuse. She is testing you to see if you will give her IOI's. When she wants you to jump through her hoops she is testing to see if she is leading and your following. She may give you fake IOIs to get you to chase her. She may try and make you apologise to her. She may ask things of you like to spend money or go get something. All she is doing is testing how far you will go. Are you working for her or is she working for you?

Now when you are in different stages of The Courtship Process, holding bags or a drink won't mean much but, in the beginning, you aren't sure if she is interested or if she is just fucking with you. So, until we are sure. We won't be a puppet on a string.

When she gives you a hoop to jump through, you grab that hoop take it off her and tell her to jump instead.

I'll give you an example:

Girl: Will you buy me a rose?
Guy: Buy ME a drink and we will see if you deserve a rose.

We aren't just going to do what she wants because she asked for it. We need her to invest as well.

Conversations and relationships are *"give and take"*. When she gives you a hoop you can jump through it only after she has jumped through yours.

Girl: Are you from here?

Guy: Do I look like I'm from here?

Girl: No, you don't.

Guy: You right, I'm actually from (wherever you are from)

You see how she had to work just a little bit. She had to invest before you invested. Remember we want this to be as even as we can otherwise, we look needy.

Guy: Are you from here?

Girl: Guess

Guy: Do you want me to guess somewhere close or somewhere far away?

Girl: Guess close

Guy: Is it (insert city near)

You see we aren't giving the answers away so easily. We are making them work just like the Cat chasing the Mouse.

Another important thing is to not react to their hoops if they are trying to be mean. If they talk about your hair or your style or what you drink, they want you to justify your choices. An Alpha male doesn't justify their choices. You ignore the comment and move onto your next story or you punish her with an IOD, so she knows you aren't interested in that kind of behaviour. She is in your world now and in your world, there are rules. She can't go around being mean and expect to get rewarded. She will quickly learn the rules. She will see the strength in you not being swayed by her comments. Leaders lead. They are not angered by the comments of Jesters.

Messenger: This is madness!!

King Leonidas: Madness? THIS IS SPARTA!!!

– 300 Movie

The good thing about using Cat and Mouse theory is that we are reversing the roles, we are making them work a little by little for your attention and approval. Remember we are doing this playfully, combining the teasing we learnt from before, looking out for IOI's to see if what we are doing is working. When they give us IOD's we give them one back? When they ask us to jump through hoops, we give them one back.

You see we are mirroring energy and attempting to bring their energy up. As they start to invest more in you, you can invest more in them. We are just making sure we do not jump fully in; they get bored and move on to the next challenge.

What we are conveying here is we also have standards. We won't just give them free rein because they are pretty. Tch, beauty Is common there are lots of pretty girls what makes her so special?

Now when we get very good at being playful and teasing, we eventually lure them into chasing us. Now when this happens, she is going to start to qualify herself to you. She will bring up reasons she would make a good girlfriend or wife. She may talk about her past relationships and how she was a great girlfriend and he was so bad (sounds like she is running a DHV story on you), she could talk about her sexual appetite or ask if her bum looks big in that dress. No matter which angle she is approaching it she is trying to get validation from you.

We don't want her to control the "frame".

Now when you have controlled the frame, people are "playing by your rules". Frame control is the unspoken rules in what you say. If someone asks, *"been in the sun today?"* it assumes it has been sunny or that you look tanned.

When they accept your frame then they are buying into your values, your morals, and your presuppositions. They are effectively accepting your leadership.

If you let her dictate the frame, then she will make it seem as if she is the prize. We do not accept this frame. We see it as mutually beneficial. You bring value and so does she.

You see most people are aware that frames are there but have never put a word on it. Frames are always there, but they become most obvious when two people disagree about something.

To give an example:

Valentine's day is near:

- He believes gifts are a waste of time and money.
- She believes that it's romantic and exchanging gifts is proof of caring.

That couple is going to have a frame conflict, and who wins or, better, how the conflict is resolved, depends on the frame control skills of both individuals.

Frame control is powerful, but it isn't quite Jedi Mind tricks in case you think you're going to be bending people to your will.

Obi Wan: "You don't need to see his identification"

Stormtrooper "We don't need to see his identification"

Obi Wan: "These are not the droids you're looking for"

Stormtrooper "These are not the droids we're looking for"

Star Wars: A New Hope

It will however prevent you from getting walked all over. You see the frame is the context in which the discussion rests. Framing, therefore, is the act of imposing a mental/psychological viewpoint on any situation and having that situation "conform" to that frame or belief.

If this sounds complex, I'll give you an example:

When raising children parents set up the frame of:

"I'm the adult and authority in the room. You need to listen to adults and authority figures. Therefore, you have to listen to me."

They do this so that children are compliant and respectful. Then during any discussion or argument, the parent refers back to the frame and says: look whatever we are arguing about must still follow the rules above.

You see how by suggesting and controlling the frame you can also limit or control the conversation.

Now the best modern-day example of a frame controller in recent history is a man who likes to play golf, has blonde hair, and was the former President of The United States.

Yes, I am talking about Donald J Trump.

Cognitive scientist George Lakoff wrote a paper that highlighted the threat he posed to the Democratic Party in 2016. He was offering advice and help. You see George was a Professor of Linguistics and Cognitive Science. He had sold half a million copies of books. Google Scholar reported at the time (more now) that scholars had cited him well over 100,000 times. He saw how Trump was framing the debate. He knew he was winning.

One thing George knew better than most was how framing influences reasoning, or how the way we say something often matters much more than what we say. He used this research to try and help the Democratic party to frame their arguments and the positions He put all of his advice in a book entitled *"Don't think of an elephant!"*. The title itself gives away the biggest clue. If you negate a frame, what you do is make the frame stronger.

In other words, if you say, "don't think of an elephant," I bet right now you can't help yourself but think of an elephant, right?

Lakoff knew that Trump was using this to his advantage with the news cycle. The more the news said he was lying the more they repeated his message.

Trump was the best at controlling the frame in this debate he constantly repeated the same message with lines like "Crooked Hillary," which according to Lakoff, was strengthening this particular frame, subconsciously causing the public to view her in that way.

Now I will leave it up to you to decide whether you think Trump was a Jedi Master or a Sith Lord, it depends where you sit on the debate but one thing we do know is that he was highly effective at controlling the frame.

There are a few techniques you can use to help you control frames.

1. Ignore it – when someone tries to comment on your appearance or says something you don't agree with you don't give it power, so you ignore it.
   Example: *Girl: Did you get that jumper from your grandad? Guy: It's so warm today, what made you wear that*
2. Label what they are doing – Label the emotion behind the words. This can be disarming and doesn't make it personal
   Example: Girl: You're such an idiot, how can you even think such rubbish
   Guy: Wow, you seem really angry man, you must feel very strongly about this
3. Use Humour – Humour can be great to deflect conversations and change the tone or to move on.

Example: Guy: everyone likes the pretty girls, especially the geeky ones
Girl: No one at work likes me
Guy: OK, everyone likes the pretty geeky girls except ones with really tiny ears like you
Girl: Ahaha
Guy Jokes aside, were you serious? I'm sorry to hear that, how come...

In the next Chapter on Safety we will speak more about Frame Controlling and using things such as mirrors or labelling when in a conversation. These tactics come from Chris Voss the former Chief Hostage Negotiator for the FBI and author of Never Split The Difference.

These are just some ways in which you can help take control of the frame and move the conversation along.

Now let's recap on what we have learnt in this chapter so far:

We know that in order to be considered attractive we must flick a woman's attraction switches. These are the things we covered in chapter one. We know we want women to think that we have survival value. There are many ways we can convey that we are of high value. We can use storytelling which humans love and there include examples of us doing things to demonstrate higher value. We can also demonstrate high value in person by making decisions or by being funny and showing we have a good understanding of social situations.

Once we start to demonstrate higher value then we should start to see indicators of interest from the woman we are talking to. Sometimes we get indicators of interest before we even speak to them. We know the different signs now.

When we are talking, we want to continue to demonstrate higher value, but we also want to give out disqualifiers. This shows that we are not easily won over and they must also work for our approval. This also helps you to speak as they do not think you are just there to chat them up the same as every other guy. We do this playfully and inject lots of humour. We want to disqualify them but also include teasing. When we tease, we use a Cat and Mouse-like game where we do not jump in their hoops, but we get them to jump through ours. We want to be recognised as of equal value at least. Even better if you can get them to chase you.

We are aware that during any discussion frame control will frame whatever discussion we are having. We are aware that we don't want to be drawn into their world and their frames always otherwise it means we are playing by their rules. We want to make sure we have a chance to also frame discussions. This allows us a chance to open debate or speak with more freedom. We are not looking to dominant. We are looking to lead but when leading there are times we also follow. A good leader knows when to step back and when to step up.

The more interactions we have with women the more fluid this will all seem. We are aware that attraction isn't a choice and we now have a range of tools at our fingertips to show we are of value. We also will not over-value the women we are talking to which is why we use disqualifiers. We do this through teasing. We want to have a laugh and make the experience of meeting us pleasant. We will never be outcome dependant. We are talking to women for the enjoyment and the experience not because we aim to always wake up next to them.

You are learning to get better at attracting women and must enjoy the process as well. Every new woman you talk to brings you a step closer to being confident with women.

The Wingman

Finally, we are aware that when building Attraction, you don't just do it by yourself. In fact, many a time you may employ the help of a wingman. Now a wingman can be part of a famous double act or even a group of guys that help introduce you to women. Over the years there have been countless examples of guys helping other guys with the ladies.

Think of:

- Ant & Dec
- Thor & Hulk

- Tango & Cash
- Turk & JD
- Cameron & Ferris Bueller
- Mario & Luigi
- Buzz & Woody
- KITT & Michael Knight
- Shaggy & Scooby-Doo
- Mr. Spock & Captain Kirk
- Ron & Harry Potter

The list goes on. Sometimes we get a little help from our friends. They can help demonstrate that we have value ourselves.

You see what you need to remember is when you are with your wingman your values are attached. Where most men go wrong is, they think that they are showing alpha-male qualities by slating and ripping into their mates in front of girls. They think this shows them in a good light.

They couldn't be any further from the truth.

Think about it like this – you are saying this guy is a loser. Yet you are hanging around with him?

Well birds of a feather flock together. So, you must be a loser as well.

You see if you were hanging out with Channing Tatum or Cristiano Ronaldo this would send your value through the roof. People would see you together and assume you were a valuable individual because you are together. Your values are linked in a way.

Never rip your friends in front of or to women. Not only does it come across as bitchy and not the behaviour of an Alpha, but it also lowers your own value. In fact, you want to do the complete opposite and say how GREAT your friends are. Wow, your friends are great? And they hang around you? You must be pretty great then for them to spend time with you.

You see the best way to do this is with an **Accomplishment Intro**.

An Accomplishment intro is where your wing introduces you and at the same time lists an accomplishment. YOU do the same for them. After all, it's hard to brag about yourself but getting your friends to do it is just fine.

"This is Jack, he wrote this book to help guys get more confident, he is super smart graduated with a first-class degree in Education, was one of the top ten students out his entire university who graduated that year, here let me introduce you ..."

Wow. You see how powerful that is. Before I have even spoken to anyone my reputation precedes me.

" Iceman: You can be my wingman any time.
Maverick: Bullshit! You can be mine." Maverick & Iceman - Topgun

It hasn't got to be as long as that, it can be about anything. All you need is something that you think demonstrates value. It doesn't have to be what you do it can be anything that you have in your life that is interesting. You want to make the story or the intro sound as good as possible. Inject it with energy. The tone will have to be infectious. Don't lie. Lies get caught. Just find something and sprinkle some magic on it.

It can be as simple as

Guy 1: turns to friend, *girls I want you to meet Cubbie, one of the most loyal men I've ever met, super-smart when it comes to electrical engineering, the man is going places.*

Cubbie: *A Pleasure* ... (Cubbie then goes into a story or asks for an opinion to get him into the conversation)

You see the introduction from you raises both values at the same time. It can be a powerful tool.

Ring announcer: The former heavyweight champion of the world...the Dancing Destroyer...the King of Sting...the Count of Monte Fisto—

Rocky: You think you have enough names?

Apollo- Be patient. We're almost done.

Ring announcer: The Master of Disaster, the one and only, Apollo Creed!

Getting The Girl

- **Rocky 4**

There are some rules to follow when you are winging. If you want to be Maverick & Goose, then you got to know how to make it work if you're going to convince her that she has lost that loving feeling.

So, we have the TOPGUN Rules of being a wingman:

1. Whoever is there first gets to choose the woman he wants to talk to. Make it clear who you have chosen to your wing
2. The sole aim of the Wingman is to help the Lead get acquire his target (fighter plane talk now). If you can find a girl yourself great but this is second to helping the lead
3. The Wingman needs to occupy the obstacles. We are talking blocking Mother hens, the boyfriend's sister and any other guys that may be tempted to swoop in.
4. Always agree with your wing. You never disagree in front of women. Always take his side.
5. Your Wing is the best. That's why he is your buddy.
6. We don't disrespect our Wing. His feelings are more important than any girls If he needs attention, we stop what we are doing with the girls and talk to him. This also makes them work a little harder.
7. We always introduce him.

Now in Topgun, there is a great scene where Goose helps Maverick talk to a girl at a Bar by helping him as they sing "She's lost that loving feeling" (QR CODE above). Now you may be thinking, this stuff only works in the movies but boy are you wrong. Back in the day when I worked promoting nightclubs in town my Wingman Jack and I (Jack Attack for short) use to have a whole host of routines, we would run together that would separate us from everyone else. You see the good thing was no matter if the girls enjoyed the routines or not, we actually enjoyed doing them. So, we would be bursting into laughter and having a great time. This energy then became infectious so even if the girls we are talking to didn't like it other girls would. It would create this self-fulfilling prophecy.

"-Viper: In case some of you are wondering who the best is, they are up here on this plaque.
[turns to Maverick]
- Viper: Do you think your name will be on that plaque?
- Maverick: Yes, sir.
- Viper: That's pretty arrogant, considering the company you're in.
- Maverick: Yes, sir.
- Viper: I like that in a pilot." Maverick & Viper - Topgun

One such routine would involve me telling a girl that Jack was really romantic. I would then tell her about this girl he was seeing and this romantic night he had for her. I would say he got the rose petals out, lit candles up until the stairs, and had some music playing for when she came in. I would tell her to imagine what it was like and get her to cuddle Jack from the front. She would rest her head on his shoulder as I was telling her this story. Then I would creep up behind and play "She's like the wind" out of my phone in her ear. It was hilarious as Jack would keep spinning around in the street with this girl. Then I would keep telling the story and Jack would do the actions to the words. Then just as it gets to the chorus he would push her away cover his eyes whilst It played " Can't look in her eyes " and I would be saying – he couldn't look her in the eyes – before finally we would both throw ourselves on the floor before her with our arms stretched out to the sky and shout " SHES OUT OF MY LEAGUE". The girl would then burst out laughing and we would be in fits and giggles dying.

You see the reason I tell this is you and your wing need to come up with stories for yourself that are original. The more time you spend together the easier it will become. It will become effortless as you know one another's movements.

Now you're welcome to steal my Patrick Swayze routine if you must but just remember.

Nobody puts Baby in the corner – Dirty Dancing.

CHAPTER 8

Safety - If they aren't comfortable then you're stuck in the mud

"Safety isn't expensive, it's priceless"

Chapter 8 – Safety – If they aren't comfortable your stuck in the mud

After the Attraction Stage, we move onto the Safety Stage.

In order to enter this phase of the Courtship Process, you are going to need to get the female by herself. Now, this can be done in numerous ways. You could have grabbed her number at the bar, work, the supermarket, or at Uni and arranged to hang out just the two of you. Great work, The Courtship process isn't designed so you have to do it all one after another in one go. Although it can work this way it's fine to have each stage at a separate time. Let's say she was attracted to you, you got the number and decided to bounce. You arranged to meet. Now when you meet up again you would go back through attraction for a while to make sure she remembers why she gave you the number in the first place. You would look out for about 4-5 IOIs then you would go into the safety phase.

If, however, you feel as if you can transition from attraction to safety in the same day/night then it's best to move from the location you met her to somewhere else. This creates a different dynamic to where you met and makes it seem as if you have known each other longer.

So, if you met at University and you are getting along you might see if she wants to go grab a coffee. There you can sit down, look for IOI's and go into the safety phase. Not everyone you meet will be free at that time which is why it is fine to do the different stages at different times. We don't want to leave it too long between the stages otherwise she may lose interest. As a rule, after Attraction tries to meet within 7-10 days to go over the attraction and start to build the safety phase. Leave it too long and you just become another guy she fancied for a while, but it never went anywhere.

Now if you met at a bar and you want to pull her away from her friends so you can run the safety phase of the Courtship process you may want to invite her to join you in the smoking area or at a quiet area of the bar. Maybe invite her to go get food with you after.

If you're in a group, you might after noticing 3-4 IOIs from the girl you want to talk to decide to address the group. You would say something like:

"Guys, I know she's a pain in the arse (nightmare, a mess, etc, a drunk or any other disqualification), but there's something about your friend I find quite interesting. You guys don't mind if I talk to her alone for just a few minutes right over there?" (point to a spot they can see that gives them safety knowing it is near the group but far enough that you can't be overheard).

What you are doing is showing you are a strong male and saying to the group – look my intentions aren't bad I'm going to be where you can see us, and you can grab her if she starts to feel uncomfortable. 9/10 the friends will be like *"yeah, of course, that's fine"* or they will ask the friend something like *"you going to be ok?"* once she says yeah then you've got the approval. They may even throw my favourite line to hear from them *"look after her ok?"* Then I will offer the girl I want to talk to my arm or hand and say *"don't worry she's in safe hands"* then walk her over to the spot and begin to talk through the safety stage. It is really important to isolate if the girl is in a relationship as she will not want to say or do anything that makes her seem like "a slut" or "a cheat". When it is not possible to isolate then here is a good time to grab their number or Instagram and set up a time to run Safety when they are free.

This may mean catching up with her and her group of friends the following week. The big bonus is this time you are known to the group so you will have an easier time. You come in go through the attraction phase again but much quicker, ask to speak to the friend alone. The friends know you so they will be like – yeah that's cool. Then you go through the Safety Phase.

If you arranged to meet up this week then there is a good chance their friends know all about it before anyway. Girls talk to each other way more about boys than boys do about girls. After all, why do you think they go to the toilet in pairs?

We build safety because dating can be a scary time for a woman. They know numerous men that may have been attractive but then skipped the Safety stage and tried to get into her pants. This is why she has built a moat and wall around her to protect herself from these barbarians. We want to prove we are a knight in shining armour, not a naked berserker screaming at the top of our lungs hurling heads at anything that comes close.

We want to earn their trust and form a connection.

The way we do this is through talking.

When we are talkative, we help to find out things about people and set them at ease. This is because with people they feel safe around they talk often and about a range of topics. What we want to do here is create the same dynamic. We want them to feel relaxed and able to let down their walls and let you in. One way we can do this is by looking for things you share. What we aren't doing is lying and saying we have always been into star signs when we couldn't tell you the difference between an Aquarius and an Aquarium. Such a thing will only lower your value when she realises you haven't a clue what you are talking about.

What we can do however is employ the methods of Chris Voss on negotiation to our conversations. You see Chris Voss was the lead FBI negotiator with terrorists across the globe. He was so successful that after his career there he wrote a book called **"Never Split the Difference"**. His goal and his work now are to help people be better negotiators and get what they need out of a discussion. He has many tools to help him with that and all of them can apply here. After all, when you are talking to a woman- all you are really doing is negotiating. You are trying to make a deal.

When we do this, we want to use **Tactical empathy**. Chris Voss defines **tactical empathy** as the deliberate influencing of your negotiating counterpart's emotions for the ultimate purpose of building trust-based influence and securing deals. It's important to incorporate emotion as a negotiating tactic. In our case, we use tactical empathy to build trust and create security.

Tactical empathy comes down to 3 aspects.

1. **The tone of Voice.** When deploying tactical empathy, we use a different voice than the one we would usually use. This is known as the late-night FM DJ voice. It is a calm and soothing voice. We then combine this with upward (inquiring) or downward (understanding) inflections. These are the important touches and what we use when employing the tools of Mirroring and Labelling.
2. **We avoid making denials or disagreements** when we are employing this tactic. This doesn't mean we forget other things we have spoken about in previous chapters. It just means that when we are getting people to open up

to us, we don't tell them they are wrong. As you imagine this will stop them from wanting to go into more detail and shut down the conversation. The aim here is to get to know them on a deeper level. The key therefore when wanting to show we are empathic is no denials or disagreements. This doesn't mean ignoring the stuff you don't like, either. You need to make them feel heard. We aren't saying you have to agree but you do need them to have their say

3. **Make them feel heard**

What we aren't doing is just blindly agreeing to everything they are saying. In fact, we aren't saying you must agree at all. We are just saying they need to be able to say their piece. You don't agree, but you don't disagree, either.

Most people men and women want to feel listened to. I am sure you have heard a million examples of men trying to offer solutions to a female's problems only to get shouted at even more. That was because she didn't want you to solve it, she just wanted to share it and wanted you to listen.

Remember, tactical empathy isn't an agreement.

Now we have two tools we can use together to practice tactical empathy and help us built safety with the women we are talking to. These are mirroring and labelling.

One tool he uses is called **mirroring**.

Mirroring is a tool you use to help the other side feel as if they are being listened to and to get them to open up.

We mirror when we repeat three to five keywords from your counterpart's previous statement, in the form of a question. We do this by changing our voice inclination to a slightly higher pitch whilst giving them an inquisitive look. Mirroring is a verbal observation.

The good thing about mirroring is like we mentioned previously it stops us from sounding like we are an interviewer but this time it comes across as being empathic. We start with a question then add a mirror.

An example:

Guy: What are you passionate about?

Girl: I like to dance

Guy: What is it about dancing that makes you passionate?

Girl: I can dance by myself or with friends, and I like to be involved with different music's and get lost in it all. It's like when I dance, I forget about my troubles

Guy: Forget about your troubles? (Mirror)

Girl: Yeah, yeah, because when you go out and your dancing I'm not bothered about work or my family. I know I can cut loose and me and the girls will dance until our feet hurt. We can dance anywhere and mostly people leave us alone

This produces great positive results Mirroring has two positive upshots. It enables the guy to rapidly establish rapport by giving the counterpart confidence that she is being listened to and heard. She feels as if you care about what she is saying, and you are taking in the information. It also leaves them wanting to feel the gap with more information allowing you to find out more about them in the process.

Now the perfect tool to go along with Mirroring is called **Labelling**.

Labelling is, in a sense, mirroring on steroids. Rather than merely repeating words, labelling involves proactively labelling your counterpart's emotions – especially things they are worried about. We are addressing their fears head-on and this creates safety. When we label, we must use proactive listening skills. When we label, we use the same few words at the beginning then a label. The important thing about these words is you aren't saying IT IS that only that's how it is coming across which gives them room to correct you without you coming across as if you know it all.

The words we use to label are: **"It seems like," "It sounds like," and "It looks like"**

An example:

Guy: Forget about your troubles? (Mirror)

Girl: Yeah, yeah, because when you go out and your dancing I'm not bothered about work or my family. I know I can cut loose and me and the girls will dance until our feet hurt. We can dance anywhere and mostly people leave us alone

Guy: It seems like you don't like when people bother you when you are dancing (Label)

Girl: that's right, when I am out with my girls I just want to have fun , like if I am at a bar maybe then talk to me but I hate when girls come up and start grinding on you talking in your ear. It's gross. Like I am there for the music

Guy: It sounds like music is really important to you (Label)

Girl: Yes! I love music, I could dance to anything, from country to hip hop, I just love when ...

By using labels, we make her feel heard and it also makes her speak about herself more. Allowing you an opportunity to get to know her. She feels safe when she shares information with you. By assigning the girl's feelings a label, you demonstrate an understanding of how she feels. This goes a long way in terms of **demonstrating empathy**. This can also work very well if she is angry or upset, you can use mirrors and labels to say what you think it is and explore the issue.

When we use tactical empathy, it allows them to share their vulnerabilities. This is a good time to share yours. It helps to build emotional connections. Even Superman himself has a weakness, so by showing you do have vulnerabilities it stops her from looking for them herself. Women are great believers in something being too good to be true. Instead of letting her come to her own conclusions, you can guide her to an area that may not be your strength or share a vulnerable story. We only do this in the safety stage after we have built Attraction.

The way we make this work is to **embrace your vulnerability** and still *be unaffected by it.*

Demonstrations are always more effective than verbal insinuations. If you can show that you can go to different places together and she will be safe this does wonders for your value. Whether it is a rollercoaster ride or simply making sure she walks inside on the pavement furthest away from the road. You are saying her safety is important to you.

Safety is the missing ingredient that allows you to convert mutual attraction into sealing the deal. As we explored in chapter 2, we looked at the different stages and we know that the reason men get stuck into the Friendzone is they get into comfort, but they can't get out of it. We cannot however avoid comfort. Comfort is necessary. We need her to feel safe when she is with us. We want her to feel safe. It is important she feels safe to open up to you, she is comfortable in your company and knows your intentions are good.

Safety helps to change her from "I want him, but I don't know him well enough" into "I want him".

Now as we know conversations aren't always led by us. When in the safety stage you may have built good attraction and asked enough questions or given statements to her that she has opened up to you. She may now decide it's your turn to answer a few of hers.

Don't worry it's not like "Meet the Fockers", there won't be any crazy former CIA Dad hooking you up to a polygraph machine. It will probably be just you two chatting away somewhere away from everyone else.

During a conversation, a woman may very well hit you with a series of questions. This is her sussing you up, trying to work out your value. They come in many forms but may sound something like this:

- What do you do for work? (success value)
- So, what are you doing here?
- Who's that? (talking about girl or guy you may be with)
- Where are you from? (determining what neighborhood or area – wealth indicator)

What she is actually trying to do is see what Survival Value you are bringing to the party. Once you offer a girl value, she will want to offer value to you back- it's human nature (this is called reciprocation in psychology). Thinking about what you bring before you think about what you can take is a good mindset. What are you bringing to the occasion?

"Pussy cost money, dick is cheap" Chris Rock

Now although it doesn't cost actual money, it does require you to bring value. If you have nothing to offer, then like TLC said no scrubs are getting in her car boy. Therefore, it is so important we form attraction by displaying value. Just because we are in the comfort stage doesn't mean we stop showing we are of high value. We continue to trigger the Attraction Switches.

When asked what you do, you want to ground your reality with theirs by telling a story of your progression from childhood or youth years to where you are today. You are taking them on a journey using all that storytelling we have learnt and shown all those DHVs we have spoken about. She may ask questions along the way. You want to encourage her to do so because she is investing in your story and investing in you.

When she begins to want to know who you truly are by asking questions such as:

"So, who are you?"– You have an answer because you have thought long and hard about the person you are now and where you want to go. When you take them on the journey of how you have got to where you are you can take them on the journey of where you want to go to. This is attractive and enticing.

When you are into the comfort building stage, we can accelerate what a woman feels and how comfortable or close to you she is by asking a series of well-selected questions.

In his book **Handbook of Closeness and Intimacy,** Arthur Aron, a psychologist at the State University of New York explores how quickly one can build bonds. In which he managed to conclude that there are ways to form deep relationships very quickly.

His study on how people form romantic relationships led to him producing ways of taking men and women who have never met before and making them feel close to one another. He performs these miracles of psychology in just an hours' time. In this hour he manages to create the intimacy levels that typically take weeks, months, or years to form, he has therefore developed a method to speed up the getting-to-know-you process.

He does this with just a set of thirty-six questions that are specially crafted to take the participants rapidly from level one in McAdams's system to level two. McAdam wrote in the 1980s about intimacy and ranked intimacy by levels. It is explained in his journal published work entitled "Experiences of intimacy and power" should you want to read it.

These questions are part of an hour-long "sharing game" in which both answer before moving on. Luckily for you, I have a few of them here for you to use. Remember it is important you both answer the questions. I would recommend spacing the asking out over a longer conversation. This should not become like an interview. You want the process to feel natural. Make it flow.

Some of the questions:

1. Given the choice of anyone in the world, whom would you want as a dinner guest?

2. Would you like to be famous? In what way?

3. Before making a telephone call, do you ever rehearse what you are going to say? Why?

4. What would constitute a "perfect" day for you?

5. When did you last sing to yourself? To someone else?

6. If you were able to live to the age of 90 and retain either the mind or body of a 30-year-old for the last 60 years of your life, which would you want?

7. Name three things you and your partner appear to have in common.

8. For what in your life do you feel most grateful?

9. If you could change anything about the way you were raised, what would it be?

10. If you could wake up tomorrow having gained any one quality or ability, what would it be?

11. If a crystal ball could tell you the truth about yourself, your life, the future, or anything else, what would you want to know?

12. Is there something that you've dreamed of doing for a long time? Why haven't you done it?

13. What is the greatest accomplishment of your life?

14. What do you value most in a friendship?

15. What is your most treasured memory?

16. What is your most terrible memory?

17. What does friendship mean to you?

18. What roles do love, and affection play in your life?

19. How close and warm is your family? Do you feel your childhood was happier than most other people's?

20. Complete this sentence: "I wish I had someone with whom I could share..."

21. If you were going to become a close friend with your partner, please share what would be important for him or her to know.

22. Tell your partner what you like about them; be very honest this time saying things that you might not say to someone you've just met.

23. Share with your partner an embarrassing moment in your life.

24. When did you last cry in front of another person? By yourself?

25. Tell your partner something that you like about them already.

26. What, if anything, is too serious to be joked about?

27. Your house, containing everything you own, catches fire. After saving your loved ones and pets, you have time to safely make a final dash to save any one item. What would that be?

Over the last two chapters, I have given you numerous tools to make sure the conversation never goes dead. You have:

- a structure for asking questions – question – answer – statement.
- You have stories you can tell.
- You have mirroring and labelling
- You have used humour and disqualifiers
- You have Cat and Mouse theory – using hoops
- You are now revealing some vulnerability

In the safety stage though we want to move away from scripted things to say unless the conversation becomes stale. This is where we enjoy the authenticity of the conversation. It is why we have so many questions to ask as we find out about them and they explore us. It is why we have introduced tactical empathy and the tools that come with it. You cannot prepare for where the conversation may go but you can know how to get the most out of the conversation.

This can be one of the best times as you have the enjoyment of going where the conversation takes you.

In Safety ,it is all about bonding and connecting.

There is no reason you should ever run out of things to say. Having something to say is much better than nothing. Remember you are a man of value. You have a voice, use it.

****

Pulling back

During the Safety Stage, there are occasions where women after beginning to feel comfortable try and test the waters. They pull back a little. They do this to see if you are willing to chase. They want you to work a little harder.

A tendency for most men is the think, ow I am so close to getting there I just need to show her I care a little bit and ill reach the promised land. This is rarely the case.

In such a case when she pulls back and you chase, you set a precedent. That being, she can have you when every she wants you. You can be picked up and dropped like a bad habit.

Now not every girl does this, many enjoying the safety stage as they get comfortable and don't play these games. Some do. It is for those that do that you must be prepared. In this instance when she pulls back. You do the same.

You are asking to be treated as an equal.

When she begins to take longer to respond or becomes a flake then you mimic it. You are showing that you don't need her any more than she needs you. This is a mutual attraction.

Now when you are together, and she begins to give you a hard time during the safety phase (make sure it's the safety phase) is you can begin to use screening questions as if to mimic you are now unsure of her.

A screening question is anything that makes it seem that as a high-value guy you want to make sure the person you are spending time with and could potentially date be right for you.

Types of screening questions:

- *So, I never asked, what do you want to be when you grow up?* – implying she has growing up to do and she is not the finished article
- *Beauty is so common lots of women are beautiful , I find beauty quite repetitive, what would you look for in a woman if you were a guy ?* – you are getting her to list traits, she will no doubt choose traits she has in trying to justify herself and you have taken looks out the equation
- *How old are you again? – followed up with omg you are so old what were the dinosaurs like or with omg you still a baby!* – it's a type of false disqualifier and she will no doubt justify her age and the merits it brings
- *Where did you go to university again?* – she either did go university and then you can say the university she went to was probably good to party and she didn't choose it for its academia or you can say ow that's where all the geeks go , *did you have to wear an evening gown for dinner?* – either way, you play off where they went and you put them on the backfoot.

Remember we are **ONLY using the screening if she begins to pull back** or give you tests. We have no need or reason to use them if the safety stage is going well. This is just a tool we can use to say – listen don't try and play these games because I can walk away as well.

If she is interested, she will sense your own pullback, stop the games and you can go back to getting to know her using all the tools outlined so far. We want the Safety stage to be authentic but at times women will test us.

People are willing to *work harder to preserve an existing investment* than they are to make a new one. This is the reason when you begin to pull back than they usually stop and come back into focus.

The less fucks you give. The more fucks you get.

Another angle you can play when they begin to test you like this is to demonstrate that you are not short of options. Here you just demonstrate pre-selection by making it appear you have options. This will enviably play on her jealousy streak where she will have to "win".

This can be done in person by when you meet her bringing along a female friend or walk to meet her with a female friend who then leaves to "go home" or "go to work". The girl you are talking to will almost certainly question the relationship between the two of you.

With the use of social media, the easiest way to do this is to upload a picture of you out with another girl onto your story on Instagram or your chosen platform. You are saying that if she wants to take long to respond or flake on you then you will just spend time with another girl. Social media is a good tool for creating jealousy plotlines.

You can answer a phone call when you are with her or laugh at a message from a girl. Remember we are only doing this when she pulls away. We are pulling away in response to her. **We do not need to do this if things are going well during the safety phase**.

Now when things are going well, and you aren't being tested or drawn into games then we have the next part of the Safety Phase. This is known as **Kino Escalation.**

Kino Escalation

When we talk about Kino Escalation, we mean how you slowly build up your kinaesthetic relationship with someone. This means you gradually over time allow them to be comfortable with not just your presence but your touch. It stops the awkward leaning in for a kiss moment and it allows you to recalibrate if someone is not comfortable.

It is a great way of slowly allowing someone to adjust to you whilst becoming comfortable and feeling safe around you. We refer to physical touching of any kind not just sexual touch. We want them to feel safe. It is important that they are happy for you to rest your arm on their shoulder or to guide them into a shop. We are making sure that along the way both parties are happy for things to escalate at a pace that suits you both.

Getting The Girl

Now we have to remember that a true gentleman and an alpha male does not take a girl out with the sole purpose of getting her into bed or snogging her face off. Ow no. He is taking her out becomes he enjoys the company of women. In fact, it's not a big deal if she doesn't sleep with him because he has options anyway. This is the mindset you must have. You are not there to spend hours walking around the park to then get ready for your big moment as you creepily lean in for a kiss. This is what happens when you don't Kino escalate. You make things such as the first kiss incredibly awkward.

If your first kiss is weak then you've probably hit your peak.

It's going all downhill from there kid. Your chance of a second kiss is as likely as getting killed by a falling satellite (1 in 21 trillion). You see women don't forgive a bad first kiss. This can be a deal-breaker for so many women. You see men have often imagined what it's like to sleep with a woman before it has happened, but women often imagine what the first kiss will be like. They have seen numerous movies where they see the first kiss as this magical thing.

Women love to take inspiration from films and books so already the bar is high sir, you are up against:

- The Princess diaries – leg popping kiss
- Rose & Jack aboard the Titanic on the bow of the ship
- Han Solo & Princess Leia in Star Wars aboard the Millennium Falcon
- Edward & Bella in Twilight in the woods by Bella's truck
- Lady and the Tramp – We all know the spaghetti scene
- A Cinderella Story – Remember good old Hilary Duff?
- 10 Things I Hate About You in the Haystack
- My Girl with Macauley Culkin – yeah it may not have been a proper kiss, but you get the point

You see what you are up against isn't just your own talent but the culmination of all the ways they imagined their first kiss would go and I can tell you it wasn't awkward. Luckily, through the use of Kino escalation, it never will be.

In the book **The Science of Kissing: What Our Lips Are Telling Us** by scientist Sheril Kirshenbaum explores in great detail the effect that kissing has on humans and the selection of mates.

This is because the lips comprise one of your body's densest zones of nerve endings, allowing you to detect more sensations than other body parts. Thanks to all those nerve endings Kirshenbaum says this makes the brain go into overdrive. Kissing is that powerful it uses way more of your grey matter than even sex.

Still don't think that kiss is a big deal.

You are wrong.

Let me tell you why Kirshenbaum in her books says that the first kiss allows the brain to do some quick calculations. Weighing up whether or not you should take things beyond the kiss and into the bedroom. "We're so aware of everything that's happening during a kiss because it's such an important part of the decision-making process when choosing a mate," she explains. "People describe 'getting lost' in sex. But that's not the case with kissing because our brains are hyper-focused on whether or not to take things further."

Kissing, or the first kiss to be precise, sets your marker for the rest of your skills in the bedroom champ. We don't want to fall at the first hurdle, so we don't give ourselves a mountain to climb. We slowly chip away so, in the end, it is just a small leap to the promised land.

The way we use Kino Escalation is just through small incrementally touches or an increase in the time you may be in physical contact so eventually, they become accustomed and feel comfortable with this interaction. We are taking away the big *"making a move"* because things will just naturally progress that way.

Kino-Escalation can be started in the Attraction phase of The Courtship process or begin in the Safety phase it will depend on the individual interaction and if the opportunity presents itself.

You see when you start an interaction with a woman the chances are you have no reason to physically touch her. So over time you can create or use opportunities to test the water. A good way to start can be with a simple high 5. If she goes ahead congratulations you have now touched her, well done Romeo. You see that's all it takes. You can be lightly touching her arm then pointing at something for her to see, telling her that her hair looks nice and fresh whilst lightly moving it from her face. You can touch the middle of her thigh as you laugh at something on tv whilst you are sat next to each other. There are many ways you can get someone gradually accustomed to your touch. The best thing is if she pulls away, you stop, build more attraction, build more safety then if you think she seems more comfortable you can go again. This is a gradual process.

Simple things like touching her arm with the back of your hand to emphasize a point in conversation send strong messages. Understand that it is natural for people's bodies to touch one another. If I was hanging out with my friends, it wouldn't be weird if they touched my arm or my shoulder because I feel safe and comfortable. This is the same feelings you want to generate. Placing your hand on the small of her back or her hip while you talk, or on her knee when sat down is a natural progression. When it's natural to touch then do so.

Some examples of Kino Escalation:

- Touching her back when guiding her
- Touching her hand when telling a joke
- Touching her when tapping it to get her attention
- Holding her hand to lead her through a bar
- Cuddling if it is cold
- Touching her shoulders if she is walking fast or getting her to stop
- Linking arms
- Holding her hand when looking at her nails or watch
- Tracing your finger over her tattoos (if she has any)
- Smelling or pulling her hair
- When she sits on your lap
- An arm around the waist when you are sat down, and she is standing
- Arm in arm
- Hands touching
- Her feet on your lap when on the sofa

All of these are ways you can gradually get used to one another's touch. You want to do this with confidence, Alpha males make such touches seem natural, effortless, and unapologetic.

You are gradually creating hoops for her to jump through whilst using this tool. You may hold a touch for longer or in a different place. Gradually you get to the point where you are asking her to jump through larger hoops. This inevitable build-up helps it appear naturally. Like if you want to show her something you grab her hand and say come over here. Then if she is comfortable whilst you look at something you may place your arms on her shoulders (If you are taller) or place your hand on her back.

Now when we feel resistance or that someone isn't comfortable, we take two steps back. We want them to feel safe during the process. It is always one step forward and two steps back.

A way you can gauge how it is going is through compliance testing. Simply put, does she comply with your requests. It can something simple such as holding your drink to holding your hand whilst you walk through a busy room. If she is complying and going along this is a good sign and it means it is good to continue to escalate.

Compliance tests –

- You squeeze her hand and she squeezes back
- You move her leg onto your lap, and she keeps it there
- You touch her and she touches you back
- You ask her to hold something whilst you do something
- You say her eyes or hair looks nice and ask her to come closer so you can see it and she agrees

Using compliance tests is a great way to see how your escalation is going and if she is getting close to being ready to be kissed. You see you don't need to wait until the end of a date to kiss. When you feel comfortable around that person and they feel comfortable around you this is a good time to kiss. Kissing only happens when the person feels safe with you.

So how do you get that first kiss?

The answer is simple – any way you like.

When you are confident she is happy with you two being in physical contact all you need is to find a moment which you think is right place your hand under her chin, behind her ear or the back of her head to support her, slowly move in, giving her the chance to pull back if she wants, if she's receptive then go ahead and plant one of the lips.

Getting The Girl

Well done you've just kissed a girl.

*Epic RPG music, level up screen, unlock bonus *

Congratulations.

Advance to the next level of The Game.

CHAPTER 9
Sex

"Women need a reason to have sex.
Men just need a place"
Billy Crystal

Chapter 9 – Closing – Getting Across the Line

"When I got here, I dominated. They thought I worked 100 hours a day. Now, no matter what time I get in, nobody questions my ability to get the job done. Get it through your head. First impressions last. You start behind the eight ball; you'll never get in front." – Harvey Specter

Born and raised in Chicago, to a broken home and made to lie to his father by his mother to cover up her infidelity not much was expected of young Harvey. He got his big break whilst working in the mailroom at a Law firm before he used it as leverage to get a step up in life. He was closing women long before he was closing law cases. Harvey Reginald Spector is known as the best god damn closer in the city and for good reason - That's because he is.

You see Harvey understands the end game just as well as Tony Stark did at the end of Avengers. It doesn't matter about the little bumps in the road or the sacrifices you need to make because, in the end, he gets the job done. When you're on your way to closing a deal, you need to take challenges in your stride. Have a witty line to disarm your opponent and buy yourself some time to get the edge you need.

You see the thing that makes Harvey such a cultural icon is his sheer self-belief.

Women want to be with him, and men want to be him.

Harvey is a throwaway to a bygone era where men oozed self-confidence and carried a room by their sheer presence. In the modern era, Harvey Spector's are rare. The sad truth is that rarity is in itself enigmatic. Human nature dictates we are drawn to these beings of purpose. We desire that which we seek is unobtainable. We want to be Harvey because we think we cannot.

By all accounts, Harvey is viewed as a charming, confident, and sometimes arrogant man. Arrogance is a fine line. One that people that are confident in their abilities often dance over like Michael Flatley himself. I have been known to have such an accusation hurled in my direction once or twice, but I can duck a jab and so should you. You see people may feel threatened by you when you are at one with yourself but that isn't your problem. When you're out here closing daily and weekly you don't care what people who couldn't close their fridge door say. You need to be above such criticism. Harvey has a no-nonsense and ruthless approach to closing legal cases long before they get to court. When you are closing you need to keep your eye on the prize. What is your goal and how are you going to get there?

Decisions > Distractions.

You see Harvey has such faith in himself because he is competent. The source of his inner belief and faith comes from his own competence. Such faith comes from Harvey being known for successfully winning cases. Harvey is a winner and he knows it.

He knows when there is an opportunity to make a deal, he will get the job done. He gets there by any means necessary. Drawing upon all of his experience, using everything he has learnt. He gets inside the heads of his opponents. The same thing we have been teaching you through the course of this book. To understand what makes a woman tick. What is she hardwired to think? How can you use this information to help better your chances of closing? This is the question you need to ask yourself when you arrive at this stage. What do I already know that can help me in this situation?

To catch a wolf, you must think like a wolf.

You see Harvey does this often he looks at things from the other side to see what angle they come after him and he simultaneously draws upon his wide range of tools and skills that he can use. But guess what so you can. Up until now, you have spent the last few chapters getting inside a woman's head. Seeing what makes them tick. Only Mel Gibson in *"What Women Want"* had more of an understanding of the inner workings of a woman's mind than you now do.

You now need to realise you have all the information you need. You just need your inner belief. Reflect on the earlier chapters where we looked at the mindset and how we can tell ourselves things to change our working mind. Use what we practised earlier to tell yourself - that you can get it across the line. Whatever that line is. Whether your line is a relationship, whether it is to have sex, whether it is to find someone to date for a while. You define your line and then get across it. You don't make excuses. I know when I define my line I always get where I want. Time you started believing you can too.

You need to **Play the Game** until the very end. You've got this far using what you've learnt don't switch off now and go back to your old ways.

"Winners don't make excuses when the other side plays the game." – Harvey Specter

So how does Harvey have such confidence? Well, it comes down to the same 3 things you are going to have.

1. A Track record of success – he has been successful before so he has every faith that he will be successful again.
2. Endorsements from other successful lawyers (Jessica Pearson and everyone else says he is the best, word travels, his reputation speaks for himself) – Pre-selection at play again gentleman.
3. The backing of a strong team – (Donna, Mike Ross, Louis he has a range of colleagues she can go to for support and advice. People that help him to close deals)- he can draw on lots of people and their expertise. I have brought together the expertise of the best people I think can help you improve your life and your success with women. It is altogether in this book for you. This book is your team. I am your vice-captain. This is where you turn when you need someone to have your back. I got you.

You see we aren't here to *"get lucky"*. We got here by our own skillset. YOU have got to this stage because you built attraction, you made her feel comfortable and now you have an opportunity to get it to the line. Whatever your line may be. There was no luck getting here. You got here for a reason.

I believe in work; I don't fuck with luck." – Harvey Specter

The closing stage isn't a sprint race, you need to get this out of your head that you must do things within a particular time frame. You want to close then great, but you need to make sure the timing is right. Whilst you are waiting to do this you employ all those wonderful tools; we have looked at that make you a good person to talk to. You are interesting and you are able to hold a conversation. This can be rare to a woman because most guys are trying to close them within the opening hour. This is where you retire to whilst the rest of them men crash and burn you are looking for IOI's and seeing if the time is right to close.

You see Harvey is a great conversationalist, he always has something to say from quoting movies and popular culture in his normal working day (who would quote popular culture aye ...) to adapting to speaking to CEO's of fortune 500 companies. He is interesting. He has tons of value. He knows this so he has no problem letting people know. What's wrong with telling people you're the best closer if you are? If a woman asks what you are like in bed, then tell her – *like nothing you have ever had before*. You don't need to go into detail you don't need to draw diagrams or tell stories. Just one line, then move on. Tell her she will have to wait to find out. Confidence is key here.

"It's not bragging if it's true." – Harvey Specter

When you are thinking of closing you need to realise that you may have to ask for the sale a few times. In Jordan Belfort's Straight Line Selling he calls this building confidence in the 3 lines. These lines are – you, the product, the company. The further along the line to a 10 you get the customer the closer to a sale you are.

Jordan says when you get a "no" what the customer is really saying is they don't trust you enough or have enough confidence in one of those 3 lines. You see a no just means you haven't built enough value yet.

He explains the three tenets of closing, such as the elements that need to line up in the moment of time when your prospect is ready to buy:

1. They love your product
2. They trust and connect with you
3. Trust your company

So, when you are trying to close a woman you may need to build confidence in the product, the salesperson, or the company you're selling from. In this case, you are all 3. The only thing separating you from closing is attraction levels and safety levels. If you are confident you are high in these 2 and you understanding the attraction switches, then all you need now is an appropriate place and time. This applies to both trying to get them into bed or to get them into a relationship.

You see according to Jordan some people are just natural closers. Why? Because they unconsciously master tonality, rapport, and control of the sale.

That's right they know what to say and they control the interaction. Exactly what we have been learning. They master the frame and they lead the conversation. They build rapport as we do in the comfort stage and they ask lots of questions without coming across like an interview.

These are the three tenets of Jordan Belfort's Straight-Line Persuasion:

1. Develop rapport quickly
2. Gather intelligence (do they have the money, is the product a good fit, are they ready to go?)
3. Control the interaction

All the 3 things we have been working on. We know how to build rapport and safety. We know how to ask lots of questions and find out about the person we are talking to. We know how to control the frame and give IOD or IOI depending on their behaviour to either encourage or discourage behaviour from them.

Now when closing we want even more information. This is known as fact-finding to know we can actually close. We are going to look at that shortly, but Jordan puts it like this:

Sell me this pen

Jordan: So how long have you been in the market for a pen for?

Prospective client: I am not in the market for a pen.

Jordan: Have a nice day.

Closers don't waste time trying to close people that aren't after products. Let the other chumps try and persuade people to buy things they don't need. Your job is to prospect the appropriate clients through a sales funnel and then show them how your product helps with their pain.

You don't convince a woman that doesn't want a boyfriend that she needs one.

A closer isn't scared of moving onto another client and they aren't scared of hearing a no. They are scared of wasting their time.

You see the worse thing they can say is no. That is it. Just a word.

You won't spontaneously combust. Voldermort won't turn up to torture you. You won't be turned into a cat called Salem by three witches and only show up on Halloween. And you almost certainly won't be defeated as a man. You see every no brings you closer to a yes.

I want you to be comfortable with the thought that you may very well crash and burn but so what. It does not matter. I make this promise to you - The more times you get to the closing stage the more chances you have of closing. That means you need to able to hit the level reset and go again.

The chances are that if you have played everything right up until now then she wants you to close.

Let me tell you 3 ways in sales you DON'T close:

1. **Wait For The Prospect To Make the First Move**

The biggest rookie moves and probably THE most popular close or should I say attempted close. This is when the naïve, young, and nervous salesman does his sales presentation, he follows it perfectly to the letter. Using everything he learnt in his 4-week training programme. He stops. Smiles. Looks and waits for his prospect to say something. ...

Fucking tumbleweed.

He is waiting. Looking. Hoping. Praying that the person will say *"This is perfect! Give me a pen, where do I sign?"*

Man:
"So Barbara, to review your order: We have two dozen cases of the extra-large rampant rabbits, two cases of the medium, and one case of the small. The whole thing comes to only £6,734, plus VAT and I'll throw in free shipping."
He smiles. Looks.
Silence.
He smiles again.
Silence.
He has more chance of being sucked down a hole on a golf course to play basketball with Bugs Bunny and Daffy Duck than he has of the customer doing his job for him and making the move.

The same applies in the close. You are the alpha male. You are the leader; you have shown you have made decisions before so make one now. If you are wanting a relationship, then you tell her.
Man:
" Listen Stacey, we've been hanging about quite a bit and although I was at first in it just to see your mom I've decided you're not too bad (a laugh or a groan usually follows – remember we take the sting out of the seriousness by using humour) *and I've given it some thought and I like spending time with you.* (aww or that's sweet usually follows) *So I have decided I am going to have to get rid of my other girls for a bit and just see you for now.*

This allows her to reply and you can see if she feels the same or she may say she is just seeing you etc.

After she says this you can take it one of two ways. You can continue your arrangement and continue to see each other or if she encourages you hit her with the:

Man:
"Great so you have won the lottery and you now get to call me your boyfriend. Have you given any thought to what picture of me you want as your wallpaper/screensaver? This is used with humour and if she seems to backtrack you

can say you were only joking and since when did she take everything you said seriously. If she asks if are serious you can say do you want me to be? If she says great or is just generally happy then well done- **you have got yourself a girlfriend.**

She wants you to take charge of the situation. She wants you to lead her through the sale to the closing process. We don't want to act like it is a big deal because you've probably done this ton of times right? Even if you haven't been here before you are going to fake it until you make it. Just like the kiss we aren't making this into a big deal where nerves will get the better of you. It's a low-pressure interaction.

Use humour along the way to relieve tension.

You are leading and they are following.

#2. Asking for their opinion The, "So What Do You Think?" Close
There is a difference between fact-finding during the sales process and asking – *what do you think?* One of them is an important tool to gather all the information you need to find out someone's pain points and offer solutions. The other is a phrase that terrified salespeople use when trying to initiate the close.
The salesman in this case thinks to himself because he has moved away from large open-end questions, to what he thinks is a closed question, that the person's answer will confirm the sale. They think they can ask for the order without directly asking for the order. They think this lowers the risk of direct rejection. What it actually does is give the other person plenty of time to think of all the reasons why they SHOULD NOT go ahead.

Doing this makes things worse, not better. Much worse.

Man:
"So, Scarlett, my team can be over on Tuesday with the swing, they will bring all the tools needed to install it for you in the bedroom. They will test it to make sure it is working before they go and also it will have safety instructions that come with it. That means the total for everything you need comes to £1,299 for the first year and then £12 per month for insurance. So, what do you think?"

Firstly, asking for a prospect's opinion is not asking them to buy anything. You are asking what they think, you are not asking for an order.

What makes this even worse is that by asking them what they think you are asking them to go through the logic of the buying process. At this stage, this is the last thing you want them to do. We get people to buy into things and buy them in general with emotions. Not logic. Logic says it is never correct to spend as much money on a car if you could buy a house with the same money. Logic says you do not need 6 doughnuts for the price of 3 because you won't eat 6. Logic says you don't need a new shirt because your old one fits perfectly and you just need to sow on an extra button. Logic tells you that although the tool on the shopping channel can help you slice a carrot in 3 different shapes in under a minute the chances of you using it are pretty slim and you don't even like fucking carrots. Do you see my point?

As we have discussed earlier in the book women think with emotions then use logic to back up those emotions. When we ask the prospect what they think, we are invariably asking them to use the wrong part of the brain to help us close. Worse you still have not asked him or her to decide.
Is it any wonder why the prospect eventually responds by telling you they want to **THINK** about it?

You just asked them what they ***think***!

If they are thinking, then you aren't closing.

"I'll think about it" is closer to a no than a yes.

If you do this when dating, if you ask them their thoughts then you are showing you are not a leader. Successful risk takers take risks. They weigh up their options and they shoot their shot. IF you are at the stage when you think you should be closing then it should be because you are confident you have correctly gone through the last two sections of the Courtship Process. The next stage naturally and logically is the close.

You are not asking for their opinion on this. You are going to lead and see what happens.

The only types of questions you should be asking in the closing stage are when you alone, preferably in the bedroom or maybe on the sofa.

- *Do you like it when guys pull your hair a little, like this?" and you say this you reach up pull a little bit of her hair and look into her eyes.*

Watch for her reactions, look deep into her eyes. She will either agree or pull away. If she agrees especially with a sharp intake of breath, then you go on ... if she pulls away then you need to build more safety and attraction. Remember two steps back.

- *"How about when a guy kisses your neck and bites on your ear very softly?" Now you use your finger and trace down from her ear all the way down to the clavicle on her neck.*

What we are doing is stimulating emotions. Charging her into an emotional state. Helping her build a picture in her mind of how it may happen. There is no logic right now only the moment.

- *"What about when a guy puts his hand around your neck?"* Here you very softly place your thumb on one side of her neck and the fingers on the other using one hand. You aren't trying to kill her Darth Vader. Look her in her eyes as you squeeze once, not too hard then pull your hand away.

You are sexually charging the conversation. This is exactly the same as Kino Escalation but now we are going sexual. The same principle applies. We take one small step forward, see how receptive they are then you go again. We are making her think about sex. We are wanting her to think about sex. To be imagining sex. You didn't think she would just take her clothes off herself.

- *"How about when a guy pushes you down into the bed like this?* At this moment you don't need to throw her onto the bed John Cena. Of course, you may decide to gently push her if you are near a bed but more likely you might just hold both of her arms and squeeze. Giving the impression you are strong and strong enough to push her onto the bed. Remember you are looking for signs she is enjoying this interaction. If she moves away or says no, then we take two steps back.

The next bit is my favourite and works great.

- You look her in the eyes, and you say," *what do you do when a guy does all of this. Looks at you then rolls over and falls asleep".* Then you move away from her, if you are on the bed you lay down flat away from her, close your eyes, and pretend to go to sleep. If you are sat down, you lay back in your chair and do the same, and if you are stood up you just close your eyes and pretend to nod off.

This bit is all about heightening the sexual tension then pulling the cork out. You are teasing and escalating. Then just when she thinks it is going somewhere you pull the plug before she does. What this is saying is – I am in control. You are showing that you can control yourself. She will either be annoyed, sexually frustrated or find it really funny. Either way your winning. That's because the next time you try to escalate you know how far you've got so it really isn't awkward if you get up to that stage. You can even repeat the whole routine then instead of going to sleep, go in for the kiss and go all the way if you like.

Remember humour and teasing and wonderful tools. Deploy them often. You are showing you are fun and not just after sex. The minute a woman thinks you are just after sex the minute she doesn't want to have sex with you. It is mutual attraction and mutual seduction; she doesn't want to feel as if you are taking her for a ride and you don't want her to feel that way. This is why Safety is so important. You want them to feel safe around you and comfortable kissing. That way when you eventually Kino Escalate sexually it feels natural and normal.

Now different women have different buying points. Jordan speaks about this in his book and that different customers need to be moved further along the lines I mentioned earlier. Some need to only trust you a 7 and some need a major 10. You won't know until you begin to explore.

I know girls that will happily close in under an hour and some that take 6 months. It is not a reflection of the woman or your ability to close, it is simply a reflection of the level of comfort needed for some.

Women have different time periods or need different levels of safety and attraction in order to sleep with you. As an average rule, it takes between 7-10 hours of spending time with someone in order to sleep with them.

Now, this is often broken up into numerous dates. It could be 7- 10-hour long dates it could be lots of shorter moments. On average a good bit of time to spend with someone is a good few hours. If you think of all the different courtship stages and how long, it probably takes to demonstrate all of your values, then you are probably looking at about 3 dates**. The Three Date Rule** should give both of you enough time to decide whether you want to sleep with each other.

Sometimes it is more. Sometimes it is less, a lot less. A few hours even. But it doesn't mean that they all go this way. All women have different buying points and they are buying you. You are the salesmen and until you have demonstrated the relevant qualities you are not going to be able to close the deal.

The three dates can be broken down into this:

- You meet a girl and build attraction and get her number. This can include socials and dating websites
- You arrange to go on a date.
- You go on date number one where you spend the time building attraction, giving disqualifiers, using Cat and Mouse theory and being fun. She is starting to like you.
- You are continuing texting, messaging, using social media. You keep building attraction.
- You go on date number 2 where you start to build safety. She is feeling secure around you and likes to spend time with you. She is becoming comfortable.
- You continue to text, call and maybe even facetime occasionally. You keep building attraction and you build safety.
- You arrange to go on date number 3. On this date you quickly go through Attraction. You go back to safety and see how secure she is feeling. You then choose an appropriate location to go to where you can close if you choose to.
- If your closing is asking to date, then you want somewhere quiet
- If your closing is sex, then you probably want your house/place or maybe a hotel if the occasion calls for it such as after drinking or dinner, etc. You need an appropriate place to close.
- You go to the place. You become flirty. You continue to Kino escalate and you begin to take things sexual. She is positively responsive, and you continue to escalate.
- She is happy and encouraging. You lead.
- You close the deal.
- Well done Harvey Spector. You are a closer.

This is just one example of how things **MAY** play out if it was to happen in 3 dates. You see 3 dates can take a month or longer to happen depending on how busy you are. In between, you are continuing to use the tools outlined in the previous chapters. You see the **Three Date Rule** is a general pattern for how things may play out, but it is not biblical. You cannot swear by it, there will be times you close sooner and times it takes much longer.

If you like her you won't have a problem waiting and if you don't then make sure you have a few girls in rotation to keep you busy.

This is where talking to multiple women comes in handy. You will have a steady stream of dates or closing opportunities at different points.

#3. The Incentive Close

The final way in which a bad salesman tries to close is through offering incentives. Incentives or bribes, to put it another way, is a way in which a salesperson tries to close the deal by stimulating a call for action. You have seen this or heard it all the time. They try and use the rule of reciprocity. I will give you something and you give me something in return.

Man:

"So, Shannon, looking at what we have on the table it is like this: We've got two dozen cases of extra-strength Viagra, two cases of the normal strength, and one case of the all-day and all-night specials. The whole thing comes in at .... just £7,666, plus VAT."

"However Shannon, if I can get that order from you today, not only will we deduct 10%, but we will give you an added box of the all-week magic pills these are so strong that you're not allowed to walk in a bank otherwise you'll be arrested for a stick-up...the best bit is it is all for FREE!"

Silence.

You can hear a pin drop.

Or more likely – your ego and your dignity as they hit the floor and roll under the table to hide away from your pathetic attempt to "sweeten" the deal

When you do this you sound like you over-charged in the first place otherwise why would you be able to throw in something for free now? You are no longer negotiating you are bargaining.

When you enter into bargaining it is because they cannot see the worth in your product. You have not helped move them along to be confident in what you are selling, who is selling it, or how you are selling it. When you begin to bargain you are admitting that the value can be altered.

Bargaining is what you do when someone does not have faith in your product. Have you ever managed to bargain for an iPhone at the Apple Shop? Did they ever budge? Nope because they know someone else will buy it for that price, they believe in their value.

Believe in your value with a woman. Know your worth. You do not beg. You do not offer false promises such as a relationship if she sleeps with you. You know your worth and what's on the table. Make it clear then let them decide. If you have built your value appropriately then they will be ready to buy.

Then it's time to see whether you are a Harvey Spector or a Harley Quinn.

A Jester or a King.

****

Fact-Finding

When the best God Damn Closer in The City walks into the room, he knows he is the best man for the job. In fact, he believes this in all cases. Not just because he has faith in his own abilities but because he genuinely believes that by closing with him the client will be better off. He has done his research before he steps into the room and if he hasn't, he has Donna or Mike do the leg work whilst he stalls. You see he does this so when he puts his offer on the table in a – take it or leave it manner. He is confident his clients stay. He routinely gives his clients the choice to leave yet they do not. So how do you make sure they think they are making the correct decision. You do your research first. You get all your facts in order then you can put on your best Harvey Spector impression and explain to them exactly the result you are going to achieve.

When we are doing our research, we need to make sure we do some **Fact-finding**

Getting The Girl

Any good salesman worth his weight makes sure to do some fact-finding before making a sale. Why? He needs to be sure he is selling the right product to the right person. He wants to identify their pain points and come up with solutions. Fact-finding helps us identify how much a prospect can afford and is willing to spend. That knowledge can help avoid or defuse objections and make a successful close more likely. **Fact-finding** can also be to explore someone's emotional state. This element of feeling-**finding** helps to unearth the issues beneath the surface which a prospective client may feel strongly about– both positively and negatively.

It is during the Safety phase where you want to gather the information that may help you with your close. For example, if a girl says she has never slept with anyone other than a boyfriend then your chances of sleeping with her whilst being out of a relationship are slim (however some of us just seem to be able to close in any situation). You need to understand things about the person that will help you combat any objections or help defuse any worries they may have. They are rightly worried that after sleeping with you that you will run away and never see them again. Have you both spoken about what you want? A great way to handle objections without speaking about them is to make statements.

You could say something like – *"When I sleep with a girl it's because I want to continue to see her for a while. "*

The frame you are setting here is that if you were to sleep together then you would continue to see her. You aren't saying it directly buy you are indirectly making statements that she can apply to herself.

Another statement you could make is – *"I am not looking for agro or drama I just want something chill at the moment I can't be doing with the headaches".*

In this frame, you are saying that you believe anything serious at the moment would cause a headache and therefore you are looking for something casual. Therefore, she knows if you were to get together it would be casual.

If a woman wants, they may question you on your statements as they look for clarity. Asking – *"So what do you mean by casual?"*

This gives you a chance to define your version of casual and how you see your current relationships playing out.

In these situations, you are doing two things. One you are leading the discussion and not turning it into an interview with an awkward *"so what do you want ..."* and two you are being clear and upfront in your intentions.

This is less likely to trigger **buyer's remorse.**
Buyer's remorse is the sense of regret after having made a purchase. It is frequently associated with the purchase of an expensive item such as a vehicle or real estate.

Now the phenomenon of buyer's remorse is not new. It belongs to the strand of psychological theory known as cognitive dissonance. This usually occurs when the mind isn't sure about a purchase and the two elements clash. Buyer's remorse only occurs post-decision dissonance, where a person is stressed by a made decision and seeks to decrease their discomfort.
It usually occurs when the buyer places a large emphasis on the purchase be that time or money they have invested. The bigger the investment the more chance of buyer's remorse.

We don't want your woman to be having buyer's remorse now, do we? We want her to feel like it was an informed decision. Not a drunken regret. You don't want to be the one guy she wishes never happened.

The more conscious we are of psychological and social influences—the ones designed to sway buyers—the more mindful we can be when shopping. Purpose-driven purchases give us agency and buying power. We regain control when we are intentional with our money and conscious about the items we allow into our lives.

We want them to feel as if they were in control, you didn't seduce her with a potion from Professor Snape's class instead you showed her why you mastered Professor Flitwick's Charm class. They are there with you because they want to be there.

With fact finding, you must also find out what her current situation is and if she is ready at the moment for anything.

Some things to consider:

- You might like a girl, but are you sure she's girlfriend material?

Getting The Girl

- Do you really like *her*, or just the idea of being her boyfriend? We don't have to explain the difference, because it's obvious that being in a relationship means you should genuinely like the person you're about to commit to.
- Is the girl you're seeing ready for a relationship?
- Did she specifically state that she's not interested in anything serious?
- Has she just got out of something serious?
- Does she want to have fun right now?
- Is it the right time of the month (You can't fight mother nature champ)?
- Are you ignoring the signs that you're in the friendzone and therefore can't be her boyfriend?
- Is she going to work a season abroad and therefore now isn't a good time to commit?
- Is she going through a divorce?
- Has she got children she must put first?

These are just an example of some of the things you should consider when looking to close you should include things that are important to you. Such as if you are a father and have children how she feels about that. Is she prepared to accept you and your family in its entirety?

There are numerous things you should find out before trying to make a close. You must decide what type of close you want and then ask the appropriate questions. Instead of asking them like an interview though make statements and see how she reacts.

You can say: *"You've just came out of a serious relationship, so you probably want something chill for now."*

She will either agree and say that's right or she will correct you.

Now if you are asking her to be in a relationship then you must also think of the time and place of the question. You don't want to be asking her at her Dads' funeral or whilst she is in an intensive care unit awaiting a kidney transplant. Timing and discretion are best applied. Wait until you are relaxed, not pushed for time, and alone just the pair of you before asking her out as outlined above. You know when it's okay to say it. You should know very well where you're not supposed to say it.

If both the place and timing in her life are right, then you have nothing to lose by asking and only something to gain. You need to take the shot and use the statements offered to see if you will be in a relationship.

"That's the difference between you and me. You wanna lose small, I wanna win big." – Harvey Specter

Remember it isn't a big deal. If they say no you don't act upset or get defensive. Do not defer to trying to convince them by using logic. Listing all the reasons you would be good together. She must come to this conclusion by herself. I have seen many guys get to this stage and when the girls say no crumble and turn into a beg. Basically, they begin to open up and pour out their heart to them and saying all the reasons they are good together. This lowers their value so catastrophically they go to the point of no return. Better to flee now and live to fight another day than to accidentally fall on your sword in your desperation for showing why you would make a good match. All it means is you haven't built enough attraction and safety. Avoid logic.

This will never convince her. What you should have done is acted as if it wasn't a problem and said you understood. Then gone and fucked someone else that night. I know I would of.

If they think you care, they'll walk all over you." – Harvey Specter

You see many men confuse lust with love. They feel because they have invested so much time in a woman that they really like them, or they must have them. You are wrong. You don't need anyone. You are an alpha male.

You don't even know if you like them until after you've slept with them. That's why it's called Cumming. Because you Cum to your senses.

This is what is called **Post-Nut Syndrome.**

The official title is something far more scientific. **Post**-coital dysphoria or **Post**-coital tristesse to give it its proper name. This is the name for the known feeling of a man after ejaculation where he feels sad, anxious, agitated, or aggressive. PCD first showed up around 150 AD, when the Greek physician Galen declared that post-sex sadness happened to every animal except "the human female and the rooster."

Getting The Girl

Spinoza, Aristotle, and Nietzsche, they write, thought it only natural that the loss of the "life force" that happens with the orgasm would coincide with melancholy. Such a thing is the true test of whether you like a woman. How do you feel about her after sex?

There is a wide range of research out there should you wish to look into why men feel sad after sex and why they have a window of clarity, but I think Dave Chapple said it best

"When a guy bust a nut, right after that, there's a window of six minutes where he does the most rational thinking he ever does."

It is in these moments and only after you've actually slept with her will you know if you actually like her or if you just really wanted to bang her. One of the many reasons why getting the bang out the way early is a good way of measuring if you think the relationship is going to go anywhere or not.

You see in order to know if you want a relationship or if you want to take it further you need to first rule out whether you just wanted to get in her pants. The only issue is you won't know until you get in there. This is why often the close may come in two parts. You may first try and close to have sex. Then you may continue to see each other for a while then you want to close and get a relationship. Success is defined by your own line. Only you can decide what type of close you are after. And only you can decide just how many times or many people you want to close during the same time period.

The Game allows for you to be speaking to several clients at once if you so wish, some may close at different times, some may flake, some may want different things to you. This is why you must be open and have the tools to be able to speak to lots of women if you hope to get the girl.

Sometimes you'll make it and sometimes you won't. But a good closer never stops trying to close new deals just because he got a no from an old one.

"Success is like being pregnant, everyone says congratulations, but nobody knows how many times you were fucked." – Harvey Specter

An important aspect as well as seeing you are right for them is if they are right for you. You need to work out whether this is someone you want to close yourself. Especially if you are looking for a girlfriend. The top 10 things to look for when seeing if she would make a good long-term partner are:

1. **She loves and accepts you for who you are**
Love means taking everything in – the good, the bad, and the unknown. It's important to be with someone that you feel comfortable with and you can be yourself around them.
2. **You think she is a cool and funny person**
If you cannot state a single non-physical attribute when asked why you love a person; you might probably just really fancy them. Lust can often be overpowering and blind us to people's faults. Good looks fade, but a great sense of humour will surely stand the test of time.
3. **When you talk, she is able to be open when communicating about how she feels**
When looking for a partner you want someone who is able to speak their mind. A woman who does not expect a mind reader and is able to tell you the truth will help you grow as a person. A mature woman doesn't play games. She communicates honestly.
4. **Confidence in who she is**
She accepts who she is and who she isn't. Someone who doesn't constantly need reassurance will help make life easy. It saves time and energy if you can grow together instead of having to help with her low-esteem. There are times we all need a pick me up. In those cases, we support our partner to grow. We don't want a woman who needs constant reassurance from other guys on socials.
5. **She is respectful to your friends and family**
It is important you share similar values and an outlook on how to start a family. If your friends approve it will make it easier for social settings. You don't want to be in a situation where you are made to choose between her or family and friends
6. **You have better chemistry than Walter White.**
Life is too short for shitty sex. You want to feel as if you want to rip their clothes off whenever you see them. Sharing a similar sex drive will help to keep sparks flying. If you share similar interests in the bedroom, it will help to stop things from going stale.

7. **Positivity is key**
   Whilst her beauty may slowly disappear being happy will stay. In bad times, positivity can help you both get through things. If she avoids drama and arguments, it means she wants things to get better
8. **She treats others with respect**
   Watch how she treats others. Her behaviour to others reflects her inner thoughts.
9. **When she speaks to you about you or herself it is in the long-term**
   She has life plans and goals beyond the next rave or going to Ibiza in the summer. The both of you should also be able to think on a long-term basis and see a future together with each other in it.
10. **Takes pride in herself and her well-being**
    They like to look after themselves this can be physically and mentally. They like to challenge themselves in the mind and body. They may go running or the gym or have hobbies that keep them fit. They may like to wear nice clothes, or they may like to do puzzles. The important thing is that they feel as if they are worth looking after. This will stop you ever waking up one day and wondering what the hell happened.

"Sorry, I can't hear you over the sound of how awesome I am." – Harvey Specter

Closing in the bedroom

There is a psychological barrier you will often have to overcome in the bedroom when you are attempting to close a woman for the purpose of sex. This is the **Anti-Slut Defence**. You see women are programmed to be selective over who they sleep with. They use slut-shaming on one another to re-enforce this socially constructed concept. But it isn't just socially constructed. It's in their genetic make-up. You see back in the cavemen times when a woman chose to lay with a man there was a chance, she would get pregnant and this made her vulnerable. This is why women put a greater emphasis on sex than men. We are at opposites. Women are better to limit the sexual partners they have to raise their chance of survival whereas men are better to sleep with more women in the hopes that one will produce an heir to protect their genetic material. Sex is viewed differently amongst the two genders.

Therefore, a woman's built-in ASD allows a girl to abstain from responsibility during a situation where there is a likelihood of sex/intimacy.

This is the:

- "We are moving too fast"
- "I don't have sex on the first/second/third date"
- "I don't know you well enough yet"
- "I don't like to sleep with guys when I am not in a relationship"

It can manifest itself in many ways, but she is trying to explain that she doesn't want to feel bad for sleeping with you. She does not want to present herself to you as 'easy' or 'slutty'. This is actually a good indication that she likes you. She wants you to like her and view her positively and not judge her or hold her in a negative light.

ASD can be a good thing therefore and it just means their safety levels aren't where they need to be. This is where you go back over the attraction and safety phases of The Courtship process.

We want them to feel comfortable throughout the close. This doesn't just mean mentally but also physically comfortable when they are there. If you are at your place, then you need to make sure she is relaxed. If she has her coat and shoes on it's going to make things difficult for later. Offer to hang it up for her. Offer her a drink. You aren't in a rush when she gets there. Just like always, you would continue the conversation. She is probably quite nervous and wondering what may be about to happen. It is your job to ease this pain. Humour is a wonderful tool for making people feel comfortable. One of the worse things people do is put on a film and not talk. You need to talk to reduce anxiety. To allow them to feel comfortable in their new surroundings.

Amateurs use Netflix and chill. Harvey Spector's gives women their undivided time until they are comfortable to relax and watch a film or maybe a better activity you would both like to try.

Be a good host, give her the tour as soon as she comes in including showing her the bedroom. Then go back to your chill-out space such as a living room. She no longer feels worried when you invite her into the bedroom as nothing has happened the last time you went. You're not there to pounce on her like all the other amateurs your there to enjoy her company. Show her where the bathroom is and say she can use it at any time. You want her to be relaxed. After you spend some time talking and you want to move to a different area then you may say let's go look at: the view from your garden, your picture in the bedroom, your new pots and pan sets. The whole point is the move her around your space, so she feels as if she is comfortable in the space.

Now, remember she is here for a reason. She clearly likes you enough to come home with you.

Keep this in mind when attempting to close. She probably is expecting you to try to close.

We must also be empathetic here you have spent time getting to know her and this might be the first time she has done this in a while. She may never have gone home with a guy from a bar before or might be worried about how it will affect your relationship at work. This can be a scary time for a woman, and she is probably riddled with nerves. For a woman going home with a guy raises her own safety concerns. It's important to address these using two methods.

1.You tell her where you live (full address), ask her to message a friend to let her know where she is. Send location on WhatsApp or check in with friends. You want her to feel safe and promoting her it makes her feel less nervous. She is probably doing it anyway but by speaking about it. Safety doesn't end in the closing stage especially if you hope to continue this into a relationship.

2.We use a technique from Chris Voss called an **Accusation Audit**

Now an **Accusation Audit** is a negotiation technique and part of the tactical empathy we discussed earlier. When we use an accusation audit we are stepping back, and taking an inventory, doing an audit of all the possible negatives, names, accusations, slanderous things that the other side might be thinking about me based on the circumstances, or the environment, or their own paranoia. All the things, that if I was able to defend myself, or had a say in then I wouldn't want you to feel them.

We are addressing the old **Elephant in The Room.** Just by not mentioning it doesn't mean the elephant in the room goes away. When we start to use an accusation audit, we can get to the bottom of all the negative thoughts someone else is thinking and help put them at ease with them. When we talk about it, we help to make the elephant smaller. The elephant in the room is diminished and eventually goes away, by you saying, hey, there's an elephant in the room.

The way we do this is by starting a sentence with "you probably think that ..." Then we follow it with whatever accusation they otherwise might throw at us. In sales terms it looks like this:

"You probably think that we are trying to sell you a lemon."
"You probably think that we don't care if you make a profit."
"You probably think we are hiding something."

By making these statements you are immediately taking each of those potential negative ideas off the table and letting the other side know that you are *not* doing those things. This typically has the effect of creating a sense of empathy and centers the discussion back to one of mutual respect and cooperation. We open up the discussion by addressing fears. The other side may say that is not how they are feeling and actually the budget is tight, or you may get other information you never would have got had it not been for an accusation audit.

When you are doing this with a woman you want to highlight her fears:

"you probably think I am never going to talk to you after this"
You probably think I only brought you here to sleep with you "
"You probably think I do this to all the girls"

In her head, she is screaming – YES, YES, YES!

But what may come out of her mouth is something like – *yeah that's right or you do don't you?*

Just like above she may have other concerns which aren't the above – she may be on her period, she may not have shaved (this can be quite common), she may not be feeling well. There can be genuine concerns and things which take into consideration. We aren't pushy and we are understanding. As always it is one step forward and two steps back.

This allows you to address the concerns head-on. You are turning those negative thoughts into a positive one. A lot of girls just need to be reassured that you are still going to respect them even though they are sleeping with you on the first night out. You are letting her know that it can be an anxious time and that she is not just another number. She feels respected and validated. She feels comfortable and safe. She feels attracted to you. This is the perfect recipe to close.

"I am against having emotions, not using them" Harvey Spector – Suits

To recap in this chapter, we have explored the art of the close. That is to go from the first two stages of The Courtship Process to the final one. Now the close is individual to each person. You must decide what your end goal is with the woman in question you are talking to. The close may occur more than once. You may close to sleep with someone then at a later date close to turning them into a girlfriend. Whilst along the way you still use all of the tools, we have learnt so far. You don't want to suddenly become this person you weren't before. They will feel tricked and cheated on.

One of the issues you will find is whether you want a relationship for the right reasons and if they are right for you. This is why you do the factfinding process. You also want to see if a relationship is right for them. You can do this by making statements and using humour to uncover more information about their situation.

You also won't truly know how you feel about someone until you have slept with them. Take this into consideration when making decisions. Sleeping with people can be a nervous experience for both of you. You must think about how the girl feels and make her comfortable. This applies both physically and emotionally.

You can use an accusation audit to list all of the things she could be worried about. You can then discuss them together. There may be other reasons she can't sleep with you that are uncovered. We are respectful at all times and apply the one step forward two steps back principle. We use Kino escalation when going sexual. We continue to use this method. You want to gradually increase things until you are able to close.

Now luckily for you, the next chapter is on about what to do when you get the Close.

Then the one after that is all about SEX.

Getting The Girl

CHAPTER 10
You've Got Them Now What?

"I swear I couldn't love you more than I do right now, and yet I know I will tomorrow"
Leo Christopher

Chapter 10 – Sex

I wrote back and said "of course I had sex before"
Knowing I was frontin'
I said I was like a pro baby
Knowing I was stuntin'
But if I told the truth I knew I'd get played out son
Hadn't been in pussy since the day I came out one
But, she don't know what
So she done roll back and told me
"Oh you a pro homie? Well I want you to show me
My mama gone for the weekend
So Saturday baby we can get to freakin'"
That's when my heart start racing and my body start sweatin'
Baby you done woke my lil' man up
I'm thinkin' how that body look naked when playing on the bed
Teacher please don't make me stand up
I wrote back like "Yeah baby sound like a plan"
Still trying to play it cool, sound like the man
But I was scared to death my nigga, my stomach turned
Talking damn shit knowing damn well I was a virgin
Fuck

J Cole – Wet Dreamz

Sex. The myth states that men think about sex about every 7 seconds, although anecdotal it Is not an accurate reflection. A more accurate representation is that men think about sex on average 19 times a day. Still not a small number by any stretch of the imagination.

Funnily enough, the same study, entitled **"Sex On The Brain"** found there wasn't much difference between the number of times a woman thought about sex.

That's right fellas she probably thinks about sex just as much as you. She just doesn't let you know.

You see sex is not physical. It never has been, never will be, this is where many people go wrong. They think sex is a physical act.

Sex is as much mental as it is physical, and it is best when it is a mixture of both. In order to have better sex, you must get into their minds at the same time as their pants.

Now Professor Xavier let's start with foreplay.

Foreplay

Foreplay begins way before you two are alone in your bedroom or on the sofa relaxing at her place. Foreplay actually begins hours and days before.

In your younger years, you probably, like most men, learnt all you know about sex from that physical performance material know as porn. You see porn isn't real. It is performed by actors and actresses, filmed for hours with specialist cameramen. The people chosen are chosen due to their specific talents. Trying to copy what you see on film there is like trying to imitate Jackie Chan running up a building. It can be done but by very few people and usually under specific circumstances. Or maybe it wasn't porn, and you had a friend that tried to tell you about a few things you could do in the bedroom to really get a woman going. What a Ponzi scheme.

The issue with this was you never got to understand how arousal works. In the many messages you get through the internet or your friends you concluded that when a penis is erect or when a vagina is wet, it means a person is horny, prepared, and ready for sex.

I am sorry to tell you that this isn't always the case. You have incorrectly assumed that a person's physical response to a form of sexual stimulation matches what is going on in their head.

Or to put it another way, you thought because she had a football kit on, she wanted to play football. This is a mistake.

In the real world away from the HD camera, the soft lighting, the special strength Viagra, and a team of editors, there are many times when desire and physical arousal don't match. In fact, physical arousal, this being the good old genital response is quite different from subjective arousal, known as being actively mentally engaged in the actual sex.

How many times do you think a woman has been laying in bed staring at the ceiling whilst someone is on top of her grunting giving it his all and she would rather be anywhere else in the world, she closes her eyes lets her mind wander to somewhere else, completely bored wishing for it all to be over. Then she taps him on the back, says *"that was great babe"* then rolls over to go to sleep thinking why did I even bother?

The answer – way more than you think.

There's a name for when physical and subjective arousal is mismatched**: arousal non-concordance.**

This refers to anytime the brain and the body don't match up in the bedroom. That's right your knocking passes like Kevin De Bruyne and your center-forward is staring at you thinking – *Ow was I meant to run for that?*

Luckily for you, we know that getting into a woman's head means she is going to have better sex. Therefore, we must aim to do this first. She will literally feel it better. She will review it better, for all intents and purposes; if you could control the exact same sexual performance, stick it in a bottle and use it for lab experiments. Your experiment would then be simple. You could use this sex sample, let's call it SEX A. If you went and use SEX A again, after being in her mind, she will tell you (and others) that you are better in bed and that the sex was actually better even though physically, nothing at all has changed.

Comprende?

You see back in September 2010 The Journal of Sexual Medicine published a study that was quite intriguing. The study comprised 50 women who were diagnosed with female sexual arousal disorder. They were struggling to feel in the mood.

The experiment gave them all a placebo drug and told them it would improve their sex life. Now a placebo for those of you that are unaware is a substance that has no therapeutic effect, used as a control in testing new drugs. Basically, it did nothing. Well, nothing medically anyway. The results however were fascinating. When given this placebo but told it was actually Tadalafil, a drug once used to treat erectile dysfunction, the study found **ALL OF THE WOMEN** reported **an increase in sexual pleasure** whilst taking the "drug".

The drug did nothing. The mind however did the rest of the work.

You see the results are not surprising when you realise that Sex is not merely physical for women; it is mental. Such a factor is so often ignored for women that they feel unfulfilled and dissatisfied. Women, at least sexually, are more complex creatures than us men. They require additional attention to reach a substantial sense of sexual satisfaction.

So how do we help them get there?

Well, it starts with the build-up.

Now the build-up can differ if you are already in a relationship or you aren't, but the same general principles apply –

- Foreplay should begin as early as possible before sexual intercourse – this can be hours or even days. If you were working away and come home to a woman on a weekend you may begin on a Thursday by telling her you've been thinking about her. That you can't wait to see her. A few flirty messages later and you go to sleep. Then when you wake up Friday, you have all day to tease her and paint her pictures with words of the things you want to do. So that by the time you actually do get home she is desperate for you to turn that imagery into reality. Use your words- not dick pics- to create sexual tension.

Getting The Girl

- If you two are dating or preparing to sleep together for the first time, then foreplay begins with your Kino-escalation. This can be rubbing her leg in the restaurant, touching the small of her back, accidentally squeezing her bum as you leave the restaurant. Sharing a strawberry with champagne, wiping tomato sauce from her mouth after she's had a hotdog (hey it looks good in the movies and it's usually mustard if it's an American film). The actual act you do should be one of a series of acts that seek to tease whilst also building sexual tension.
- We are never in a rush to get to the actual intercourse; this is just one part of the sexual experience. Describe in words some of the things you like to do in a nonchalant manner to see where her desires lie. Ask her to talk about the things she is into. Ask her to describe in detail what she likes about those things and why. The important thing to do here is to do so tactfully. If you are preparing to sleep together for the first time, she may be uncomfortable with such conversation, in that case, we don't talk about that as we want her to feel like she wants to rip your clothes off not that she is uncomfortable.
- The sexual conversation should always be light and not heavy, you want to make it personal to the person you are talking to and not generic
- When kino-escalating for sex aim to cover a woman's most erogenous zones - The most important erogenous body zones on a woman are the mouth, followed by the nape of the neck, the nipple/breast, the inner thigh, the back of the neck, and then the ears. You want to start by slowly and softly kissing these areas, pulling away then going back. You are bringing a broth to simmer and not boil over. The aim is to give her shivers down her spine, and she grabs the back of your neck pulling you in. This is when you know you are doing a good job
- When kissing it is good to pull away after a few kisses, look her in the eyes with a fierceness then go again. The look will raise her temperature and the element of control showed by you separates this moment from all the other men that rush to the sex.
- A study in Human Andrology 2016 concluded that extragenital erogenous zones are present in a vast majority of women. Of which, 12% of women said that they can orgasm following stimulation of these zones. This is without even touching her vagina. Pay close attention gentleman there is more than one way to skin a cat.
- Build up the sex as both an image and with your actions. As you begin to see what makes her tick bring these into alignment

- The aim is to get them to think about you and sex in the same vein of thought. What amateurs do is they talk about sex with people they've never slept with and it comes across painful. They say things like *"do you like to go on top or bottom?"* or *"what's your favourite position?".* You have no need to ask if you have every intention of finding out. When you talk this way, you come across the same as every other guy she's met that wants to sleep with her. You aren't talking about sex for your benefit **you are doing it for hers.**
- During foreplay, you are teasing, whilst also trying to find out what she likes so you can do this for her. You are taking an interest in her sexual preferences for her benefit.

This is all-important because of the difference in attitudes towards intimacy and sex between the sexes. Men are, by and large, physical first, and emotional second. In other words, *"if you are close to me, if you have sex with me, then you love me and I will love you back."* This is known as the **Proximity Effect**.

On the opposite hand, women, hold emotions and feelings first before the physical interactions second. She will respond to you physically and sexually once she feels you are emotionally invested. When she feels as if you care and not just for your own sexual gain. We spoke about the power of imagery in the earlier chapters when we looked at female fantasies. We know what ways we can behave to make ourselves seem more attractive and we are aware of how to make women feel safe. We continue to employ these tools through a relationship (even a brief sexual one) because not only does it increase our rapport with the woman, but we will also have better sex.

Therefore, if you want to have great sex then think about the build-up. How long is your foreplay process? Extend it. How many different ways do you currently employ to create sexual tension? Do you fact find information about their sexual desires and begin to add this into your move pool? If you know a woman likes to be choked then try it, if she likes her hair pulled then try it. You see talking about sex and what you currently do rarely helps your sex life but getting her to talk about her interest in sex will almost certainly help you to have better sex together. The more you know the better it will be.

Therefore, when you think of sex, ask yourself if you think she is into It mentally first and if she isn't how can you change this. Work on the mental before the physical.

Getting The Girl

You see being in someone's mind mentally can work as a combat or bonus multiplier. You go from an X1 to an X1.5 or X2 with every action you take. If you were a 5/10 in bed without being in her head, then with a 1.5 multiplier you're now a 7.5/10. Work smarter not harder boys. The more mentally into you they are the easier the physical task becomes.

My top suggestions for helping with foreplay after they are mentally engaged:

1. **Fail to prepare, then prepare to fail** – prep the room or the place you are expecting to have sex in. Make sure it is clean and tidy. Fresh sheets go a long way (although when you become a real champ, you'll be swapping these after every session). Candles and soft lighting combined with music can help set the mood.

2. **Will you welcome to the stage, the one, the only... Magic Mike! –** There is no race to take her clothes off or your own. Slowing things down increases anticipation. If you have ever seen our boy Magic Mike drive women insane it is because he understands the principle of anticipation. He heightens the emotional response. He knows that the mind can be more powerful than the physical. Take your time when removing your own clothes as well as hers. Have confidence in your body regardless of how you look. The person who gets undressed in the dark appears like he isn't confident in his own skin. Remove one article of clothing at a time from her and appreciate the new body parts it reveals. As you take off her jumper to reveal her t-shirt, she has her arms exposed. Begin to kiss these and appreciate the body before you remove the next layer. You want to fill her with confidence, and this happens when you appear to marvel in her body. If you are built like a Greek god yourself then she will do the same. Help guide her hands around your body. Let her explore all the parts of you other than the sword between your legs.

3. **Slowly, Slowly, Catchy Monkey-** Our brains know two forms of pleasure.

   One is the **Anticipatory** - Pleasure experienced in anticipation of something we want. Think of how you feel when you are waiting for amazon to drop off a new book (one like this) or a new video game you have ordered. This is the feeling of pleasure anticipation.

The other is **Consummatory** - Pleasure experienced when you actually get what you've been craving. That feeling of immense joy when you load the game for the first time.

When it comes to physically having sex, building up sexual tension, and achieving heightened states of pleasure is all about anticipation, and anticipation falls right at the center of sexual pleasure.

4. **If you don't ask, you'll never know** – Don't be afraid to ask if they like something or what they like whilst doing it. Feedback is good it helps to improve performance.

5. **Grooming** – You want to always be ready for war solider. You should be clean, prepped, shaven and ready to go. Remember sex doesn't always happen inside the bedroom. Are you ready for a night stealth mission? What about going behind enemy lines (at the in-law's house)? War can be a dirty business comprising of lots of little battles in order to win the war. Make sure you are prepped to fight if the situation demands it...

"Ok ma what's your preference
Nice and slow
Or fast and breathless
Pull your hair girl, bite your necklace

Getting The Girl

Let me show you what a nigga from Louis blessed with
Hey, I'll make you spring a leak
When I'm done I flip the mattress
Change the sheet (Gotta change them)
I'm like a radical one
I vibrate a little more than your mechanical one
(From your titties to you thong)
Either way mama I'm a make you do it or do it
(Girl I'm about to make you come)
Guaranteed when you fuckin with me
('Cause I go on and on and on, on and on and on, on and on and)
Ladies if you feel me
Grab them Thangs fo Biggie"

Biggie Smalls – Nasty Girl – Nelly Verse

Female anatomy and the orgasm

Way back in 1950 the Germans, being efficient as they are, made a wonderful discovery. Now, this was after world war 2 were the birthplace of many great inventions began. The war helped lead to many great inventions such as The computer, Superglue, Penicillin, Satellites, Radar, Jet Engines, and the ballpoint pen. However, many women would argue that man's greatest discovery happened just after the war. Ernst Grafenberg made the miraculous discovery of a spot inside the vagina, which, when stimulated produced immense sexual pleasure. He was a Gynaecologist, not just a man who had a passion for exploring vaginas in his spare time, may I add. His discovery was so good he named it after himself. Here the G-Spot was found.

<u>Where Is The G-Spot?</u>

A question that has plagued mankind for years. If you ask a woman, they will tell you even if they draw a map and gave the guy a Sat Nav, they still wouldn't find it. Luckily, I have a diagram just for you.

Finding the G-spot is can be tricky for most and it's certainly harder than finding the clitoris, but it isn't impossible.
It presents itself as slightly raised with a small bump like spots on the inner, upper wall of the vagina. It is not in the same location on every female but hell, half the fun is discovering between you.

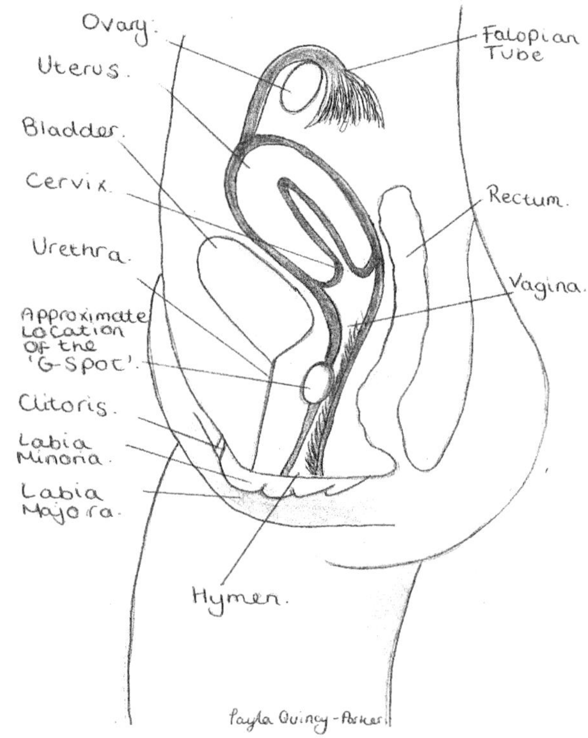

Call yourself Captain Jack Sparrow and tell her you're looking for her buried treasure. The eye patch is optional. The Hook technique however works wonders.

<u>Where is the Clitoris (Clit for short)?</u>

Made popular by modern porn and the go-to for most females when looking to stimulate themselves the clitoris is the pleasure center of the vulva. Many see it as a magic button that can help unlock the next level of a woman's pleasure. A bit like the Maze Runner.

Just like the G-Spot if there were a GPS device that could show you where to find the clitoris, we'd probably all be a lot happier. The thing is, lots of people don't know where the clitoris is, and many of us are too afraid to ask for directions. But you're not an idiot if you aren't sure where or what the clitoris is, because it's not as straightforward as it seems.

Getting The Girl

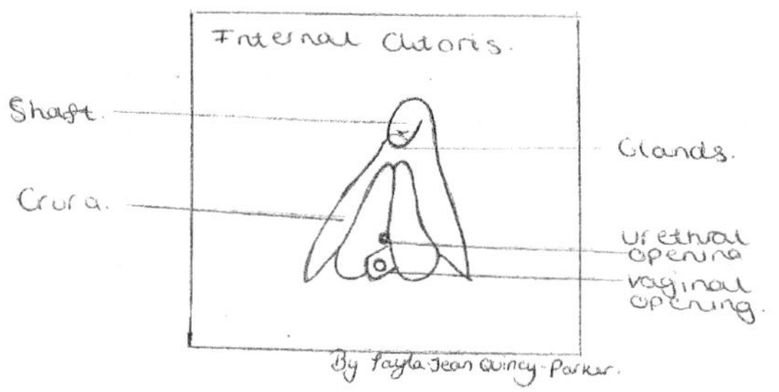

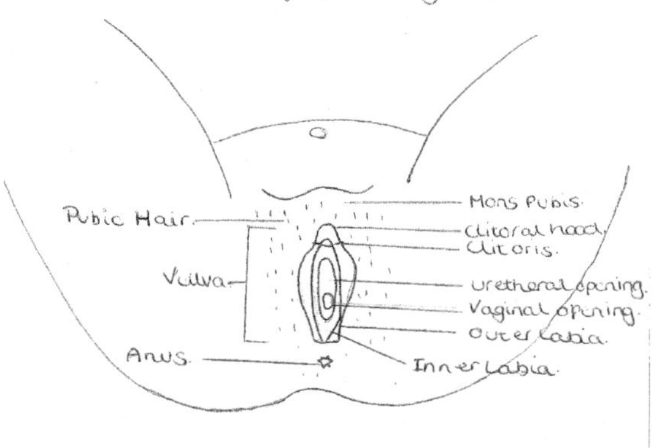

The easiest way to find it is to look at the top of your vulva. It is tucked inside the inner labia, underneath its own protective hood. It can be easy to find on some and harder on others. It comes down to each person being unique. I will give you a hint gentleman it's usually under a slight hood, hidden from sight. The clitoris can vary in size – from that of a pea or as large as a thumb. We only ever see the tip which comes out. The easiest way to find it is during arousal it becomes hard and swollen. Just like a dick.

It may resemble a tiny area to us from the outside, but it is much bigger and goes inside the vagina. The clitoris is actually shaped more like a wishbone.

The clit can be one of the easiest ways to help a woman to climax. You can do this by rubbing directly, with your hands or using the clit as part of other types of sex such as oral or penetrative or by making it part of a wider tease.

The clit is often the easiest way to help bring your partner to climax so get used to finding it and using it. It is ok to ask them for guidance on where it is. If they are not sure, then you can go exploring together.

<u>How men can use the Clit to help the lady in the bedroom</u>

You have hands – Use them

Most penetrative positions give you the option to use your hand to stimulate the clit. Do this to help raise the sexual experience. If not ask the woman to do it herself. This brings a *"We will get there together"* dynamic.

Pillows are for more than sleeping on
If a pillow is placed correctly it will allow the female to grind on it whilst you are behind or in front. This way you get clitoral stimulation without needing your own hands.

The sofa is for more than NETFLIX and Chill
Having sex in different places makes it easier to reach the clit. This applies to both you and your sexual partner. In positions from behind the sofa can make it easier to reach as it offers support.

Just because you're on your back don't mean you give up Jack
When your partner is on top you can use your hands to glide her hips forwards and backward. This sliding up and down motion helps move the pelvis to stimulate the clitoris. After all, you didn't do all those push-ups for no reason right?

Gunfight at the O.K Corral
The final way you can help stimulate the clit is by using the reverse cowgirl position. You can have penetrative sex whilst also reaching around to help stimulate the clit. You can also sit up slightly to help with the reach.

There are many different types of orgasms a girl can have, and they all happen in different ways. Now as much as you would like a step-by-step guide to giving all of these, I need to keep a few tricks up my sleeve and leave room for a follow-on book, right?

For now, the most important thing for you to do is to try the above and learn the female anatomy. Learn to get into her mentally before physically and all of the below happen far easier.

The orgasms a woman can have are:

<u>Different types of orgasm</u>

1. Clitoral
2. G-Spot
3. Penetrative
4. Squirting

5. Anal
6. Erogenous Zones

Make it your journey to explore these together and see how many you can achieve. It can be rather fun.

Exploration

Born in Genoa in August 1451, Christopher Columbus knew since his teens that a life of exploration was for him. After failing to win patronage from the French and English courts of the day he eventually found sponsorship in Queen Isabella of Spain.

On the 12th of October 1492, he set foot on the Bahamas and so began his discovery of the Americas. The New World , as it was known, was the starting place for many great things. You see without Christopher's appetite for exploration and without a willing woman then many great things would have remained hidden to the world for many years.

Now it is time to do some exploration of your own in the bedroom. It is time you tried something new.

Exploration in the bedroom during sex is best done with someone with who you have a regular sexual relationship with. It is a way to keep things fresh, exciting and to supplement your normal sexual routine.

There are different ways you can explore the bedroom and I shall offer just a few. There are of course many books you can purchase which offer a more in-depth analysis of how to better your sex life. There are : **Better Sex: A Step- by-Step Guide for Beginners to Improve Your Sex Life** by Evelyn James**, TRANSFORM YOUR SEX LIFE** by Paula Ann & Damien Old, and of course we have **Kama Sutra & Tantric Sex** *by Emma Bright***.**

Tantric sex if you remember correctly was in American Pie 2 practiced by Finch in his pursuit of Stiflers mum. Now Tantric sex is a slow, meditative form of sex where the end goal is not orgasm but enjoying the journey. With Tantric sex, the aim is to move energy around the body for different purposes.

That's right gentleman , there is more than going as hard and as fast as you can in the bedroom.

Lovemaking

Now lovemaking may not be as fashionable these days due to the rise of BDSM and the growing influence of that market but it is no less enjoyable. BDSM play can also be enjoyable and I will talk about how you can bring elements of that into the bedroom later but for now I will explain how bringing in a bit of love-making can help to mix up the bedroom and bring joy to both.

You see when we make love, we slow things down to a sensual level. We are in no rush to climax or bring our partner to climax. It is the sensual exploration; it is the passion kissing in between strokes as you whisper into their ear. Lovemaking may well be a dying art to many but all the more reason to master it. You will be surprised how many women can testify they have never made love, but they have had a lot of sex. Think about it this way you don't even have to be good you just need to be remembered.

For love-making positions of intimacy are required, missionary or a spooning position which brings you close together where kisses can be exchanged are wonderful. The aim is to bring closeness to you both, this can be done with interwoven fingers, brushing their hair, kissing on their neck.

Kissing is the best part of making love. You share your passion through your kiss. Making love is when you bring together safety and attraction to form a deeper connection. Try it every now and then she'll be pleasantly surprised and so will you. What's the worst that can happen, Romeo?

Girl relax, let's go slow
I ain't got nowhere to go
I'm just gonna concentrate on you
Girl are you ready?
It's gonna be a long night

Throw your clothes on the floor
I'm gonna take my clothes off too
I made plans to be with you
Girl whatever you ask me you know I can do

I'll make love to you
Like you want me to

And I'll hold you tight
Baby all through the night
I'll make love to you
When you want me to
And I will not let go
Till you tell me to

I'll make love to you – Boys to Men

Rough Sex

On the opposite end to the lovemaking, we of course have the more common rough sex. This is most often displayed in modern-day porn and has led many to believe this is the norm. Now there are many people that do indeed enjoy rough sex, but I feel it is best to explore it verbally first. This helps to establish comfort levels. After such approval is given then you are free to explore.

Rough sex usually refers to the animalistic regression of sex back to a display of physical prowess. We are talking about when one removes themselves from the situation and goes back to their carnal desires' initial emergence and uses this as the fuel for their sexual experience. This usually results in: hair pulling, spanking, biting, nail clawing, throwing them around the bedroom sex.

Rough sex although can be similar to BDSM it remains in its own category for now as are almost certainly talking about your ability to be physically dominant in the bedroom with just natural things right now. These usually result in the removed positions such as doggy style where people can pull hair, bite and scratch whilst performing sex.

In - Game of Thrones – Khal Drago uses this as a sign of his power. It is his way of showing he is in charge. Some people love resulting back to this form of sex as a form of escapism from the world and its constraints. They see it as naughty and like to do things that are rebellious. It plays on people's natural tendency to do things that give them a natural high. This is the opposite of making love as this tests safety levels and raises anxiety which can heighten the sexual experience.

It's important to make your partner aware of these things before sex as they can often leave marks and although made with love as part of an agreed-upon style of sex it is best to discuss these before. Many people love this type of sex, but it shouldn't be your only or your go-to style. It's important to be able to mix things up.

You let me violate you
You let me desecrate you
You let me penetrate you
You let me complicate you

I broke apart my insides
(Help me) I've got no soul to sell
(Help me) the only thing that works for me
Help me get away from myself

I wanna fuck you like an animal
I wanna feel you from the inside
I wanna fuck you like an animal
My whole existence is flawed
You get me closer to God

Closer – Nine Inch Nails

BDSM

When we say BDSM we use the term as each letter can refer to a different aspect of the sex. The B refers to bondage and disciple. The D to domination and submission. The SM to sadism and masochism.

Now, this type of sex grew in popularity from the hit book and film series 50 Shades of Grey. For those of you unaware 50 Shades of Grey tells the story of Anastasia Steele and Christian Grey. They become acquainted when Anastasia interviews the wealthy businessman for her college newspaper. Christian is a dominant force; he is rich powerful and he begins to date, Anastasia. Slowly introducing her to his sexual viewpoint and his fantasies surrounding BDSM. Such was the popularity of the book it was translated into 52 languages and the trilogy has sold over 125 million copies.

In the book, Christian has a playroom where he uses dominance and submission, often tying her up before he moves onto other interests such as whips and so forth. This is what most people think of when they hear BDSM.

How BDSM works in the real world is a large emphasis on informed consent. This is the most important thing such as when having rough sex as there are situations where people can get hurt as a result of the play itself BDSM often involves varying degrees of pain, physical restraint, and servitude.

Either the man or the woman can be dominant, or you can swap depending on who wants to play the role. It always has one dominant and one submissive.

Due to the nature of how extreme this sex can become lovers who indulge in such play often introduce a safe word.

As mentioned at the beginning of the **Exploration** such forms of sex are best done with regular sexual partners as you begin to work together. Either in or out of a relationship. You wouldn't expect to do these things with women you are sleeping with for the first time or just for a short while.

Many women will not want to try these extreme forms of sex and this is something that must be taking into consideration. Remember sex is but one part of a healthy relationship and sometimes you have to make compromises. It is important to communicate fully and throughout to ensure both are enjoying the experience and anything new that you try.

The best safe word is usually unrelated to sex, such as 'Pineapple Juice'. This makes it easy to know when to stop or things are going too far and that leaves little room for interpretation.

A traffic light system can be an easy way to monitor how both parties are enjoying themselves.

Red: means stop. Saying this will mean you want your partner to stop everything they're doing immediately. It should be used when you're not comfortable, things are getting too much, or you no longer consent.

Amber: means slow down. Maybe you liked what they were doing but then it became a little too much. Yellow is basically saying "calm down a little bit". It can also mean you are starting to reach your limit.

Green: means go for it. Use green if you are enjoying what your partner is doing or they are enjoying what you are doing. I mean you are happy for things to continue.

Remember when being or asking your partner to be a submissive lover it is about trust. The best way to start is with basic sensory deprivation.

Start with using a blindfold to deprive them of their sense of sight. This heightens other senses and can increase the sexual experience. It plays into the teasing from earlier and also the sense of anticipation.

The next sense to deprive them of is their ability to move. This can be done with rope, handcuffs, restraints, or all manner of things to tie someone up. You can tie their hands, feet, or to an object.

You can find lots of BDSM toys to use online and It's good to explore these together to find out which ones to use.

Just one night full of sin
Feel the pain on your skin
Tough, I don't scream mercy
It's your time to hurt me
Yeah (Oh, oh, oh)
If I'm bad tie me down
Shut me up, gag and bound me
'Cos the pain is my pleasure
Nothing comes better
Yeah (Oh, oh, oh)

'Cause I may be bad but I'm perfectly good at it
Sex in the air, I don't care, I love the smell of it
Sticks and stones may break my bones
But chains and whips excite me

Rhianna – S & M

Phone sex

Now our boy Ozzy in American Pie had to do this the old-fashioned way by talking down a landline phone and describing exactly what he wanted to do to his girlfriend in France. Now we have come a long way since then and the impact of video calls and facetime has meant that you don't even have to be Shakespeare with words to have the pleasure of phone sex with your other.

Phone sex should only be used when you can't physically get to your partner after all why wouldn't you want to just do it?

Phone sex can become awkward and cringey if scheduled too often and often best works after a long day or night away from your partner when it can be spontaneous. Now I do not recommend ever calling your partner and just start to try phone sex. Remember they must be mentally in it and also the time and situation must be right for them. You may be all alone in the shower but she could be having afternoon tea with her mother and auntie and the last thing she wants is you whispering down the phone or worse you to pop up on facetime and scare her aunt out of her seat. Discretion is key here.

Phone sex only really works in long-term relationships, there isn't much need to short-term ones and they are best if it is a long-distance relationship. Where possible you would always rather just wait and see your partner in person.

If you're doing it the old-fashioned way verbally then describe in intricate detail all the things you would be doing if you were there. If you're on video, then you have a lot more options at your disposal. Choose carefully and tastefully.

Baby you know that I miss you
I wanna get with you tonight but I cannot baby girl
And that's the issue, girl you know I miss you
I just wanna kiss you
But I can't right now
So baby kiss me thru the phone (kiss me thru the phone)
I'll see you later on
Kiss me thru the phone (kiss me thru the phone)
See you when I get home

Soulja Boy – Kiss Me Thru The Phone

Using toys

Jim and Michelle were certainly experimental in American Pie and whilst I wouldn't recommend getting your partner to stick a trumpet up your bum (unless you are really into that stuff, not for me , mind) you can however use other objects know as toys to enhance the sexual experience.

The first thing to be mentioned is toys do not take away from your ability as a lover, they are not there to replace you and they aren't a reflection of how good you are in bed. Toys can help to bring new things into the bedroom and can be an add-on to an already great sex life.

You don't have to be intimidated by using sex toys nor does your partner. You can discuss the type of things you might like to try and what you are into before. You don't even have to wander into a shop to buy them as they can all be done discreetly over the internet.

Toys aren't for everyone, but they can be great fun.

The best way to start using toys is to start small both literally and in the sense of something you don't see as intimidating. The best for this can usually be something like a vibrating bullet. This little device vibrates and can be used by you or your partner to stimulate their clitoris. This can help aid them during sex to reach a climax or be used outside of sex for foreplay. How you use it depends on you and your partner.

After that, we have things men can wear that vibrate that help offers this experience during normal penetrative sex then we go into a range of other toys such as those used for anal or different kinds of sex.

The important thing here again is communication. Communicate how you are bringing them into the bedroom what you want their uses to be and how often you want to use them. The focus is on pleasurable exploration. You are **using them together**. They aren't there to replace anyone or anything.

Threesome

The last one in exploration is what our man **Stiffler** managed to achieve at the end of American Pie 2 with the two blonde chicks. Now you have to remember this is most men's fantasy, but it is very few women. As with all of the above you have to make sure you want to do so for the right reasons.

The wrong reasons are things such as wanting to sleep with another woman but with permission. This will only seek to hurt and upset your partner probably leading to alienation and the eventual breakdown in the relationship.

Unfortunately for you in my experience threesomes most often occur outside of a relationship and they are not planned. However, if you were to plan them inside a relationship then there would have to be very clear rules.

You would have to outline exactly what is allowed to happen and what isn't. You would need to introduce safety words like mentioned above and be prepared to stop immediately.

You must realise that introducing someone else to the bedroom also bypasses all the attraction and safety you have done so it can be a very nervous experience on both sides. Your partner's feelings must be considered along the way. Your expectations of them and what they will or won't do must be clear and their consent to what they want to do. This works the same way with them and you.

As a general rule, the best way a threesome can work in a relationship is if the girl chooses and wants to bring a girl into the bedroom and the same way for a guy.

You wouldn't like it if your partner said *"Hey here is Tom he is going to be joining us in the bedroom"* so don't do the same to them. It needs to be low pressure. You may suggest it and discuss it when it's you two then it is up to her whether she wants to act on it. For many girls, they are curious but only in certain circumstances such as on holiday or with a complete stranger. You must remember that things such as threesomes are extremely rare and although popular in porn very rarely happen in real life. If, however, you must persist then speak to your partner about it.

You will probably have more chance of waiting for a star to fall through.

Reviews

The final section in Sex. The one I recommend the most and I think is the one used the least. This is to review your performance with the person you are sleeping with. Now I am not talking about a good old *"How was that for you?"*. I mean a genuine review where you sit down with the person you are sleeping with and ask them what they like and don't like. Now I know Mel Gibson could see inside women's heads but the rest of us usually need them to tell us.

A sign of a confident, Alpha-male is one who can openly and honestly talk to a woman about sex and how he can improve without having his ego bruised. You see if every woman you slept with gave you just one tip, think how much better in bed you'd be now compared to when you began? Worse imagine if you go no better in bed as you went on. You see the point.

One of the best things you can do is speak to the woman and ask what they would like differently. You see if you genuinely care about them you want them to have a good time. It may also encourage them to do the same and ask you so you can tell them how it can improve for you. You open up an honest line of dialogue.
You see I know there isn't a single criticism that I could get in the bedroom that would affect my sense of self but a few pointers on how to get this particular woman off and she will be telling all her friends how she spent a night on Mount Olympus with a God.

As you get better in bed you have more and more tools you can use. You will read a woman's signs better and better. You will have techniques you can draw upon that work. Certain moves you do that you know work really well. Sleeping with different people teaches you different things if you are prepared to listen and talk. Then as learn more and more you become better and better. Then once you are confident in your abilities you can put this into place. Every woman is different, and they like different things just because one woman preferred it one way doesn't mean another will.

Let's take the guessing out of sex and start to get honest reviews to improve your own performance. Whenever I ask a woman what she likes she usually says, *"no one has ever asked me that before"*.

Time to start making some changes if you want to be known as a legend in the bedroom my friend.

To summarise you can do many things to ensure you have a healthy sex life. Trying new things is best done with a regular sexual partner. You have many things you can introduce but they should always be done in communication. The important thing is that you are both comfortable with what is happening. Sex begins in the mind way before the physical, by making sure they are mentally into you it heightens the sexual experience. In order to heighten the sexual experience, you use teasing and building us suspense. You want to take your time.

When women are emotionally involved, they enjoy sex better with you. When it comes to the act of sex there are many ways you can approach it. Choose which one is best for you and your partner. Practice makes perfect. But doing the wrong practice over and over again isn't helping anyone. Feedback is key to improvement do not be scared to ask how things went and try new things. The more times you have sex and with different people, you will learn new things and see what makes different women tick.

Improve one step at a time and next thing you know you'll be your own little Demi-God with your own Devil Dick that keeps women running back every time.

Getting The Girl

CHAPTER 11
What Makes A Relationship Work?

"When someone does something wrong, don't forget all the things they did right"

Chapter 11 – What makes a relationship work?

We must first begin with a word of caution. Relationships can be wonderful, enhancing life experiences for many. When you meet a person, who pushes you to be the best version of yourself and supports you in its entirety they can be fulfilling times.

I have been involved in many relationships. Usually other peoples.

Here is the other side of a relationship.

You see, living together, a label, a wedding ring, none of these things protect you from infidelity. You could be the most loving, caring, best partner anyone can ask for and they can still fuck someone in Ibiza on holiday.

You must be aware that being in a relationship and getting such a label is not the end goal. This is just the start of another journey. You speak to anyone you person who has been in one long enough they will tell you that you need to work hard at them. They aren't easy.

You must continue to try and make effort and add value. If you don't then usually your missus is going to get bored and begin to look elsewhere, that's where a certified sweet talker like me comes in and whilst you're working away trying to put food on the table, I am helping her change the bedsheets.

Such immortal words were never truer. Remember this – **YOU CAN'T TURN A HOE INTO A HOUSEWIFE.**

So, don't try. I have seen it happen to good friends and I have helped many a woman embraces her inner Rhianna and be unfaithful. The woman that spends her time seeking attention from every man will never change.

One of the biggest issues men get from relationships is they chose the wrong woman in the first place.

Date Eights

Burn this immortal phrase into the front of your brain it will save you a lot of agro my friend.

Tens are great fun; they are wonderful to sleep with and to show off every now and then. But to settle down with? An absolute nightmare.

Now an easy method for selecting women is to date a woman that you think is an eight out of ten on your personal hotness scale and for good reason. You see a woman that is an eight on looks, usually makes up for it in other departments. She has had to develop herself to be a better well-balanced human being. Not being able to get by on just her outstanding aesthetics, she usually had a lot more to her. She will usually be offering a lot more to you and the relationship, than those pesky tens.

Tens are great to have fun with but rarely make good partners. They know their worth and often make your life difficult. They will constantly need attention or try and test you and get you to jump through hoops. Such a relationship will only ever be such a strain as you constantly feel the need to keep up.

Now I am not saying you can't date a ten. You certainly can. It can also work. What I am saying is that you shouldn't aim for those that you think are a ten because you feel as if the best partner is the one who is best looking. You see what you want from a relationship is often much more than you want from a sexual partner.

You see when I say a ten, I don't mean the entire package I am talking about the male hotness scale which we usually rank women on. This shallow but effective barometer only tells us a slither of information we actually need about choosing a great partner. Should we fancy them? Absolutely but we also need more than good looks to make a relationship work. Too many men choose a woman because they perceive she is the "best looking" they've been with or out of their current options, but that person was never right for them. They were completely incompatible.

In order to make a relationship work at least give yourself a fighting chance by selecting people that you may be able to make a good go at it with.

There are certain things you should strive for in a relationship that are universal but only you know your absolute deal-breakers. Those things you can't stand, or you absolutely must-have.

Getting The Girl

You have to remember there is no such thing as perfect only perfect for you. As you become older you realise that not only do you have lots of flaws but so may your partner and that is fine. You must learn to live with the fact that you will both make mistakes, but as long as you have each other's best interest at heart then you'll get by.

Some of the things you can look for in a healthy relationship:

1. **Praised when you do well.**
   Men have infamously tender egos. Men, in a bygone era, use to get on and do things without much recognition, as it was just what they did. However, in this new era where a man's place is blurred, often he isn't sure what he should do. The roles have become blurred and his purpose isn't as clear. In order to help you navigate the world and a relationship, it is healthy to get reassurance when you do things right. It helps us to know we are doing well in our relationship and we are continuing to offer value, just like at the start.

   We like reassurance about ourselves: our career paths, our efficacy as partners, our sexual prowess, our attractiveness if we did a good job fixing the sofa like you asked, if we didn't mind picking you up from town after a night out or if we remembered your mother's birthday. You see it's nice to hear from your partner what they like about you just as much as how you can improve. We know we need to improve, and we try out best to do so. That's why it's also nice to know you are doing some things right. If a woman is happy to give you praise it means she cares about your feelings and wants you to feel good. This is a good sign of a healthy relationship

2. **Sexually compatible**
   This doesn't mean her role is to do everything you want in the bedroom. Don't be silly (keep dreaming champ). It does mean you have a sexual connection. Relationships usually work best when you both feel as if you have a good sex life. You both enjoy mostly the same things and are on the same wavelength.

   Men also use sex as a means to communicate. They say through their bodies – I love you; I want you. Women however often prefer to communicate with words. She wants to hear you say the words for you to tell her you desire her. It is important both of you are aware you communicate differently. Often, a man will initiate sex just to make see if the woman is still sexually available to him. Does she still fancy him? Has he still got it?

What he is looking for is validation. Therefore, you need to ask yourself the question- Do you have sex regularly enough?

After thinking about yourself it is also time to think of her. Think of all the ways you can communicate to her verbally all of the things you want to be communicated physically. Tell her how beautiful she is, talk to her about how much you have missed her. ***Men often show and women want to tell***. Be aware of the differences in order to make a relationship work.

3. **Emotional Intimacy**

Do you feel as if you can confide in her your emotional state? Can you be honest and share when the day is stressful. Now of course you don't want to come across as a person who is constantly moaning. Don't be that negative guy who seems as if the world is against him. That certainly isn't how an Alpha behaves. He takes challenges head-on. But every now and then life becomes a little too much. Are you able to open up to her emotionally and is she receptive? She isn't judgmental. Doesn't berate you for how you are feeling. You get the impression that she genuinely cares about your emotional state.

Can you do the same for her? Can you listen to her and only offer solutions when she asks for them? Sometimes we as men want to solve problems when a woman just wants to feel listened to.

As much as you want to be sexually intimate it is important you can both be emotionally intimate.

4. **Space**

Does she afford you time to pursue hobbies and interests that are important to you? Often men give up all the things dear to them in order to spend their time with a new partner and turn resentful at the fact they made the sacrifice in the first place. Work out quickly what things you would be prepared to give up and what things you wouldn't. If you play for a pool team on a Thursday night, then is she supportive or does she give you grief every week you walk in the door?

Does she have hobbies of her own and do things that don't involve you. Both of you will need space from one another from time to time. You need to support her when she wants to try new things. If you can't give her space, then you cannot fairly demand it.

Relationships usually last better when each of you understands you cannot be with each other all the time and it is ok to do things by yourself or with other friends. But women will naturally want to spend more time together than males. This is something to be aware of and one of the differences between the sexes. You may both approach the same problem in different ways.

Author Deborah Tannen has written brilliantly on the masculine and feminine divide between independence and intimacy. This being that the male is drawn towards independence and the female towards intimacy.

We have to go back to the Caveman times again to see how our brains are hard-wired differently. Deborah talks about how men and women differ in this regard. Traditionally, when women needed to solve a problem, they would go further into the tribe – connecting with close friends and family and discussing their issues. By contrast, when men have a problem to solve, they would leave the tribe to be alone with their thoughts.

So, when things are going wrong don't be afraid to ask for space and when she tries to get closer or spend more time it's her way of trying to fix things. The best way to avoid confusion is to communicate clearly. Most relationships break down for lack of communication. Tell each other why you want space or explain to her why you need to gather your thoughts.

5. **You share goals and a vision of the future**
   Now her goals and your goals can be separate from one another but if you don't support each other in what you want to achieve it will never work. You will always feel like one person is holding the other back. There are other things that are important such as if you both want to start a family. If one does and the other doesn't this can often spell the end of a relationship before it is done.

   You see *the person you should be with is the person who you like who you are around them.* Do you feel as if they bring out the best or the worse in you?

   Will they be there for the bad times as well as the good. If this book teaches you to get the girl, then make sure it's the right girl. The one for you.

   If you couldn't care less about relationships and want to play the field, then that's good for you, enjoy whilst you can young stallion, but it would be a valuable lesson to pay attention to the next few sections.

You see relationships won't heal you and being single won't kill you.

Choose carefully and choose wisely.

Now onto what happens when relationships don't work and someone begins to cheat. Why do they cheat and what do I mean by cheating?

Well, as for what I mean let me define it for you now –

Infidelity or cheating is the breaking of trust that occurs when you keep profound, meaningful secrets from a committed primary partner.

This means we aren't just talking about the physical act but also the emotional, the keeping secrets and other grey areas of cheating. This encompasses online, in person, it allows the individual couple to also tailor it such as those that are in an open-relationship or maybe into more kinky things that mean that they may have multiple sexual partners, etc.

Now men and women both cheats. But they both do it for different reasons. Let me explore those now.

Reason Men cheat

Men are now, always have been and always will be physical creatures. Men are stupid. Come on guys we know it. Most of our brain is kept inside our pants. We just can't help ourselves. Almost all male cheater comes down to a physical response to an emotional stimulus. She had great breasts. She had a great bum. She looked fit. Men will cheat on opportunity whereas women's cheating will be more planned. It is no wonder we always get caught; we leave the club arm in arm with a woman at the bar whereas when a woman cheats, she meets him at her house in a separate taxi. Men are stupid when it comes to cheating and the reasons we offer are just as stupid.

"Every guy wants to have sex with other women so I just took my chance" Whilst this may be true, we can also control ourselves. It may feel at times like we are fighting against human nature and that's because we are. As you are by now aware It's a man's biological imperative to have sex with as many women as he can. However, when you realise the hurt this can cause then you must weigh up whether you think your actions are worth the potential fall out of the relationship. I can't answer that for you. Only you can.

"If I got enough sex at home, I wouldn't need to cheat". A very common one. The only way to combat this is to talk to your partner about your sexual needs. It can be very frustrating when you have all your pent-up testosterone and your lacking sex, but you may be better suited by approaching and talking to your partner. If she doesn't listen, then get rid. You aren't suited. You may be able to put up with it for a while but eventually, your varying sex drives are going to drive one of you to cheat. Better to end it sooner rather than later.

"If my wife hadn't gained so much weight then I wouldn't have gone elsewhere, she doesn't make the effort anymore" One of the key reasons I mentioned when selecting a woman to find one who takes care of themselves. It is not uncommon to stop finding your partner attractive. If you can help support them to get back to their best, then do so. This is always a better option than looking for greener grass. However, if you have tried everything and she just doesn't want to go back to her best then it's probably best to move on. In an ideal world and in the movies, people stay with each other no matter what but that isn't how it works in real life. If you don't fancy your woman then you have a real big problem. Men are visual we know our attraction switches. The same as you turn hers on by emotion, she turns yours on physically.

Men cheat due to physical reasons but there is another rationale behind their motives, I will explore the most common now:

1. **Immaturity** He has never been here before so doesn't know how to act. He just isn't old enough and ready enough to settle down. He still has things to prove to himself and to others. Although he has begun his sexual adventures there are other things he wants to try along the way. Unfortunately, if you aren't ready for a relationship fella then no woman is going to convince you. You must be mature and emotionally ready for one. It doesn't matter who the girl is and how beautiful she is, if you aren't ready then you will cheat.
2. **He is finished in his head, but he is a coward,** so he has decided it's time to end it, but he is scared to do the deed. He wants to keep his options open and instead of telling her, he decides to cheat and let her do the ending. He is looking for someone to put him out of his misery.

3. **He is done but he isn't moving on until he has found someone** Although he knows it is finished, he doesn't want to be alone. So instead of breaking things off, he will just wait until he has a new ship to jump to. Some men just can't be by themselves.

4. **He is number one** When you put yourself first repeatedly then sometimes you lose how your actions affect others. You start to view monogamy as constraining and want to break free from those shackles to do as you will. This is similar to immaturity. You just aren't ready to settle. Best to wait until you are or be open with the girls you are seeing to save future heartbreak. His primary consideration maybe for himself and himself alone.

5. **Revenge.** You want to get back for how she has wronged you. You want her to feel the pain she inflicted on you. Revenge is often a good motivator for men to cheat.

Reason women cheat

There is no easy way around its gentleman and contrary to popular culture, the memes you have read on the internet or your own desire for it not to be the case, women cheat just as much as men. The research states that just as many married women cheat as married men. Research suggests that 10 to 20 percent of men and women in marriages or other committed (monogamous) relationships will actively engage in sexual activity outside of their primary relationship.

This is of course relying on self-reporting as we don't yet have cameras in every bedroom although OnlyFans is trying to turn such a goal into reality. So, it's safe to assume the numbers are under-reported.

Women often cheat due to a lack of emotional connection in a relationship. Whereas men are physical and hard wired to spread their seed to better their chances of survival women are not. This is why we express such shock when we hear it was the woman that cheated not the man.

Some of the most common are:

- **They feel as if they are not appreciated**. No woman wants to feel like a babysitter. When men do not act like alphas and leaders, they regress to toddlers form expecting the woman to do everything for them. Your job is to bring value to the relationship and show that you can do things for yourself. Do not give them a reason to seek external validation to show she can be appreciated...***Remember a shoulder to cry on is a dick to ride on.***

- **The partner isn't intimate enough on an emotional level.** If you won't allow her to talk about how she is feeling, then someone else will. Now we aren't expecting you to turn into Jerry Springer but every now and then be prepared to let her get it off her chest. As mentioned above you may think by having sex with her you are showing that you love her, but she doesn't see it that way.

- **Loneliness.** Another reason why it is important she has hobbies and friends is, so she actually has stuff to do. If you are always working away (through no fault of your own) or when your home, you never find time to do things, then trust me, she will find a way to fill the big gap in the bed. The best way to overcome this is to ensure you spend time together just you two. It is about quality time not quantity.

- **Unreasonable expectations**. When a woman lives her life on social media or watching reality TV her perception of what is normal becomes distorted. She expects expensive gifts or for you to serve her in every way. For starters, this is not what an alpha male does and second, she is the wrong woman for you. It is time she started to realise that films, TV shows and memes aren't real life. Make it clear from the outset you are not an ATM nor a servant. YOU will support her where possible, but you aren't there to finance her.

- **Traumatic Childhood.** Unfortunately, not everyone has the same starts in life, some people come from homes that do not allow them to see how a normal functioning relationship works. Such times make it hard to have relationships. If you truly care about this person encourage them to seek help such as counselling or to see a clinical psychologist. They need to heal first before they can move forward.

- **Sex.** The easiest one and the one we all think. The sex at home just isn't happening or it's not hitting the right spots. Women love sex as much as men. If they aren't getting satisfied at home, they will seek it elsewhere. This is why reviewing performances is so important. It helps to make sure they are enjoying themselves and knowing how to improve. Often, they will cheat with EX's where they know what the sex is like.

You see women cheat for more emotional reasons than physical ones. She isn't just going to be running off with the guy who is better looking or is in better shape. They have a bit more class than us gentlemen. Also, we know this isn't what draws them in. As we have spoken about in the entire book a woman's attraction switches are different. They stimulate her emotional response, and these are the same thing that makes her want to cheat.

If you are a strong person of value and you can control the frame in most conversations, then you won't have much to worry about. You will still have to be a clear communicator; you will still need to find out how you can improve but you shouldn't be worrying at every turn that your girlfriend is going to run off with someone else.

Knowing these things helps you to identify the signs so you can stop a relationship fail before it does. Providing you want it to survive that is. They aren't here to make you paranoid or anxious. If you follow everything we have spoken about and continue to offer value, then you have very little to worry about. You just must realise that when you move to a relationship you must shift in how your mind works and how you can keep it going.

You don't suddenly change and become a beta male. You don't stop looking after yourself. You don't stop being a protector of loved ones, but you do now need to communicate regularly with her, so you know how things are going.

You won't be worried about being replaced because you are the only original.

You see in order to be irreplaceable one must be different.

You are different because you are not like all the other Beta males she has met. Remember this. You have value.

Reputation destruction -

Unfortunately, when relationships do break down you must be prepared for the reputation destruction. You see Mr. Jordan Mr. Peterson, the author of "12 Rules for Life: An Antidote to Chaos, explains how decades of scientific research shows men and women generally opt for different methods of displaying aggressive behaviour.

Funnily enough, after a relationship breaks down or you get caught cheating your former spouse is going to be feeling quite aggressive.

Whereas men displaying aggression physically. Most men are aware that an argument with a man always has an undertone of physical violence to it. They know that if they can't settle it with their words they can always resort to fists, this isn't the approach that women take.

Women won't try and beat you physically, well not most of them, because they know for the most part, they won't win.

They instead aim to ruin your reputation. ***The tools of a woman are gossip, rumors, and scandal.***

Watch how women tear other women apart using the same tools, you only have to look in office politics to notice it is the women that will gossip behind backs whilst men confront things head-on. You are most likely to get a passive-aggressive email from a female employee than a male. They use their words like weapons. Poison dripping on every syllable.

Female aggression, therefore, manifests itself in a different way. In the social media age, it allows for women's aggression to have a far reach. She only has to post a Facebook status that she knows is rooted in lies in order to become the victim. To cast doubt on others or to try to tarnish their image. The words and actions we now associate with a female displaying aggressive behaviour include excluding, ignoring, teasing, gossiping, secrets, backstabbing, rumor spreading and hostile body language (i.e., eye-rolling and smirking). Most damaging is turning the victim into a social "undesirable".

It is through these tools that a woman can obtain power, to please her desire for control, for achieving greater social status and popularity. She uses them to mask her jealousy, fear and attempts at derailing the competition (other women). You must be aware of these and understand that they will be used against you. You must rise above and know that such attempts won't hurt your self-worth. You won't indulge the falsehoods.

Now the research on this is huge Richard E Tremblay is a Canadian Professor of Psychology at the University of Montreal. He was awarded the criminology equivalent of the Noble Peace Prize known as the Stockholm Prize in Criminology. He has received the Jacques Rousseau Award from the Association francophone pour le savoir, and in 2003, he received the Innis-Gérin Medal from the Royal Society of Canada. He was also given the Order of Canada. He has over 100 publications of research into this area. He is the premier world expert on aggression both male and female. There are numerous papers he has written on this and the difference between males and females in aggression.

Women use the tools to try to destroy you after the relationship has ended. Do not allow such things to get to you.

"Lions do not worry about the opinion of sheep"

Women can be cruel in their use in this especially amongst teenage girls. The effects of these **social aggressions** can have long-lasting effects. Often, they are more damaging than physical aggression. The weapons they use on one another can easily turn on you.

We are aware of them and we will guard against them. We must be strong gentlemen. We often need mental toughness to deal with the weapons women throw at us.

They can use children, money, houses, or anything they can as leverage against you during the breakdown of a relationship. Do not play their games. Remove yourself from the situation. Material things can be earned again. It is not worth the headache.

Suicide is the single biggest killer of men under 45.

If you are ever struggling, then seek help. Seek help from friends. Family and professionals. The more help you get the better.

Many factors make men more vulnerable to suicide. Men are often under pressure to appear strong and not show signs of weakness. Being alpha does not mean we don't turn for help if we need it. Even the strongest of us need support at times. If you need to talk about issues and have mental health concerns, then do so early on.

During stressful times men often turn to risky behaviour such as substance or alcohol abuse which increases the risk of suicide by up to eight times.

A relationship breakdown has a bigger impact on a man's suicide risk than a woman's – divorced men are three times more likely to commit suicide than their married peers, whereas divorced women show no increased risk.

This is why we must cover what happens when relationships break down just as much as what to look for and what makes them go well. You may have one relationship or many. It doesn't matter but what you must do is also look after your own health. This being physical and mental.

Mental health can affect all of us in many different ways. At six-foot-nine, 275-pound the heavyweight champion of the world Tyson fury was a giant of men. A man who had just risen up the boxing ranks to become the best heavyweight boxer at the time. Yet it was not the physical form outside but the mental from within that brought him to his knees.

Back in November 2015, Tyson Fury was on top of the world after dethroning long-reigning heavyweight king Wladimir Klitschko. He went on to achieve all that he and his father have dreamed of ever since he was a boy. He became the heavyweight champion of the world.

He had won all the fights he needed inside the ring, but it was the fight outside that he was losing. In just two years the Gypsy King had fallen hard. His struggles with mental health issues led to his misuse of alcohol and drugs. So severe was his slide, that his weight ballooned to almost 400llbs. It seemed as if his legacy was at an end. The king's reign was over.

Yet there was hope still within him and he set himself a challenge. To take on the most-feared puncher in current heavyweight history. Deontay Wilder.

After out-boxing Deontay for the fight, In the final round, the Bronze Bomber landed a punch that sent Tyson to the canvas. It was all over. Or so we thought. Yet something within Tyson refuses to give up. Refused to stay down. And in a moment that epitomizes his current comeback, he got up and finished the fight.

The judges had it as a draw. The rest of us had it as a Tyson win.

He went on to beat Deontay in their next fight and showed the world that anyone can come back from a loss. Especially one of the minds.

"I fought back from thinking about suicide, mental health, depression, anxiety. I wanted more than anything to show the world it can be done. Anything is possible with the right mindset." Tyson Fury

Tyson Fury came back to be the world heavyweight champion of the world and wrote a book on mental health struggles to help anyone who is in a dark place. There is always hope.

I hope you all your relationships are successful and part on excellent terms, I hope you meet one woman that you may spend the rest of your life with, but I also want you to be prepared if that isn't the case. If you're worried about suicide you can call the Samaritans free, at any time on 116 123. If it is an emergency, then use your emergency number such as 999 for the UK.

Now I know what you're thinking, jeez Jack that went a bit serious, didn't it? Well yes, but relationships usually are serious, and I want you to be seriously prepared to make it work but also seriously prepared for if they don't.

I know that after your relationship ends you have all the tools to find a new one, after all, I taught you them. So, you go back to the beginning of the book and you start again.

I just want to make sure you are prepared for the time just after a relationship where things may not be so good. Trust me they will get better.

Now you can avoid all of this heartache by just never having a relationship and just using other people's girlfriends...

Or taking your time and being really selective over who you settle with (even then it can still not work)

But if all else fails then remember the magic potion for a broken heart:

"The best way to get over someone is to get under someone"

Jump back on that horse cowboy. I didn't help you understand the secrets of The Game to only play once now did I 😉

CHAPTER 12

It's A Numbers Game - Practice Makes Perfect

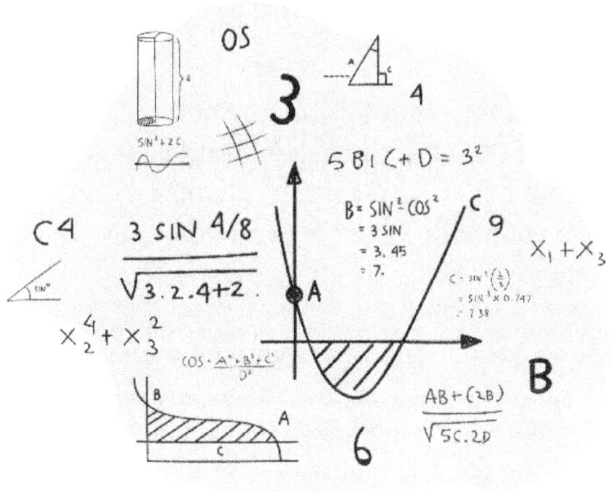

"Casanova: Casanova, the philosopher? Who devotes his life to the perfection of experience? Yes, I know him.
Francesca Bruni: No, Casanova the libertine, who devotes his life to seducing women.
Casanova: Well, we're obviously talking about the same person."

Chapter 12 – It's a numbers game

Finally, we come to the last chapter. We have been on one hell of a journey together. It's like you just completed Skyrim or finally got your Blitzball team together on Final Fantasy 10.

We now have all we need to transform your life like Marty McFly and the Doc in Back to The Future. In fact, the last time we saw a coming of age this good, it starred Emilio Estevez and Molly Ringwald (The Breakfast Club). The point I am making is- everything you need to begin to slowly take back control of your life you have now learned. You have begun to unpick the different areas in your life that you can improve.

You see the book was never just about talking to women. Yeah, women are great, but it was about much more than that. Just like Mr. Miyagi had to hide the lessons to becoming great at karate behind the guise of washing a car, I too had to slowly uncover ways to improve your life by showing you how they can be used to help you be successful with women.

You see why all of what we mentioned works with women you want to date it also works in other areas of your life. It is not limited to just trying to help your chances of meeting Meg Ryan at the top of the Empire State building. The skills you have learnt to hold a conversation, work just as well if you are trying to ask your boss for a raise. You can use mirroring to help build rapport and establish mutual ground. As your boss begins to feel listened to, he will feel that you have the company's best interest at heart. This will then allow making them more likely to see things from your perspective. If not then you can always ***"make them an offer they can't refuse"*** knowing you are prepared to walk away, as you know your self-worth.

The tools we have learned can help you in so many aspects of your life.

They can help when you are looking to make friends or at a networking event. You can use an opener to engage people and stop you stood on the sidelines, anxiously playing with your laptop bag.

The ways we have set out to help you transform your body will help you live a longer life so you can actually enjoy all of the things you want to. Then I will be happier seeing you make the most of your time on earth than Red was when he found out Andy escaped in The Shawshank Redemption.

We have explored how you can begin to hack your mind. Changing your thought process to inspire yourself, to fill your own psyche with confidence. You can find your own motivation to achieve whatever goals you have set out. You can begin to turn your fears into your weapons aye Batman.

When you use to be scared to talk to strangers now it doesn't hold such a fear factor. The ability to talk to new people is an invaluable life skill.

As you begin to build a personal brand, soon your reputation will positively proceed you. You will have social value and others will be more receptive to the ideas you have. You will notice that as others see your inner strength and your wealth of knowledge, they come to you for advice.

You see all of what we have looked at extends into all areas of your life. As you begin to master these things watch as things get just a little easier. Being able to quickly build rapport, friends or sell yourself is a skill not many can master.

So how long does it take to master all of this Jack?

Not as long as you think.

10 thousand hours

What does it take to become an expert or master performer in a given field? 10,000 hours of practice. Or so you thought.

Although popularized by Malcom Gladwell in his bestseller *Outliers: The Story of Success*. It's catchy, easy to remember, and more or less **completely false.**

That's right it doesn't take anywhere near this.

The rule which was based on the research of Anders Ericsson on musicians of expert level is a very basic oversimplification. Even though you have heard this many times, it doesn't make it true.

You see in the original research from our pal Gladwell he uses a few pieces of research. With just one being Ericson's studies on violin students. It was Ericsson work that is often quoted. That is because he found that on average students used about 10,000 hours of playing time by the time, that they turned 20.

Gladwell also used the 10,000-hour figure to estimate how many times the Beatles practiced. Not sure he spent that much time in Liverpool gigging with the lads so it's safe to assume he managed to pluck this number out of the air as well.
He did the same when trying to justify his figures by attempting to give an answer as to how many hours Bill Gates put into programming before, he created Microsoft. Now I wasn't with Bill. Neither was he. Now the only one who actually knows how many hours he put in is Bill and nobody actually asked him. So, we will have to remain sceptical as to where he got this figure from. Unless of course another Bill and a bloke called Ted to lend us a telephone box to go back in time and find out. Maybe Doctor Who can help if the infamous 90's rockers are busy.

So basically, according to Gladwell if you do anything for 10,000 hours - you become an expert?

Well for starters the figure chosen is arbitrary. The average isn't the same as how many hours some of every best violist used. It could take some of them far less and some of them far more.

Also, although they were really good, who decides if they are experts?

We get into a whole different ball game when we start questioning what makes an actual expert is it just a professional or is it the top 1% of a certain subgroup. Defining an expert- in itself - requires an expert with certain expertise. See what I expertly did there.

He also didn't count for the quality of the time spent and only the quantity of the time. I am sure we would all agree that an hour one to one coaching with an expert would help us progress in a field more than 5 hours with a novice.

The quality of the training given is paramount. Also, the amount of quality instruction be it direct instruction or tutelage with self-discovery will play a role. There are just too many variables to tie down how many hours it takes a to become an expert.

Hey, I know some people that have been having sex for decades and are still crap in bed.

Since the 10,000-hour rule isn't based on solid science, what do we know about practice and how to master a craft? A few things we know for sure are that not all learning or practice is equally helpful – and not everyone starts from the same place. Here is one of its major flaws when trying to provide an arbitrary figure for what makes an "expert".

It focuses on the quantity of time practicing, not the quality of the practice – and not all practice is equally helpful.

That being if you spent 10,000 hours aimlessly speaking to women would you improve? Yes, you would. By a bloody lot.

But you don't need to spend that amount of time because:

- You aren't starting with no prior knowledge
- You know how and what to say now
- You know how to behave
- You have no intention of being a world-renowned expert you'll probably settle for being pretty bloody good
- And also, the research in itself is flawed as they just chose a random number based upon one group and how long it took those individuals to play the

violin! Now I am sure you may play on a few heartstrings in your time but it's not quite the same and won't require 10,000 hours.

The good news is it is going to take you far less. It will take you just 63 times to gain this skill. That is, it.

63 reps to gain a skill. Do all of this just 63 times and it is yours.

You need about 63-65 repetitions of use of a skill to build a new neural pathway, so it becomes easy to use. So, you can call on it at will. This is like your muscle memory. When things become automated. When you no longer have to think about what to say or how to say it.

When I say a neural pathway is formed, I mean the things in our brain actually physically change. Neural pathways, comprised of neurons connected by dendrites, are created in the brain based on our habits and behaviours.

The more we do something then the number of dendrites increases with the frequency of a particular behaviour.

These pathways are like roads that allow us to quickly zip messages along neural pathways. The roads in our brain get better. It is like going from the Victorian steam train to the Japanese bullet train.

Neural plasticity is conceived as the ability of the brain to reorganize neural pathways that are based on new experiences encountered throughout the course of life span development (Huttenlocher, 2002). Neural plasticity can occur at multiple levels, including molecular changes, cellular alterations, shaping of neuronal structures and interconnections, and reorganization of functions (Cicchetti & Curtis, 2006; 2008; Whitten, 2013).

To explain this simply when brain cells communicate frequently, the connection between them strengthens and "the messages that travel the same pathway in the brain over and over begin to transmit faster and faster." With enough repetition, these behaviours become automatic. It means you don't have to think about it. Like decoding words to help you read a great book like this, thinking what each peddle does and how to change gears when driving your car (forgetting where you were the last 30 minutes as you stare out the window), or even thinking about how to balance and squeeze your breaks when riding a bike. These are just a few examples of complicated behaviours that we do automatically as a result of these new neural pathways that have been formed.

So, it seems like you can teach an old dog new tricks scooby.

In order to form a new habit or to change the way we have spoken to women so far; we must do it more often. With the new tools you have learnt. Just 63 times. That is, it.

63 conversations. That is all you need. Just 63 times. Then the skill is yours - for life.

We are what we repeatedly do. Excellence then is not an act, but a habit."
-Aristotle

Now all your times before reading this book don't count, I am afraid. That's because you didn't know what you were doing before.

You had no strategy. You were winging it like Joey's acting career in Friends.

Now, however, you have a plan. A sequence of very fortunate events. Call me Lemony Cricket. A man on your shoulder whispering in your ear helping you with a series of very fortunate events to help you get to your desired outcome.

You know where to lead the conversation. What attraction switches to be ticking. How to make a good first impression, in person and online. What openers to use. How to build attraction. Cat and Mouse theory, false disqualifiers. How to build safety. Mirroring, labelling, tactical empathy. How to close the deal. What to be prepared for when having sex. What to consider when thinking of a relationship. You are better equipped than Arnold Schwarzenegger in Commando.

We know way more now than we did when we started. All we need to do is put it into practice. That is why it is a numbers game.

For the foreseeable future work on just internalising the skills. Think of it like recalling your times tables. The easier you can do this the more working memory you free up. You see the brain can only hold between 4-7 pieces of information at any one time. **Working memory** is a cognitive system with a limited capacity that can hold information temporarily. **Working memory** is important for reasoning and the guidance of decision-making and behaviour.

The more things you have to remember the less information to solve more complex problems. This is why remembering things for quick recall frees up the brains computing powers for other things. Think of it like when you use to Disk Fragment your old computer. The good old – CTR ALT DEL – closing programmes and tasks you don't need.

This is what we are aiming to do. We want to internalise all of the thoughts and processes so that you free up more brain space to better make decisions when you're with a group or an individual woman.

It doesn't matter if you make it pass the opener, it doesn't matter if you can't close. You are just trying out your new tools and becoming use to using them. It's all practice.

And practice makes perfect.

Mentors

Imagine how much money you would have in your bank account 20 years from now if Warren Buffet himself sat you down and mentored you on all he knew about the stock market. He spent his time to help show you everything you need to help build a company as he has at Berkshaw Hathaway worth about 400 billion dollars.

Imagine if Cristiano Ronaldo himself offered to coach you how to play as a winger. Showing you all the drills, he has used to improve. Talking through his decision-making. Explaining why he does what he does on the football pitch and how.

Imagine if Bill Gates said he would teach you how to computer programme. He offered you a placement at Microsoft meeting him once a week to discuss everything you are learning. You can spend time with him personally working on your self-development. Just imagine the worlds on Minecraft you could create.

Since we evolved from primates, we have embraced the role of mentors in development. Mentors help us to alleviate the need to start fresh all the time. It helps us to avoid making the same mistakes they did.

It is the Dumbledore to our Harry Potter, the Boss to our Big Boss, the Professor Oak to our ...well it depends what you named the character, but you get the point.

Mentors allow us a way to get hard-won information without doing the same hardships. *"Don't stick your hand in that poisonous cobras mouth Ben"*.
What took them years can take us just weeks to learn. They help to speed up the learning process and keep us in check.

Before the rise of the University phenomenon, the craftsman and apprentice scheme were how most people learnt their way in the world. In the centuries before the internet, many would choose a profession and be apprenticed to a master. This master would in return for their service offer to teach them all they needed to be a success. They helped with the passing on of knowledge.

Often this knowledge was kept secret like the guilds. So, outsiders couldn't steal this information without having undergone the correct training. Or in most RPG's read a scroll that gives you the necessary skill points to level up. To become King Arthur, you are going to need a Merlin.

Did you know that Bill Gates had a mentor?

Yep. Some bloke you may have heard of. Called Warren Buffet. Yeah Waffen Buffet taught Bill Gates all he knows about investing and that is why less than 20% of Bill Gates fortune comes from Microsoft today. He owns less than 2% of the company yet is still worth over 100 billion dollars.

Then we have Alexander the Great. He had a mentor. Some famous chap called Aristotle. Yeah –Aristotle the famous philosopher. You know the one who was taught by Plato. The other great Greek Philosopher. Yes, that one.

But did you know Plato was taught by Socrates, the father of western philosophy? You see the power of the right mentor can do wonders for your ability to speed up the learning process.

Use this book as your mentor. Refer back to it often. Use it to help you learn what you need to make your life as successful with women as you wish.

If you have further questions, then reach out to me on my channels which will be listed at the end. I will try my best to help you where I can. If you need a mentor, a coach, someone to help you stay in check then reach out and we can see what we can do.

However, everything you need is in the book. You just need to have confidence in the method. It works. Trust me.

There is method in the madness.

Crash burn Phoenix

The process for learning skills, like all things, will involve success and failure. There will be times when you crash and burn but just like the phoenix, you must rise from the ashes.

The Game is best played in real life. It is the best way to try out your new tools. As mentioned, I have prepared you for Tinder and social media but do not use this as a crutch. The success rate for Tinder for guys is 0.6% to get a match. That means you are likely not to get a single match out of your 100 free swipes.

Now everything I showed you will raise this probability. By enough to give you a fighting chance but the best chance you'll have is out there in person. This is why it is a numbers game.

Say you speak to 100 women and out of those 100 women one in five give you their number. That means you now have 25 numbers. Out of those 25, you message you may only get 5 that actually meet for a date. Another one in five. Out of those you meet you may only sleep with another one out of five. That means just one out of the 100 you spoke to you will close. In the beginning, this is probably how it will look for you.

Until your Game becomes tighter you are going to need to prospect and nail down your sales pitch.

At my height, I could be regularly talking to 45 women at once. Seriously. I knew that they wouldn't all go anywhere so I kept my options available. It meant I was never desperate to close and it also gave them the impression I wasn't desperate. After all, how can you be desperate if a girl flakes on you if you just message another and take her out instead?

You see when we say talking you aren't messaging constantly all day. You are a busy guy. YOU have things to do. You message when you can.

If you want numerous regular sexual partners, then you need to consider what is a number you can actively juggle and ensure that it suits all parties considered.

Getting The Girl

There are many things about the Game you will only learn after you become accustomed to The Courtship Process and how it works. There are many elements that are personal to you.

You could want just one girl for now and forever. You could want to do a 30-girl month as my Uncle David use to when he was a DJ. That is up to you to decide.

Remember true mastery of The Game isn't about gimmicks or giving away free drinks or buying a woman's approval. Any sucker can do that. It is about bringing value. Ticking all the attraction switches.

Remember that in the end all that matters are if what you are doing is making you happy. The rest is all just numbers.

The only numbers that count are the ones you choose to make important.

You set your goal and you achieve it.

Alan Shearer is the Premier Leagues' all-time leading goal-scorer with 260 goals. If you ask me - those are rookie numbers 😉

#GoalsPayTheRent

Giacomo Casanova

The infamous Giacomo Casanova lived from 1725 to 1798. He was a man of great intellect, far more than he is given credit for. Beyond his ability to dazzle and beguile women he also spent time with Voltaire, Catherine the Great, Benjamin Franklin and Mozart. He entered University at the age of 12 and left at 17 with a degree in Law.

His careers were just as varied he was a gambler, an astrologer, a commissioned officer in the Republic of Venice, Secretary to The Cardinal of Rome, an Author, a spy and many more.

A well-cultured man he managed to travel around Europe from Madrid to Moscow. Finally settling a librarian where he wrote his legendary memoir, the innocuously named *Story of My Life*, though he died of old age poor his life was rich. He was often surrounded by women and enjoyed them from the moment he first lost his virginity. Although a late starter by modern standards, he was 17 when he finally did it.

Whilst studying to enter the church his first sexual escapade was a mark of things to come. His first sexual conquest was to two well-born teenage sisters, Nanetta and Marta Savorgnan. He found himself alone with the adventurous pair one night sharing two bottles of wine and each other in equal measure.
Thus, began a life-long crusade to experience all that women had to offer. Of all types and calibres. To learn to love them and enjoy them in ways others only dreamed of. ***"I was born for the sex opposite to mine,"*** he wrote in the preface of his memoir. ***"I have always loved it and done all that I could to make myself loved by it."***

Casanova loved women which were taken, those that were married or betrothed. He felt great joy in having those things he cannot

By his own accounts, Casanova's body count totalled 122 women. It seems I am 3 times the man he was in some respects yet not nearly measured up to him in others.

Casanova lived a life many aspire to, yet many would not wish. Make your life memorable and choose your purpose. I wish you all the success in your life. I hope you have found all the work and research I have brought together useful.

You are a person of incredible value and it is now up to you to give people the opportunity to see just how great you are.

I have every faith in you and know that you can use what you have been taught to improve your life.

See you on the other side gentleman, the weather is lovely over here.

If anyone asks where I am- **tell them I had to go, see about a girl – Robin Williams – Good Will Hunting**

Best wishes, as always,

Jack Hickey

Be the flame, not the moth."
— Giacomo Casanova

"If you have not done things worthy of being written about, at least write things worthy of being read."
— Giacomo Casanova

"The sweetest pleasures are those which are hardest to be won."
— Casanova, The Story of My Life

About the Author –

Jack has had a colourful life, full of excitement. He graduated as an Inspirational Student from his university in the Class of 2015, and he was chosen to be part of the top 10 students from the fifty thousand that graduated in that year. He has a degree in Education, and he uses this to help explain complex issues in simple terms. He has previously been a nightclub promoter, bar manager, teacher, politician, and author. Jack decided to write the book to help bring together over 15 years of experience in dating and research. “He’s been from Number Ten to dating tens”.

Jack now works in Public Relations and Marketing, specialising in: Corporate, Scale ups, Scale downs, Pre and Post acquisition businesses helping them develop long term growth. Basically, he gets paid to have dinner, lunch **and Close**.

Contact information – Stay Up to Date – Drop me an email to sign up for a monthly newsletter with updates and extra tips.

Social Media – Instagram - @Gettingthegirlbook
Email – gettingthegirl@hotmail.com

For questions reach out to the social media platforms. I hope I can continue to help you on your journey.

If you need a coach drop me a message and lets, see what we can do.

References

Chapter 1

Baker , R (2015) Sperm Wars: Infidelity, Sexual Conflict, and Other Bedroom Battles

Noble , K – Website (https://www.kezia-noble.com/) 03/03/2021

Mobbs D, Hagan CC, Dalgleish T, Silston B, Prévost C. The ecology of human fear: survival optimization and the nervous system. *Front Neurosci*. 2015;9:55. Published 2015 Mar 18. doi:10.3389/fnins.2015.00055

Jasieńska G, Ziomkiewicz A, Ellison PT, Lipson SF, Thune I. Large breasts and narrow waists indicate high reproductive potential in women. *Proc Biol Sci*. 2004;271(1545):1213-1217. doi:10.1098/rspb.2004.2712

Rhodes, G., Proffitt, F., Grady, J.M. *et al.* Facial symmetry and the perception of beauty. *Psychonomic Bulletin & Review* **5,** 659–669 (1998). https://doi.org/10.3758/BF03208842)

Chapter 2

Costa PT, Terracciano A, McCrae RR. Gender differences in =pPersonality traits across cultures: Robust and surprising findings. *Journal of Personality and Social Psychology*. 2001;81:322–331. [PubMed] [Google Scholar]

Chapman BP, Duberstein PR, Sörensen S, Lyness JM. Gender Differences in Five Factor Model Personality Traits in an Elderly Cohort: Extension of Robust and Surprising Findings to an Older Generation. *Pers Individ Dif*. 2007;43(6):1594-1603. doi:10.1016/j.paid.2007.04.028

Jensen-Campbell, L. A., Adams, R., Perry, D. G., Workman, K. A., Furdella, J. Q. and Egan, S. K. (2002). Agreeableness, Extraversion, and Peer Relations in Early Adolescence: Winning Friends and Deflecting Aggression. *Journal of Research in Personality*. 36*3*. 224-251.

Ogi , Ogas (2011) **A Billion Wicked Thoughts: What the Internet Tells Us About Sexual Relationships.**

Chapter 3

Hip to waist Ratio – Facial Symmetry and more PPT - https://www.unl.edu/rhames/courses/ppoint/beauty-212.pdf

Greene, R., & Elffers, J. (2000). *The 48 laws of power.*

Greene, Robert. The Art of Seduction. New York, N.Y. :Viking, 2001.

Chapter 4

Behind the Smile' Perception study

Gan EH, Pattman S, H S Pearce S, Quinton R. A UK epidemic of testosterone prescribing, 2001-2010. Clin Endocrinol (Oxf). 2013 Oct;79(4):564-70. doi: 10.1111/cen.12178. Epub 2013 Apr 5. PMID: 23480258.

Chapter 6

Gray, John, 1951-. (1992). Men are from Mars, women are from Venus : a practical guide for improving communication and getting what you want in your relationships. New York, NY :HarperCollins,

Geher, G., & Kaufman, S. B. (2013). **Mating intelligence unleashed: The role of the mind in sex, dating, and love**. Oxford University

Chapter 7

Aron, A. P. (Eds.). (2004). Handbook of closeness and intimacy.

Bolmont, M., Cacioppo, J. T., & Cacioppo, S. (2014). Love is in the gaze: An eye-tracking study of love and desire. *Psychological Science, 25,* 1748-1756.

McAdams, D. P. (1982). Experiences of intimacy and power: Relationships between social motives and autobiographical memory. *Journal of Personality and Social Psychology, 42*(2), 292–302. https://doi.org/10.1037/0022-3514.42.2.292

Perper, T. (1985). Sex signals: The biology of love. Philadelphia: ISI Press.

Stephens, G. J., Silbert, L. J., & Hasson, U. (2010). Speaker-listener neural coupling underlies successful communication. *Proceedings of the National Academy of Sciences of the United States of America, 107*(32), 14425–14430. https://doi.org/10.1073/pnas.1008662107

Walsh, D. G., & Hewitt, J. (1985). Giving men the come-on: Effect of eye contact and smiling in a bar environment. Perceptual and Motor Skills, 61, 873-874.

Abrahams, Matthewf.. Perceiving flirtatious communication: An exploration of the perceptual dimensions underlying judgments of flirtatiousness. Journal of Sex Research. 1994. 31(4): 283-292.

Fink, Bernhard; Nadine Hugill and Benjamin P. Lange. Women's Body Movements Are a Potential Cue to Ovulation. Personality and Individual Differences. 2012. 53: 759-763.

Lakoff, George. (2004). Don't think of an elephant! : know your values and frame the debate : the essential guide for progressives. White River Junction, Vt. :Chelsea Green Pub. Co.,

Hinsz, V. B., D. C. Matz, and R. A. Patience 2001 Does Women's Hair Signal Reproductive Potential? Journal of Experimental Social Psychology 37:166-172

Chapter 9

The Science of Kissing: What Our Lips Are Telling Us Hardcover – , 2011

by Sheril Kirshenbaum (Author)

Chapter 10

Fisher TD, Moore ZT, Pittenger MJ. **Sex on the brain?:** an examination of frequency of sexual cognitions as a function of gender, erotophilia, and social desirability. J Sex

Res. 2012;49(1):69-77. doi: 10.1080/00224499.2011.565429. Epub 2011 May 24. PMID: 21512948.

Younis, Ihab; Fattah, Menhaabdel; Maamoun, Marwa Female hot spots, Human Andrology: March 2016 - Volume 6 - Issue 1 - p 20-26 doi: 10.1097/01.XHA.0000481142.54302.08

Chapter 11

That's Not What I Meant! How Conversational Style Makes or Breaks Relationships – Deborah Tannen (2011)

Chapter 12

Cicchetti, D., & Blender, J. A. (2006). A multiple-levels-of-analysis perspective on resilience: Implications for the developing brain, neural plasticity, and preventive interventions. *Annals of the New York Academy of Sciences*, 1094, 248–258.

Cicchetti, D., & Curtis, W. J. (2006). The developing brain and neural plasticity: Implications for normality, psychopathology, and resilience.
In Cicchetti, D. & Cohen, D. J. (Eds.), *Developmental psychopathology: Developmental neuroscience* (Vol. 2, 2nd ed., pp. 1–64). Hoboken, NJ:

Stiles, J. (2008). *The fundamentals of brain development: Integrating nature and nurture*. Cambridge, MA: Harvard University Press.Google Scholar

Whitten, L. A. (2013). Translational neuroscience and potential contributions of functional magnetic resonance imaging (fMRI) to the prevention of substance misuse and antisocial behavior. *Prevention Science*, 14, 238–24

Printed in Great Britain
by Amazon

26754643R00183